Enlightenment Codes

For Cosmic Ascension

A Sacred Journey through Creation

First printing: 2021

Cover illustration: N. Van Der Auwera

Graphic design: www.graficus.alziend.be

Photographs: J. Hayward

Illustrations: S. Di Nitto, N. Van Der Auwera

Photo backcover: www.jannekewalter.nl

ISBN 9789464517309 (pbk.)

Library of Congress registration number: TXu 2-294-817

Contact the author directly online:
www.sabrinadinitto.com
www.enlightenmentcodes.com

Enlightenment Codes

For Cosmic Ascension

A Sacred Journey through Creation

Sabrina Di Nitto

To Our Human-Divine Nature

Gratitude overflows me as the womb of our Cosmos lovingly envelops me. The delight of a cosmic emotional haven to embody life on Earth again radiates from my heart. The touch of the golden strings of our Sun and the silver rays of our Moon nourish, nurture, and protect me. And above all, they illuminate my path.

To Earth on which I walk as I radiate my Divine Essence, I bestow my divine potential.

As soul mates, we agreed to assemble on this planet to share love, laughter, bliss, and tears, recognising the love and strength in one another's eyes.

And as we meet, together we weave a matrix of love, compassion, and strength for the times ahead.

Table of Contents

Table of Contents

Acknowledgements

I honour my eternal friends Thoth and the Light Beings of the Venus Light Path for their accompaniment, extraordinary magical co-Creation, and confidence in bringing forth the Enlightenment Codes.

I extend my deepest gratitude to all the Primaeval Creational Light Beings of the Cosmos and the Earth. I especially thank Amun Ra, Amunet, Nun, and Nunet, for their moving presence, dedication, compassion, and softly whispered utterances during this exploration through Creation.

I offer deep appreciation to my family for their love and compassion. To all my treasured friends, thank you for your unconditional, loving presence. I am grateful to all my life teachers – past, present, and future. I thank my dear friend John for his unconditional friendship, unwavering support, and encouragement in the revision of this Light Tablet.

I convey my recognition and affection to each of you who fully expresses your eternal essence or will do so. Remain close to your soul and remain at home there.

And I would especially like to acknowledge Luke Faulkner, whose stunning compositions have moved my heart again and again while channeling and writing this book. Thank you for your companionship and for sharing your divine potential with the world.

Preface

The Primordial God of the Seen and Unseen

Here you stand before Amun Ra and Amunet. They have the energy of a devoted mother and father who stare at you with soft, warm, and gentle eyes. Their gazes acknowledge you are of eternal, Divine Essence. You are their Divine Child, and they will co-create with you. Amun Ra[1] and Amunet express their gratitude in advance.

In your hands lies the Book of Light, the Light Tablet. Together, all three of you connect with it. They ask you to feel from your heart the light it radiates. They ask you to see the unique codes of light you will contribute to this Light Tablet. For you, too, are a divine seed of life incarnated on this Earth.

Together we offer this Light Tablet to Amun Ra and Amunet. We grant them the New Earth Star. We guide the Earth in her ascension process through the Axis Mundi. You will represent this Cosmic Axis Mundi[2] as you travel through these codes of light.

You extend your hands to Amun Ra and Amunet. The Earth will climb your body and ascend into their light. Through this offering, you open yourself to Oneness with yourself, with all temples, with all Light Beings, with all life on Earth, and with the Earth itself. You come into harmonic resonance with All That Is.

Behold your precious endowment to Amun Ra and Amunet.

As equals, you stand together within the Circle of Light. You resonate the same frequency, the same love. You carry the same deep appreciation for one another. We are all divine. Through this sacred initiation,

---

1 Amun Ra was known to the Egyptians as the Supreme God, the Sun God, who embodies the Central Sun's Light, the first manifestation and Creation of Source and All That Is. He not only created himself, but he was the creator of the multiverse. Mut is his consort. She is also a Mother Goddess worshipped in ancient Egypt. In the ancient Egyptian language, her name literally means Mother.

2 In contemporary mythology, the terms *axis mundi, cosmic axis, world axis, world pillar, centre of the world*, and *world tree* denote any mythological concept representing the connection between heaven and earth or the higher and lower planes.

we give birth to our light. We anchor on Earth as seeds of light. This is our gift to the Earth, for we are all midwives of Earth's ascension into the cosmic realms. We are midwives of our own ascension into the Cosmos. We are Divine Creators.

Amun Ra and Amunet hold the Light Tablet in their hands. It contains the blueprint of the love you birthed for yourself and the world. It radiates the highest frequencies of Divine Love that flow from your open heart.

This Light Tablet is an offering for Amun Ra and Amunet. This offering is precisely what they wished for. They utter, "Thank you, beautiful Light Being."

The Primordial God of the Creational Waters

The primordial waters of Nun and Nunet procreate eternally from their bodies of love. By doing so, they foresee the Cosmos as teeming with life: the infinite divine sparks of these new-born souls breathing continuous life into the Cosmos.

Nun and Nunet are here with you. They manifest themselves through an ascending wave of blue-indigo etheric water. Warmly welcoming and blessing you, they envelop and weave a circular string of their liquid light around you. By adorning you with another twelve liquid-light petals, they bestow upon you *the unveiling blueprint of the Thousand Petal Lotus… the Flower of Creational Waters.*

This geometric pattern of twelve petals encircles a central petal and deepens multidimensionally according to the Fibonacci code, up to the 144th dimension.

Nun and Nunet say, "We offer this Light Tablet, a divine blueprint of 144 dimensions embedded deep within the Earth. This blueprint mentions that we will assist you in activating and grounding each temple in this 144th dimension in Inner Earth."

As the coefficient of light increases, the etheric light temples and the inner-Earth light temples to the 144th dimension will realign to function as One Light Body. You will witness the cracking of the entire Earth Light Body into its soil, bedrock, magma, and all inner layers. All inner multidimensional temples will then come into Oneness. Then, significant shifts in the Temple of Love,[3] the Temple of Mother Earth, can manifest.

The sacred geometry of the horizontal and vertical octahedron will ignite the Maltese Cross,[4] Earth's ascension wheel enabling Divine Love to radiate all over the Earth.

Illustration: The Maltese Cross.

The Maltese Cross, when in balance, ignites and unfolds the spherical Love Body of the Earth. As it spins, all insecurity, fear, lack of love, and dismemberment carried by the Earth for tens of thousands of years move towards the Earth's crust. All old energetic layers collapse.

A new Blue Moon will emerge. It supports the Earth. It will imprint her new blueprint and prepare her to resurrect herself as a Sun.

The Alpha α and the Omega Ω energies encompass the beginning and the end. We begin our journey with the Blue Moon Goddesses. She brings forth an era of Oneness for Egypt, for the Earth, and for you. You witness the birth of the blue moon energy on Earth.

We invite you to play and imagine the Blue Moon in your hand. As you swivel it, bright-yellow Venus Light desires to break through. Venus Light gives birth to itself through blue moon energy. The Blue Moon is our gift to Egypt, to the Earth, to you.

Blue Moon, the Earth Star's Sacred Midwife.

---

3 The Temple of Love is referred to as the Holy of Holies on Earth. Each sacred site has a Holy of Holies where the Divine seed of life resides. The core essence of the Earth is love.
4 The Maltese Cross is a cross symbol, consisting of four V or arrowhead shapes that meet at a central vertex. It is a primordial geometric structure present as a sacred geometric building block in the expansion of the multiverse. This structure expands matter and supports growth and development on microlevels and macrolevels.

Introduction

Suggestion for the reader

This Light Tablet contains countless layers of multidimensional consciousness streams, each resonating in phase with a particular layer of consciousness within you. Some of these layers may already be lively within your awareness. Others, slumbering impatiently within inner depths, await your touch.

I suggest allowing this enveloping Light Tablet as it leads you on your journey, flowing in surrender to these multidimensional floods, these shape-shifting forms of sacred geometry. From your innermost surrenderings, these enlightenment codes nourish you becoming you.

Trusting in what John Keats describes as negative capability--the art of allowing beauty to be beautiful, stillness to unfold ever further--you contemplate these codes to come home yourself, to open your heart to the golden light now present, as always, within your cupped hands.

About the Enlightenment Codes

The River Nile reveals the silhouette of a pregnant woman with nourishing breasts, carrying her baby. Adorning both banks along the river, the Creational Nile Temples have positioned themselves both within and outside the pregnant womb. This sacred architecture reveals the structure of the Cosmic Axis, the staircase to heaven, bringing us home again.

The sequence of the temples follows the four quarters of the moon cycle. This sequence allows our divine seed of life to blossom in its full, divine potential. The solar and lunar essences initiate us in numerous initiations, shedding light on our Unseen eternal Divine Essence. They allow us to experience life from our I Am Presence.

By travelling spherically through space and time, the deities, using portals and Stargates, lead us through the most primordial initiations. These predate even Egyptian, Atlantic, and sometimes even Lemurian times. With Isis as our Divine Mother, we shape and sculpt our Light Body into a Divine Light Being. We plough through Inner Earth, the Creational Nile Temples, the higher dimensions around the Earth, and multitudes of stellar constellations and Cosmic Birthing Temples. To remember our Divine Cosmic Creational Mothers of Existence, we stretch our consciousness far beyond our known Cosmic Womb.

Birthing oneself in the Light of Amun Ra, the Supreme God, fulfils the purpose of the Enlightenment Codes. The Light Being of the Nile Temple Valley is a Cosmic Midwife aiding us in this process: understanding that Divine Love permeates the Cosmic Womb. It runs like a thread through the initiations. A Foundational Desire for Life thrives within us. All Light Beings desire that we show our divine potential. They ask us to birth ourselves in the Divine Light and to shine upon them our Heart Light.

Enlightenment Codes Light Tablet

Thoth Hermes Trismegistus and the Light Beings of Venus Light Path have brought forward this Light Tablet in co-Creation with Star Consciousness. Star Consciousness has midwifed the Earth in this current incarnation. It has always been present throughout Earth's existence. At certain times it has been present with luminous intensity. At other times, it has been at a further distance. For example, when the Earth went through the dark night of her soul.

Star Consciousness seeded the Earth with these Enlightenment Codes so that when the time was right, these codes could again emerge, re-align, and activate the Earth as a Star Consciousness into the cosmic grid. Thus, the Earth emerged out of her exile. Time had slowed. Dimensions became denser. Energies vibrated at lower frequencies. During these thousands of years, the energies of the Divine Heart were barely tangible. Throughout history, humanity has tried to live up to these Enlightenment Codes. But the time was not right. We never truly succeeded.

At present, we enter the Cosmic Day and the Aquarian Age.

It is time.

In this Light Tablet, Earth reconnects with her cosmic counterparts to unfold within all her seeds, to birth them from the Unseen exile into the Seen. As she undergoes this process, so do we. As Light Beings we move from our Unseen into our Seen divine potentials, preparing the way for ascension for both of us. You will be guided on a sacred path through Creation to rekindle *your Eternal Bliss, your Foundational Desire for Life, your divine spark, your Divine Love.*

This Light Tablet, multilayered and multidimensional, enlightens the ascension processes of the Cosmos. This is Earth's ascension process, and our own ascension path towards our I Am Presence. Earth's Light Body is being submitted to a transmutation process of disintegrating the old Light Body and transitioning towards her new Star Blueprint. The Light Body of the Ancient Earth is gradually disintegrating. Meanwhile, she connects with her new soul incarnation in a different divine verse. We travel Earth's inner layers and stretch into the outer, etheric structures, in our Cosmos and the Creational Worlds beyond the known.

The alignment of the temples and the pyramids plays a vital part in activating the temple seeds. The latter embark on their unfolding journeys. Thus, in full bloom, they mirror their cosmic counterparts. By doing so, they activate Star Consciousness for you and the Earth. They fulfil the Hermetic Principle of *As Within, So Without. As Above, So Below,*[5] completing her ascension.

The Egyptian Gods coronated with a Sun Disc or Moon Disc will initiate you as a Creator into the Seen and the Unseen. Amun Ra depicts the sun and moon essences as the passageways for the unborn seeds to unfold their divine potential, their Divine Heart Light, and their I Am Presence. If you choose, they ignite within.

On a planetary level, the bandwidth of all alignments reaches all the individual temples. These all merge into One Temple body. On the mi-

---

5 Emerald Tablets of Thoth Hermes Trismegistus

crolevels in our body, they restructure us on molecular and macrolevels. They unite all our parallel soul incarnations into our heart. They realign us with Source. As human beings, we merge and consecrate our divine feminine and divine masculine energies into One Pillar of Light.[6] In our heart, our central sphere, where All That We Are resides, we ignite our Golden Diamond Heart, the primal expression of our *divine spark*.

All the deities and temple Light Beings,[7] those who guide you on our journey, anchor their primaeval essence and original cosmic codes into the akashic records. They ask human consciousness to free them from the past modes of perceiving and depriving them of their true Divine Essence.

During this sacred journey, the Divine Light Beings initiate you to access the nucleus of a soul, its prime expression, one's own Heart Light. When we access the nucleus, we let go of all the various manifestations to which we adhere. We no longer need to hold on to anything beyond ourselves. We must release ourselves and reside only in our Divine Heart. It is the Divine Heart that liberates us to be in the I Am Presence, to embody the divine.

About the Path of the Venus Light

The Light Beings of Venus Light Path are Creational. They are the first emanations of Source and co-create with Source to manifest the Source Codes. Situated at the threshold of source consciousness, in the vesica piscis to All That Is, these Creational Light Beings bring All That Is into manifestation. As weavers of worlds, they weave the Source Codes into matter of all density levels. To accomplish this, they use prima mater essences such as sacred geometry, vibration, liquid light, ether, plasma, crystalline light, colour, and life force. As a result, on cosmological and quantum levels they create blueprints infinitely

---

6 A Pillar of Light is the Central Axis of our toroid. It represents also the microlevel of the Axis Mundi, the place where all codes are rendered at the end of our incarnation.

7 Every temple, pyramid, menhir, dolmen, in short, every sacred place as a physical expression on the three-dimensional Earth plane, is animated by a soul, a spirit. In the case of the Egyptian temples, we call them Temple Light Beings: the souls animating the temple.

foreseeing multiverses and universes. On a cellular level they create humans, animals, plants, and microorganisms. These cosmic sages contain the wisdom of all blueprints on which Creation is based.

The essence of Venus Light comprises various colours and vibrations: blue, rose, yellow, and white. Magically, these are the same colour essences belonging to the sacred heart of Yeshua and Mary Magdalene. They, as universal avatars, carry the codes of Creation within them.

As cosmic midwives, the Venus Light Beings midwife all seeds of life dwelling within source consciousness. They find themselves within our Cosmos and beyond. Within our Cosmos, they envelop our Cosmic Womb. Their essence also resides within the various segments on the level of the etheric fabric, for they are weavers of existence.

They create harmonic resonance. Even more so, they *are* harmonic resonance. They carry this divine potential within their beings. With this, they bring all that has been created back to this frequency. The Earth has suffered much during the last tens of thousands of years. This has weakened her frequencies. The Venus Light's mission is to lift the Earth back into harmonic resonance, to interconnect her with higher dimensional vibrations. This cosmic harmonic grid will include all of Earth's inhabitants, if they wish. As soon as our cosmological environment restores its original high-frequency state, it projects that state into the solar system, the galaxy, and beyond. As a result, a high-frequency environment thriving on harmonic resonance gives us the chance to reincarnate into our divinity, as we did in ancient Lemuria.

At present, we depend mainly on the opening of certain portals. These provide us with cosmological information at specific times. Once the Venus Light lifts the Earth back into the higher vibrational tones, though, we will find ourselves in a solid gridwork. It is more crystalline, through which an enormous amount of information exchange occurs within the celestial bodies of a higher vibrational order. It is a quantum update for Earth, for it will receive a constant influx of necessary light codes.

Through the Venus Light, our stability, solidity, and light frequency increase substantially. For the higher Light Beings, this would result in the Earth becoming again a place where they, too, could reside in their vibration. Divine love and compassion would then expand exponentially. Now the vibrational values are too low, the energy, still too dense.

In essence, harmonic resonance offers a deep connection on all levels in Inner Earth: between temples, Light Beings, humans, plants, and animals. It deepens everything on Earth while connected with the Temple of Love at Earth's core.

When everything returns into harmonic resonance, an energetic dilation occurs. The high-frequency permanent *state of being* awakens the Divine Light. The Earth and all who inhabit her transmute into Divine Love and ascend. The latter projects on the cosmic scale.

The Light Beings of the Venus Light Path show themselves as pure, pristine, ethereal, silk-veiled, luminous, loving, and factual. Because they are androgenic and whole, they carry within themselves the realised divine masculine and feminine natures. While these two energies are in balance, they foresee Divine Creations that match the highest levels of Divine Love. They remind us that we carry our divine seed of life within us. All that we are and all that we require resides in our seed of life.

Their mission is to accompany all seeds of life in this Cosmos birthed by the Cosmic Creational Mothers of Existence. The Light Beings of the Venus Light Path are the divine mothers who – with diligence, love, and nurture – balance us and, where needed, meticulously reweave the etheric fabric. Most of all, they desire to see us bloom into our full potential. They are ambassadors for developing our divine potential by harmonic resonance. Through co-Creation with all moon and sun grids throughout the Cosmos, they assist all seeds of life in expressing their Unseen essence and emanating their Divine Heart Light.

By unfolding our divine potential, we connect with All That Is. We experience life through our I Am Presence. We then embody the Hermetic Principle: *As Within, So Without. As Above, So Below.* They assist us in becoming All That Is, the I Am That I Am, in becoming Creation. They remember us as our Divine Creators, and only we can unfold ourselves into our full potential.

The Venus Light Beings will guide you in this sacred journey through Creation to unfold your essence and divine potential. They will assist you in unveiling your seed of life and reigniting your divine spark so that the end and the beginning meet, and the circle is complete. For at the beginning, you entered this Cosmos as a divine spark within your seed of life. That is the state in which you will leave this cosmic realm. You will journey through Creation with them. They will show you the Master Blueprint of how to complete Cosmic Ascension. And so it is.

In Eternal Bliss.

COSMOGONY

Part I

The Creation of Worlds

Unseen Creational Forces

"Now you will always remember me,"
Cosmos Light Being says,
"for we are One. You are me. I am you."

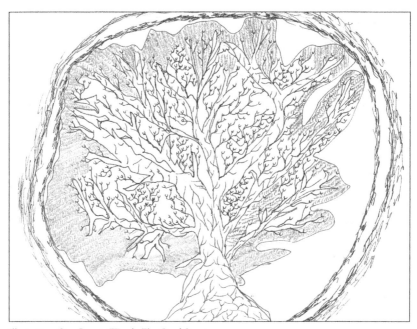

Illustration: Our Cosmic Womb. The Coral Structure.

Venus Light Path

Deep in your subconscious, this memory wades like a flame asking to be rekindled. Here the remembrance lies of our Cosmos: a womb, a birth temple we have all resided within since time immemorial. In this Cosmic Womb, spherical in its sacred geometry, impalpable energies have developed from primaeval energy. Some walk the path of light and others the path of shadow. Together, they are divinely loved by the Light Being animating our Cosmos.

Multidimensional, Cosmos resembles a seed of life dwelling in a Cosmic Womb surrounded by a membrane. This membrane provides a stationary phase in the Creation process. It is filled with etheric liquid light containing two sources of energy: in the upper part, Creational blue-essence light, in the lower, Creational yellow-essence light. We will refer to them as the Venus Light.

The Venus Light is the essence emitted by the Creational Light Beings. They sit at the throne of God. Established there, they weave worlds into existence. These Venus Light Beings are cosmic midwives. In the membrane enfolding the Cosmic Womb, the yellow-essence light provides fertile soil, a favourable environment for divine seeds of lives to unfold from within. As a divine seed of life, you too have travelled this same journey. This tale is engraved deep within your soul.

When you enter our Cosmos and abide for a limited time in this membrane, these rich, yellow waters of liquid light – the golden essence of your seed of life or divine spark – become attuned to our Cosmos. Your vibrational information attunes to the data resonance of our Cosmos. As this exchange of vibrational codes takes place, your divine seed of life begins its unfolding journey to its full potential. It activates its blooming process well and gently. It develops and prepares itself in a rhythm unique to your divine seed of life.

Once your divine seed of life feels the preparatory phase is complete, the blue Venus Light creates electroactivity and powerful vortices. With electrical impulses, the blue Venus Light opens the dimensional space of the yellow Venus Light around your divine seed of life. This allows it to emerge. This envelops it with additional codes of the blueprint it needs to blossom to its full potential. A first DNA ladder of white light emerges. It draws the blueprint of your primaeval Central Axis. This electric-activity then unlocks multidimensional space within the yellow-essence light. It paves the way to arise from this yellow Venus Light.

Once the primordial Central Axis develops and your seed of life acquires the right vibrational attuning for life in our Cosmos, the Light Beings of the Venus Light raise you from this yellow Venus Light.

Love permeates All That Is. On its way to its full completion, your seed of life enjoys the guidance of the Creational Angels. They animate the Venus energy to the bottom of the spherical geometry. Here the incarnational journey in our Cosmos begins. Accompanied by a sphere of yellow-blue light, you undergo an alchemical process. It manifests as an emerald field. This impulse further prepares your seed of life to descend into the Cosmos. Primaeval angels such as Thoth welcome you. And so you leave the membrane and enter the Cosmic Womb itself.

Honeybee Energy

The structure of the Cosmic Womb is a coral fan with a trunk and a grid of many branches. These bask in liquid light. Here, the energy of honeybees permeates all levels. Honeybee energy radiates an unconscious inner drive to reach full awakening and full bloom. Therefore, the intense activity present in the Cosmic Womb revolves around preparing for the blossoming, fulfilment, and full completion of the Cosmos Light Being.[8]

In the manner of any seed developing into a full-fledged fruit, the Cosmic Womb provides a Central Axis around which everything spherically grows in the shape of a toroid. Through whom this is constructed, will be elaborated later. The Cosmos develops in a fractal way from its Central Axis, at its core. This growth manifests itself in the manner of a coral fan.

When we travel through the trunk of the fan, we perceive carnelian and rose liquid light, imbuing and nourishing the whole structure. The divine seed of life is placed in the centre of the Central Axis. Here energies rotate increasingly, mimicking the movement of a potter's wheel: the energy of Khnum the Ram Head God. The divine seed of life rotates with it, and through this, fine white filaments emerge from its core essence. These rise upwards, and in its upwards journey, they mirror the texture, the light codes, and the core essence of the Cosmic Axis. They replicate within in its body.

---

8 The Light Being, the soul of our Cosmos, our Cosmic Womb.

The Cosmos Light Being says to you, "As Within, So Without. As Above, So Below. Once you incarnate into my vast womb, I want you to remember me, who I Am. I want you to know where you are, for souls can become forgotten, lost, dismembered." She keeps spinning, developing you and your filaments so that you fully reflect her. You are her. She is you. "Now you will always remember me," she says, "for we are One. You are me. I am you." You take it all in, every wave of vibration. You long for it to attune into your body to find your way back home.

You must remember.

Structured Crystalline Light

The divine seed of life is now contained at the root of the coral fan. Clear white-crystalline light illuminates it. The light radiates up through the trunk, and then throughout the Cosmos. The light's moving rays resemble resplendent sunbeams reverberating upwards from the depths of the ocean.

These crystalline rays of light create crystallisation that matches, holds, and dwells within all the dimensions present in this Cosmic Womb. While this crystalline light is prestructured for our Cosmos, specifically with sacred geometric patterns uniquely designed and composed, these prebuilt designs allow the divine seed of life to materialise into all the various densities of matter viable in our Cosmos.

Here, a blueprint develops to hold all the various levels of density and matter. Thus, the divine seed of life will have everything in its hands to realise its gifts. This Creation tale shows that we carry everything within us to bring ourselves to full fruition, to unfold and reveal our true selves, our divine potential, and ultimately our I Am Presence.

Once the divine seed of life has received the complete crystallised blueprint for embodying matter in all density levels, it rises through the trunk. The trunk resembles the Central Axis of a toroid field. The inner wall of the trunk contains all the information currently active in our Cosmos. The trunk represents the cosmic central processing unit, or rather the cosmic mainframe. When you touch it, you feel its multilayering, made of pastel-coloured plasma textures. You hear high-pitched, shrill sounds radiating from it. This plasma is multidimensional matter. It is moving, indicating that it constantly encodes what is unfolding in the Cosmos. Everything occurring in our Cosmos - in any multiverse, universe, galaxy, star, planet, or Moon - is immediately inscribed on this inner wall. This cosmic inner wall is the cosmic scroll on which Thoth and Seshat inscribe your soul's journey. As the divine seed of life rises before the inner wall of the trunk, the pastel-coloured textures become a matrix of coded lines. They form a web throughout the trunk. They encode the divine seed of life as it moves upwards. Thus, imprinting takes place with the most current information existent in our Cosmos.

The structured crystalline light races through the filaments of this matrix. The light encodes this memory deep within your soul. You witness the first imprint your new-born soul receives. It contains the blueprint of your unique energy signature. You have received the Cosmos star map, the Master Blueprint which you must follow when you incarnate here. Cosmos Light Being says, "I imprint this on you because I love you, as I love all the divine seeds of life incarnated in my womb. I am your Divine Mother. You know that I am with you always, wherever you are. The structured crystalline light further develops the unique blueprint of your seed of life, to provide the major components of Creation and to allow the vibration to self-sustain through prestructured geometry unique to this Cosmos."

With these heartfelt words, she leads you up through the coral trunk. You float, feeling the ethereal essence of Divine Love flowing through your ethereal veins. You observe the numerous coral branches along the trunk through which you are travelling. Within the wall of the coral trunk, you are the blueprint of all energies already living in the Cosmic Womb.

The Light Being of the Cosmos withholds nothing. She wants the divine seed of life to reflect her. A vibrational match between each divine seed of life and the Cosmos is required to evolve at the same pace, side by side. This level of equality is beautiful. It offers a new perspective of love and nurturing by all the Creational Light Beings involved in our soul journey.

You continue to ascend until you find your destination. Through osmosis, you leave the trunk to incarnate on the branch where you begin your embodiment journey in matter. You position yourself in our Cosmos: embedding and developing the first blueprint of white horizontal and vertical strings into a spherical sacred geometry. Cells divide for a new beginning.

Also here, in the Cosmic Womb, the Venus Light remains at your side. It supports your unfolding from within, throughout your entire soul journey.

Alpha α and the Omega Ω

This cosmogony involves an Omega Ω and an Alpha α dynamic. The coral fan is the Omega Ω yearning to fully unfold. The seed of life is the Alpha α energy fundamental to achieving this bloom. The coral blooms from within. Her branches, housing all the souls incarnated in our Cosmos, are increasingly occupying more space. This growth happens fractally, like a tree, from the core to the branches outwards, where the seed of life adheres. During the attachment process, the seed of life nourishes itself with the rose-essence light of love infusing the coral-branched matrix. Within the coral's sanctum, the rose-essence light of love foresees sustenance. The manifestation of universes, galaxies, and all antimatter can now occur. The seed of life unfolds until the entire essence within blossoms into the desire of the Omega Ω to manifest her full potential. When the crystalline energies reach into the waters of Venus, the seeds of life[9] are gifted with the choice to respond. Creation emerges from a primordial desire to exist. Choice is the premise of existence.

Choice is the basis of existence. When you forget our Creation tale, you also forget we once chose to exist. When you relinquish your sov-

---

9 The divine spark is the golden light animating a soul. The seed of life is a further development into a manifest form of the divine spark.

ereign right to choose, all your divine nature is reduced to dormant potential veiled deep within your subconscious. During eons, many of us have lost this primordial vitality and truthfulness about our divine nature: that once we chose to exist, we have the choice to be the Creators of our existence at any given moment. When we regain this momentum, we reverberate back to the Creation of our seed of life. We experience the choice we made at one time: Our Foundational Desire for Life. When we are in touch with the Divine Love for existence, we can then rekindle our slumbering inner flame and our birth right.

As you journey through the sacred grounds of Mother Earth, as you wade through the etheric tissue of her multidimensional sacred sites, we, the Creational Light Beings, invite you to revisit all choices returned to you. We inspire you to remember and to pursue your heart. You can choose to rekindle your divine spark, to rekindle your Foundational Desire for Life, to rekindle what you originally embodied in the Cosmic Womb's membrane. We Creational Light Beings guide you into the silence of your I Am Presence.

Cosmic Moon Cycles
The Cosmological Creational Process

You embody your Heart Light and have passed the initiation into being a Creator.

The Enlightenment Codes thrive on a cosmological foundation. They are emanations of Source Codes. They embody the birth process of the divine potential of All That Is. The Creational Nile Temples allow these Enlightenment Codes to flow through their essence. There, they restore and embody their divine potential. From this alignment, they initiate all who co-create with them into Oneness.

The First Quadrant: New Moon, the waxing crescent up to first quarter.

The Unseen, Amun, is where all seeds of life reside and stir in the unconscious to be Seen. This quadrant symbolises the journey out of the darkness, the unconscious, the beyond, and the taking of first steps into the Light. A seed of life embarking on this journey of enlightenment carries within it all the unconscious wisdom. A seed of life leaves with a sense of completeness, fulfilment, and Oneness. During the journey, the seed of life learns to balance itself between the different worlds and stay close to itself. The seed of life is accompanied by the Moon's and Sun's energies. These energies, as two spheres in a vesica piscis formation, will bring the seed of life to fruition. A seed of life embarking on this journey may be a primary divine spark. Or it may be a seed of a primary divine spark, one of its many soul extensions. The seed may also signify an incarnation or a life journey. The New Moon and the first quarter embody new beginnings, a new cycle of being born.

The Second Quadrant: First quarter, up to waxing gibbous, Full Moon.

As the seed embodies more and more light, it feels nourished and unfolds its petals to blossom entirely. It is essential now that it remains firmly anchored in its core and remains true to the unique codes of its divine spark. When a seed goes through this process in a centred manner, it reaches culmination and embodies the Sun, Ra, in the heart. At Full Moon, when the lunar and solar energies merge in the heart and transform it into a heart gate, the seed comes into full bloom. The seed has embodied its feminine and masculine energies. As they, too, merge, the seed itself becomes the birth canal. The Creator has awakened within. When the birth process completes, the Sun's and Moon's spheres merge into one another as One Sphere. Each seed, each animated life, is a carrier of the divine spark. Thus, you also birth yourself into Oneness. You unlock your full potential.

In the Full Moon phase, you merge with the Sun and the Moon. You become the gateway through which Creations manifest themselves. You become the Creator. You manifest yourself and your Creations. While you embody your Heart Light, you have passed the initiation into becoming a Creator. In this process of embodying your Heart Light, both Amun and Ra co-create with the Cosmic moon energy. Amun and Ra allow the most profound secrets residing within you – your true gifts, your divine potential – to unveil themselves and emerge. You have come into full bloom. You have reached the pinnacle of this cycle. This is the ascension process toward budding your seed of life. You find its result in Full Moon.

The Third Quadrant: Full Moon, waning crescent, the third quarter.

Throughout the waning phase, you feel fulfilled, saturated. You turn more and more back to the inner world rather than the manifest. You gradually give retreat to your Light into the unconscious realms. You de-manifest. You allow your Unseen side to come more to the forefront. You are in a constant birthing process of what you find in the Unseen. You bring what you find to the Seen.

The birthing process is a constant process of ascension, descension. Both processes allow you to unveil your highest potential. The third quarter reveals embodying the middle line between the Seen and Unseen, the hidden space in between. In this in-between space reside all seeds awaiting enlightenment and still needing to emerge.

From the third quarter onwards to the New Moon, a new process starts. The new process connects to these unborn seeds residing within you. Here we listen to their whispers. Through listening, we understand which divine potential wants to emerge at the New Moon's beginning. The more you evolve in your journey from Full Moon to New Moon, the more the enlightened seeds that came into fruition install themselves within yourself on deeper levels. They form a foundation of fully blossomed seeds. They have unfurled into the unfolded petals representing a base, they encircle you. As you unveil more and more of your divine potential, you allow your *Pillar of Light* to emerge.

Your *Pillar of Light* awaits in the centre of the moon cycle. The Sun nourishes you to unfold each petal residing within you so that your *Pillar of Light emerges*. This moon cycle in the Creational Nile Temples is devoted to unfolding all petals. You unfold your Thousand Petal

Lotus so that your *Pillar of Light will emerge:* the Scroll of Maat,[10] your Scroll of Truth. The full blossoming of your divine potential is the only thing your soul desires. The Moon in co-Creation with the Sun enlightens every phase. Co-Creation nourishes each seed of life emerging and unfolding its divine potential.

The Fourth Quadrant: third quarter, waning crescent, New Moon

The I Am Presence and the eternal soul reign in the fourth quarter. For the dark side, the Unseen is also the Cosmos and all beyond. The seed evolves back into the Unseen. The Unseen holds all secrets, wisdom, and knowledge we cannot see but eternally feel stirring within our unconscious.

From there, when we have ignited the I Am Presence, a new beginning commences. This happens when the Cosmic Axis Mundi dissolves and transmutes, and the *Cosmic Pillar of Light*[11] emerges. We all then evolve together into a new beginning. The moon cycle is devoted to growth and enlightenment in individual ascension on our own Jacob's Ladder and Cosmic Ascension.[12]

Both an ascension and a descension process can take place in the moon cycle, from waxing to waning. Every Creational Nile Temple goes through the moon cycle. Every individual goes through the moon cycle. Also, the entire Nile Valley as One Temple body goes through this moon cycle. This moon cycle is intrinsic to the Cosmos on many levels where evolution is required. The moon cycle has numerous levels of deepening. As you undergo the cycle, you descend more and more back into your One divine spark.[13] The moon cycle spirals you down into her and your centre, where you find your Cosmic Ascension and your *Pillar of Light* emerges.

---

10 Maat or Ma'at the ancient Egyptian concepts of truth, balance, order, harmony, law, morality, and justice. Maat was also the Egyptian Goddess carrying the ostrich feather. She embodies these concepts. It was said she governed the stars, seasons, and the actions of mortals and the deities who had brought order from chaos at the moment of Creation.
11 The transmutation of the Axis Mundi allows the Cosmic Pillar of Light to emerge. The manifested worlds that came into being will dissolve and transmute.
12 Cosmic Ascension leads us through the Cosmic Axis, the Axis Mundi, to achieve complete ascension. Here we do not limit ourselves to merely ascending through different dimensional levels. Cosmic Ascension can be experienced in a physical way, where one is no longer incarnating in the Cosmic Womb or as an attained higher state of being, a state of enlightenment.
13 The One divine spark is the first animated form, a consciousness that can procreate itself multidimensionally into numerous divine sparks, each leading a different form of incarnation in a different level of density. When coming into Oneness, we all return home to our One divine spark.

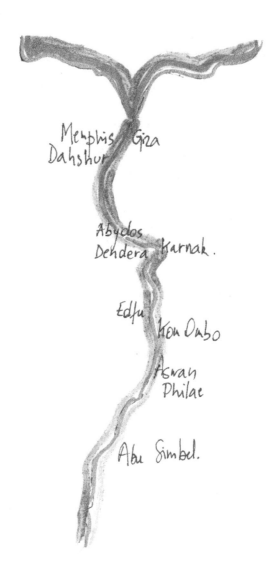

Map of The Creational Nile Temples.

Part I

New Young Moon

I.1 Temple of the Cosmic Moon Overture, Dahshur

Illustration: Dahshur Pyramid.

Arrival of Cosmic Moon Midwifery Forces

Each New Moon, as a crone, offers universal moon codes
to allow the Earth to alchemise it into its unique soul light.

The Light Beings of the Dahshur Pyramids welcome you by rolling
out a path of bright rose light of love for you. They already know you
are here to initiate the Enlightenment Codes for Cosmic Ascension.
You are walking this path with all the Divine Light Beings surrounding you. As you move steadily on this path of love, you feel a bright
star in the sky, shining its light upon you. This light envelops you in
a cylindrical column of light. Here you are, bathed in this starlight.

Starlight's light codes enfold and prepare you for your sacred journey through Creation.

You turn your attention to the pyramids, teeming with activity. And while you are enveloped in this column of light, a larger circle of white light emerges. It luminously bathes all three pyramids. This Circle of Light carries the same starlight. It is an emanation of your own Circle of Light. You are radiating it.

You connect to these triad pyramids through the Circle of Light. Intuitively the middle one attracts you: the White Pyramid. The starlight descends. The starlight creates a toroid field around all three pyramids. The White Pyramid towers at its centre. The emergence of the toroid field creates a living organism of consciousness, a light being of its own, the newly awakened Light Being of Dahshur.

In principle, a physical temple is a physical[14] dwelling for a light being animating it. Each temple maintains a constant within the higher dimensions. When the soul conduit between the higher dimensions and the physical sanctuary is damaged, a sanctuary loses its spiritual force. This has happened in many sacred places around the world. In this event, the temple is unable to fulfil its soul mission on the earthly plane. This pattern is very much the same for human beings. When we align with our multidimensional soul matrix, we express ourselves as determined by our divine potential.

You create with the help of Sothis' Star. You do not understand why this is happening. You are a sacred witness. You allow that which will be created to be given life. In surrendering to the divine, you are creating. Yes, you are a pure channel of the divine. Now, you see an energy exchange happening between the White, the Black, and the Red Pyramids, aligning them. A symbol of eternity is gradually installing itself, with the White Pyramid as its centre. It is reconnecting the triad in eternity. You feel you can detach from this white Circle of Light. You walk around in this sacred field. The energetic imprint now remains stable. It no longer moves with you. You know that Creation has happened.

---

14 Physicality expresses itself in various forms of density. Sometimes, the material, the bricks, are not present anymore. The etheric blueprint of the sacred site, however, still is. This etheric blueprint level of material density can also be considered as a physical dwelling, but in a more etheric form.

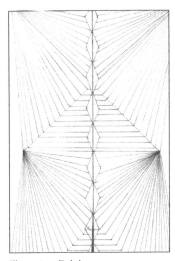

Illustration: Dahshur.
Pyramid Alignment with its
Multidimensional Temples.

As you observe the entire process, the Circle of Light develops white light walls in the form of a cone. Within this structure, you see preformed crystalline structures emerging in the form of a honeybee grid. As this sacred geometry expands, descends, and truly assumes its entire space, you also feel the entire pyramid area deepening into the Inner Earth. The structures connect with their Inner Earth temple, their sacred multidimensional temples. Remarkably, as they deepen, they move as One. They unite as One and thus come into Oneness. As they attune to one another, you feel an enigmatic presence deep within the core of the Earth. A cosmic summoning of three Cosmic Creational Mothers of Existence, far beyond our solar system. A call to awakening has just been sent out as this triad has come into Oneness.

This Cosmic Moon Grid awakens its ancient Earth *Moon Gate.* It has been dormant for eons. Here in this sacred space in Dahshur, between these three pyramids, a vortex emerges, swirling and spinning like an upwards-facing cone. Interlocking rings form, creating a concentric field ever enlarging until it includes the entire Nile Valley. The field answers the call to re-ignite its energy essence to re-create with the trinity of all existence. The trinity of pyramids of Dahshur awakes the consciousness in the Earth. In our collective unconscious they awaken the Cosmic Creational Mothers of Existence.

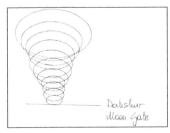

Illustration: Dahshur. Moon Gate.

The Cosmic Creational Mothers of Existence have called upon this Cosmic Moon Grid to become operational again so that the Cosmic moon essence, as midwife, brings the Codes of Enlightenment. Woven through the cords of eternity, the memory, or energetic imprint of these hidden structures – the Earth *Moon Gate*, the Cosmic Moon Grid, and the three Cosmic Creational Mothers of Existence – has been ever present. They wanted only to be awakened for the Aquarian Age, to bring us back to a level of consciousness so deep that it will allow us to attune to our souls and our divine selves again, to become who we really are, now, here on Earth: Divine Creators, Universal Solar Angels of Light.

Orion's Transmutational Energies

Illustration: Dahshur.
13th Pointed Black Star of Orion.

The blue moon energy emanating from the Cosmic Moon Grid carries the energy signature of Orion.

They are known for merging the above and below, the within and without. Folding existence, until dimensional space narrows, and energy intensifies and becomes high frequency to eventually transmute. We find these energies mainly in environments prepared for transmutation.

The hourglass, as the stellar structure of Orion, can be pictured as two triangles with the two tops above one another. If you project the process of transmutation onto this sacred geometry, you fold the top pyramid onto the bottom one, and you get one, single triangle. When you continue the process of condensing the energy by folding one corner of this triangle onto the other, decreasing shape and space, a Black Star with twelve points manifests, generated by an additional, thirteenth, circumventing point. This thirteenth point of the Black Star turns around so rapidly that the energy field fractures, and all fractured energy particles expand forcefully and dissolve into a new level of density, or into light.

Prerequisite for Cosmic Ascension

Illustration by Matt Nelson (Unsplash).

The Sacred Union of Cosmic Moon and Sun

This moon essence, which introduces itself, is not merely our Moon's energy but a composite energy of all moons in the entire Cosmos. It permeates through a cosmic grid of its own, with a different resonance and vibrational frequency than a Sun grid or any other grid. The Cosmic Moon Grid comprises several subgrids. The whole forms an intricate network of moons. These co-create and transmit energy from the planets and suns they connect with. Together, as a group consciousness, they form an overall toroid field.

Illustration: Dahsur.
Sacred Union of Solar and Moon Essence.

The Moon Gate installed in Dahshur resonates with this Cosmic Moon Grid. A Moon is a Sun extinguished of its solar essence and represents *the crone.*[15] The archetype of the Maiden, the Mother, and the Crone represents the evolution of celestial bodies. The triple-Goddess[16] principle translates into a planet, a Sun, and a Moon. As a planet, you go through all the processes to arrive at full fruition being a Sun. As of then, the Sun can choose to take a functional role as a Moon. The silvery moon essence is similar to the human ageing process, also becoming more greyish silver during this transition. In this phase, we embody all the codes of wisdom and take the role of nourishing and guiding.

This Cosmic Moon Grid interconnecting to many moons, resonates with the Moon Gate in Dahshur. Here the successive phases of the Moon are crucial in this triple-Goddess principle. A Moon embodies a distinct energy in each phase. At the New Moon, the birthing process begins. It is a cycle of nourishment. When a celestial body (here the Earth) moves through the moon cycle, the Full Moon completes this nourishment process. Upon completion of its nourishment cycle at Full Moon, the moon essence withdraws from the Earth. In the withdrawal process, the universal moon codes integrate into the Earth this Moon is assisting. By withdrawing, the Moon allows the Earth to be sovereign. The Earth imbibes these moon codes and discerns how it will integrate them on a unique soul level.

Subsequently, a new cycle starts with a new phase of emanation of codes. Each New Moon, as a crone, offers new light codes to allow the Earth to alchemise them into her unique soul light. The principle of the beginning and the end, the Alpha α and the Omega Ω, represents

---

15 The crone represents a collective unconscious primal archetype that conveys wisdom, inner knowing, and intuition. It guides us through life processes and going within to bring forth the light for transformation.

16 The Triple Goddess, these three archetypes are often described as the Maiden, the Mother, and the Crone, each symbolising a different phase in the female life cycle.

rebirth. A New Moon nourishes, gifts, and aids in birthing something new by offering light codes. The Sun also nourishes the Earth with light codes. The Moon carries within it the Alpha α and the Omega Ω principle because it provides the light codes, and once *all the codes are in,* it withdraws its light to allow seeds of life to flourish.

The vesica piscis of a Moon and Sun creates a birth canal wherein planetary consciousness, the Earth, births new light codes.

The Hermetic Principle behind the Sun and Moon Disc

You find yourself on a Circle of Light on the outline of the Moon Gate at Dahshur, with the Blue Moon Goddesses surrounding and accompanying you. They contemplate, their heads elegantly inclined downwards. The Circle of Light connects you, and every Goddess while they integrate and anchor your connection deep within the Earth into her Temple of Love. And while this moon cycle is anchoring itself deeper and deeper, the moon cycle widens more greatly on Earth's surface. Then it rotates in clockwise and counterclockwise directions, inducing a weaving process of rising light strings.

Simultaneously, a widening of the Moon Gate towards the Cosmos occurs, taking the form of a cauldron, inviting all moons connected to this Cosmic Moon Grid to bless the Earth and contribute their moon codes. As this moon cycle opens and forms a receptacle for all moon codes, the two vertical light strings intertwine and rise into the Cosmos. They culminate in a membrane. It resembles a cosmic, white sphere: the outline of the Cosmic Moon Grid. This grid is present in a distinct evolutionary part of the Cosmos where moons thrive. Thus, the spherical shape of the Cosmic Moon Grid does not follow the full spherical shape of our Cosmic Womb.

This moon cycle receives the universal moon codes as it interconnects with the two light strings rotating in alternating clockwise and counterclockwise directions in this Cosmic Moon Grid's membrane. As the universal moon codes funnel down through the light strings, a process of specification and recoding to Earth's unique energy signature occurs. We witness a cosmic download of universal moon codes predestined for the Nile Temple Body. These now-specific moon codes slowly approach the moon cycle and establish concentric energy circles. These widen the moon cycle's circumference even more. The moon cycle dilates with a sigh to receive these moon codes. From inside this moon cycle, a light chamber for alchemisation of moon and Earth codes emerges. Here all moon codes fuse further with Earth codes. This fusion moves through the entire Earth body to a predestined position within Earth's centre. All predestined positions interconnect and build a new-born Inner Earth-Moon Grid around the Inner Earth-Sun Disc in Earth's centre. This Inner Earth-Moon Grid around the Inner Earth-Sun Disc continuously aligns with the cosmic sky. When it is fully aligned, the Earth will ascend.

Each Moon belonging to its Cosmic Moon Grid connects to the planets and Sun in its respective galaxy. This intricate Cosmic Moon Grid system provides the Inner Earth-Sun Disc with information about cosmological changes. Thus, the Inner Earth-Sun Disc can evolve simultaneously with these changes. It can become more and more a reflection of the Cosmos. In other words, the Inner Earth-Sun Disc mirroring the cosmic sky reflects the Hermetic Principle: *As Within, So Without. As Above, So Below.* When the Earth completes this reflection, this Hermetic Principle can come into existence. The Earth then shifts her timeline from planet to star.

As the Inner Earth-Moon Grid receives this cosmological information, it rotates like a safe lock and attunes the Inner Earth-Sun Disc to cosmological coordinates of all multidimensional layers of the Cosmos. The Inner Earth-Sun Disc is complex. It is a complete representation of the Cosmic Womb. According to the conveyed cosmic moon codes, each Inner Earth-Sun Disc movement brings about tremendous changes within the Earth. The inner Earth dimensions shift. Earthquakes occur. Most do not even disturb Earth's surface. While on Earth's surface, everyday life goes on and on, the Earth's body undergoes constant changes. These simultaneously occur in the Cosmos. The energetic or vibrational effects are deeply felt on Earth's surface, though. We become aligned with the Cosmos itself. More important, if we choose to align with this consciously, we can achieve Cosmic Ascension on Earth.

When you align with the changes in the deep inner layers of Inner Earth, you align with the Cosmic Womb. The total energy of the Cosmic Womb is present within the body of our Earth. When we travel in Inner Earth, we travel the Cosmos. Consequently, living here on Earth offers us Cosmic Ascension if only we have eyes to see. For example, if we would like to travel to other universes, divine universes in the Cosmic Womb, we first find a corresponding representation within the Earth. This representation reflects the Hermetic Principle. Thoth asks us to bring our attention to the Earth body and the Sun Disc present there. He guides our attention to the Inner Earth-Moon Grid that aligns to Earth's South Pole or the lower point of Earth's Central Axis. The lower part of the Inner Earth-Moon Grid stretches downwards, forming a downwards cone within Earth's southern region. Its shape is similar to a spinning top. It influences the shift of the Earth Axis. The Earth follows the movements of the Cosmic Moon Grid, and cosmological codes nourish that grid.

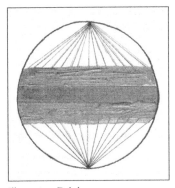

Illustration: Dahshur.
The Inner Earth-Moon Grid and Earth-Sun Disc.

When you bring your attention to the upper part of the Inner Earth-Moon Grid, you find it also has a spinning top toward the north. The ensemble forms a double conic shape. The Inner Earth-Moon Grid around the Earth-Sun Disc represents an alchemisation chamber where the Inner Earth-Sun Disc becomes aligned with the Cosmos.

This double conic shape within the Earth is the spinning top. It constantly aligns the Earth to the Cosmic Moon Grid. This alignment follows cosmic moon phases. The Moon ignites all moon phases within the Earth. Each moon cycle encompassing these eight phases brings down new moon codes within the Earth and her Inner Sun Disc.

This cycle deepens the Cosmic Moon Grid codes within the Earth and aligns her Inner Sun Disc with the whole of the Cosmos. Accordingly, cosmic moons are aiding the Earth to fulfil the Hermetic Principle.

This is the prerequisite for Cosmic Ascension to solar consciousness.

Thoth Hermes Trismegistus is known as the deity with a Sun Disc and a Moon Disc. He has these double features. We also know Sothis as a Goddess connected to the stars, but also to the Moon. Khonsu is also known as a Moon God. Thoth will guide you in initiating the moon and sun essences within yourself. This is what Amun Ra encompasses, the Seen and the Unseen. Thoth holds the knowledge of the Hermetic Principles and understands the prerequisites for ascension to occur. He knows we will obtain Cosmic Ascension when we work with both sun energy and moon energy.

New Moon, Harbinger of Cosmic Ascension

As the New Moon makes its appearance in Egypt's sanctum, a silvery robe of maternal and mystical energy engulfs the area. The Cosmic Moon Grid is invoked because the time has come for the Earth to rekindle her seeds. The Cosmic Moon Grid takes the form of a cone made of silvery concentric rings. These become wider and wider as they approach the Earth. The Cosmic Moon Grid's essence penetrates in light strings into the area of the pyramids of Dahshur. The rings themselves, though, encompass the entire spherical surface of the Earth. These rings emanate an energy awakening all temple seeds on Earth and within Earth's soils and waters. The light strings penetrating Dahshur carry within themselves the imprint of awakening. Awakening descends in the energetic form of a flower. The flower's petals are unfolding. From Amun to Ra, this blueprint signals the unveiling process from Unseen to Seen. The Moon translates this same process into the four phases from a New Moon to a Full Moon. As the energies holding this blueprint descend, all Egyptian temples encode this blueprint for the temple seed. Each temple seed, housed safely within the Holy of Holies by past temple builders, now receives the blueprint upon which it can further blossom. Ancient times return in even more powerful forms. The temples will unfold their full potentials in unseen ways. In the process, they will receive the new codes of the Aquarian Age. You can see that unfolding in Egypt, around the Nile delta and the river itself. New temple seeds manifest in the depths, even where there are no physical temple remnants. The call of the Cosmic Moon Grid has awakened them. The concentric rings encompassing the Earth are rekindling all Earth temple seeds. These seeds receive the signal of what is happening in Egypt but have yet to be activated themselves. They go through only a short activation process. No initiation process, though, occurs yet.

Meanwhile, as this energy steadily descends and the moon codes interleave their ways into the temples, they integrate the Nile River into their energy fields. A deepening process even more profound occurs. The Nile waters surrender and open entirely. They allow the codes of the Axis Mundi to reemerge from the depths. As a mirror of the Axis Mundi, the Nile River takes over its codes and translates and mirrors the ascension process into the Earth of the Cosmic Axis. This Cosmic Ascension occurs when the Axis Mundi transmutes and allows its inner Cosmic *Pillar of Light* to emerge and express itself fully. Through this energetic transfer of the Axis Mundi codes into the Nile River, the Earth can resonate with the ascension evolution of the Cosmos and contribute to it. Cosmic Day finally dawns.

Blue Moon Heart Gate Initiation

The Red, the White, and the Black Pyramids are now aligned with one another. They continue fusing their energies. They slide into one another to become One Pyramid. This One pyramid carries the golden-yellow light around its apex, Sothis Starlight. As you align with this One Pyramid, you behold a portal in the form of a keyhole. The portal gives you access to all three pyramids at once. The One Pyramid indicates it will align you with its apex.

You now enter the portal. You behold three separate blue-light gates. Each represents a pyramid. As you pass through the three light gates, a horizon of bright-blue liquid light appears. You take in an infinite, vast path of liquid blue light. You feel an invitation to walk this path. You step into the blue liquid light waters. With every step you take, you slide more and more into liquid light. Soon you are already knee deep.

In the far distance, you perceive the Sothis Starlight guiding you. This Starlight makes you feel cherished, nurtured, and cared for. Your body is now fully immersed in liquid blue light. You still perceive the Sothis Starlight shimmering.

Even as it becomes more challenging, you continue walking. As if you need to force your way through thick layers of plasmic fluids, you feel resistance when moving your body. You come to know that these plasmic layers of liquid light represent your old energies. These energies crystallised and were extracted from your body. They hindered you from effortlessly birthing yourself through this blue-moon energy. The crystallised energies form a cluster positioned right before you. Sothis reaches out to you and says, "Reach out your hands towards this cluster and hold it. Feel its meaning and how it has served you in the past. Also feel your inner guidance, saying it is now time to move on. Honour this cluster of energy for having assisted you in this lifetime and for its care and nurture. Please, raise your arms and allow the cluster to infuse itself with my Starlight."

You witness the cluster dissolving into liquid blue light. You have cleared your path. You reply to Sothis, "Thank you for being my guide and friend on this journey." As you utter these words, you feel her energy permeating your body. She answers, "My light is with you. My light is within you. I will be by your side every step of the way."

As you continue to walk, the base of this liquid lake of light descends even more. You walk into your inner depths, your inner fears. The bottom steepens downwards. You can no longer walk. You slide inwards into your abyss. You find yourself in a pit of pitch-black water far from the surface. The Starlight rays are merely visible. You hear only your heartbeat. Light-blue water creatures appear in increasing numbers. Curious, they approach you. Their bodies resemble pale-blue floating veils swaying in the liquid-light water. You hear your heartbeat. You hear them whispering to you. They speak a language you do not understand. As these water creatures float, circling around you, they mutter words. Their sounds penetrate you.

The language they speak is not from this planet. As you listen to the whispered words, you feel your etheric body growing larger, taller, stronger, more expansive. You gain an energetic structure of light-blue essence. It surpasses your current three-dimensional etheric body. In your heart, you notice the yellow light of Sothis Star. The yellow light calls you to merge your heart with her light. You have expanded your consciousness through the blue moon energies, allowing you to outgrow this pitch-black pit you fell into. This pit symbolised your old and outdated fears. You have outgrown them. As you continue to grow, the light of Sothis is becoming clearer and brighter.

As you rise through these waters, you are approaching closer to Sothis Star. Your head reaches the water surface. You break through the water barrier. You lift yourself out of the water and continue to expand and see you have arrived in front of the One Pyramid of Dahshur. The pyramid's apex is situated at the level of your heart. It radiates Sothis Starlight. You allow her Starlight to resonate with your heart. You exchange light codes. Her Starlight absorbs your unique codes. They blend into her star body. She prepares your unique codes initiated by her essence. A yellow-golden disc appears uniquely for you. To receive it, you extend your hands towards the pyramid's apex.

When you touch your yellow-golden disc, its dense energy vibrates. Inside the disc, your inner eye beholds spinning movements. You gently guide the disc into your heart. As the disc hovers within your heart area, a second disc appears in the region of your shoulder blades. Two yellow-golden discs envelop your heart. These discs belong together. They co-create. Each rotates in a different direction and positions itself uniquely in relation to the other, aligning itself at various angles when necessary. Each will open your heart and transform it into your heart gate to integrate Light Codes yet to come. We thank Sothis and the Light Beings of the Venus Light Path for preparing our hearts with blue moon energy to embark on this sacred journey.

We love you. Thank you.

I.2 Temple of Emergence of Cosmic Love, Sphinx, Giza

Illustration: The Sphinx.

Unveiling Blueprint

The key to open your heart to the next phase
in your soul journey: Cosmic Love.

During the waxing crescent, the seeds receive additional light codes. These enable each to continue its development according to its blueprint. The unfolding results in intricate patterns. The Sphinx prepares you and each temple to evolve with the codes from suns, planets, and Star Consciousness with which these moons interconnect. Within a universal unfolding pattern, the Sphinx invites each Star Consciousness to transmit its light code to help each distinct temple unfold in its unique way. Cosmic codes also diffuse through the universal moon codes. They resonate with each temple.

The Sphinx is an earthly portal. Even though he is a lion connected to the Sun, moons are also extinguished solar consciousness in the form of the crone ship. Therefore, the Sphinx conveys both sun and moon codes throughout the Nile Valley, as he gazes at the sunrise. The Sun blesses all seeds to grow and unfold. The Sun also bestows stellar gifts for the temples and all who are recipients of the Cosmic Moon Grid. The Sphinx has taken on a nurturing role by nourishing all temples with their unique codes of stellar consciousness. Similarly, the Sun bathes all temples and beings in his light, warmth, and universal life force to support their unfolding into full potential.

At the Sphinx, you receive all the stellar codes. They originate from the stars you most fully entrain with. They come to full fruition in your own unique way.

The Sphinx watches over all the double cone shapes entering the Earth sphere through the Earth-moon cycle. They descend through the sacred grounds of the Sphinx. The Sphinx itself is also a gateway into Inner Earth. From there and through the Inner Earth network, the codes fuse with the temple seed. Each cone shape entering the Earth has its intelligence. It knows which seed needs to go to which specific temple. Each seed is predestined.

The Sphinx has a second distinct role. He infuses each cone entering the globe with his red-essence Earth codes. By adding Earth energy to it, the temple connects at a deep level to the Temple of Love at Earth's core. This deepening allows the Creational Nile Temples to always be in refined alignment with the Temple of Love's[17] desire and evolution. They connect by Earth codes – Codes of Love – and resonate with one another. The stellar codes, on the contrary, are needed to initiate the temple on a more cosmological level. The Sphinx adds stellar codes. These are unique to the Earth. Then, the stellar codes nourish the temple seed. The Temple of Love refines this process by discerning even

17 The Temple of Love, is the Earth Temple in the heart of the Earth. The core of Eart's womb, where all souls incarnating on Earth receive her divine blessing.

more precisely which stellar codes are most appropriate. A recoding to a more refined, specifically intricate level of uniqueness occurs.

Mirror of Axis Mundi's Roots

The Sphinx transmits the unique stellar codes through an underground circuit. The circuit connects all the Creational Nile Temples. Cosmic Light transports these stellar codes through the Cosmic Moon Grid to the moon gate and then on to all temples. These stellar codes alchemise. Though they do not yet thoroughly intertwine, individually, they blend into golden light strings within each temple at an inner-dimensional level within the Earth. At this level, you find the Holy of Holies and the temple seed. Here is a specific chamber where this double cone shape – the vessel holding stellar and Earth codes – is received and planted around the temple seed.

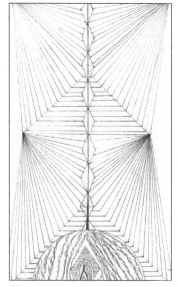

Illustration: Temple Seed.

The temple seed resides within this double-cone vessel. The seed integrates the stellar codes through strings of golden light. Thus, it receives guidance on unfolding its potential and temple mission to be accomplished on Earth: which energy to radiate, and how to do so. In this conical vessel, the various stellar codes do not intermingle. Each remains unique: from one another and from the unique essence of each. Each, though, interacts with the temple seed. Each in its moment nurtures and encodes the temple seed.

Each double-cone vessel moves down from the Sphinx and into an Earth arterial network encompassing the entire Nile Valley. The codes radiate their essences from the moment each double cone enters the Inner Earth Temples. The emitted codes resonate with all other temple seeds and induce change within them. With this, the entire Nile Valley comes into Oneness at a deeper Inner Earth Temple level. The whole Nile Temple Valley resonates with each double-cone vessel related to its specific temple. Information flows freely in this rooted underground network. The uniqueness of each temple and a universal information grid now ignite and activate. Each can now evolve in Oneness according to the divine potential of each temple. The Creational Nile Temples form One Temple body.

Cosmic Key of Life into Your I Am Presence

Hypnotically glancing at the Sun, the Sphinx asks you not to stand in front of him. He wants to align himself. And so you stand next to him and also stare at the bright light on the horizon. Your heart, the Sphinx's heart, and the heart of the Sun are all aligned in one triangle. As soon as this alignment takes place, the Sphinx invites you to enter his body. He says, "Come and be in my heart." You notice a magenta-coloured crystal in his heart space.

You move with your consciousness into his body. Like a cat, he purrs. He pulls himself together and curls around you, enveloping you, hugging you. As you lie next to his heart, you feel it pulsating. His heartbeat gives you a sense of calm and peace. The throbbing rhythm makes you sink into your own body. The further you sink, the more he invites you into the depths of his being. The seat in his heart pulls you in as if he has become a vehicle. You are now in the driver's seat. As you embody his heart, you feel this magenta essence. You continue sinking until his heart entirely absorbs you. His heart now envelops you as if you were in a magenta tulip whose petals surround you. Your head tilts towards your breastbone. He pushes you even further in. With your mind's eye, you sense in your body an entire system of veins. His heart essence, in this tulip shape, ignites this vein system in your body. The codes of the Sphinx's heart rewire you. The magenta essence now seeps through your entire body. The magenta concentrates in your Central Axis. From there, numerous strings wind themselves around your body at an even deeper level. These new heart codes now envelop you from within. This prepares you for something not yet clear to you.

The veins, permeated by magenta essence, form an antenna system. They leave your crown and feet. This necessary coding will enable you to resonate with his heart essence. He confirms: the activation is complete. He gently asks you to step outside.

Outside, you look to the west. The Sun is at your back. Suddenly everything becomes dark. The ground sinks beneath your feet. Nothingness engulfs. Everything disappears. You can still feel the Sphinx's presence, though. You know he is here. This presence is the only thing you perceive. A golden chariot appears from nowhere. Its wheels look like suns. Its propellers are of blue light. They have the same density as crystals. The entire structural axis of this golden chariot is of crystallised blue light. You touch the golden chariot. It feels cold. It tingles. While walking to its front, you behold three white-winged horses awaiting. You touch them. You feel their feathers.

You look into their black eyes. You make their acquaintance. Then you retreat into the chariot. A golden seat welcomes you, and you settle down into it. As soon as you resonate with this chariot, you perceive a presence next to you. It is Horus, Falcon God, he who carries a feather from Amun Ra. He says, "Come, we have something to show you." He speeds you out into the solar system and even further into the universe. It feels as if these winged horses are not making any effort. The place you are going to attracts you. The chariot glides with ease and grace to your destination. Your head feels light, spinning. The chariot's energy is of a sublime frequency, and the energy of Horus makes you even more dizzy. You pause at the outline of a vast plane. Even from a distance you can still catch a glimpse of the Earth. One horse shows you this vast plane is in our multiverse.

You draw your attention to a place where the same blue essence in the propellers of the chariot wheel is present. In this plane, a string connects seven blue spheres. At the head of that string sits a winged sphere. This structure closely resembles the blueprint of an angel. Horus says, "The blueprint is ready. Now let us proceed." The horses take off with great force. They start at the bottom of the string, then spiral up to the string's top, where the winged sphere awaits them. They follow the path of the ascending kundalini. You spin and spin around this axis until you arrive at this last sphere. Then you pierce the winged sphere. The two strings you have wrapped around the axis of this cosmic shape now lead you back down to the bottom of the shape. You suddenly recognise it. You have activated the Staff of Thoth Hermes Trismegistus. One string moves downwards to the left, the other to the right. You and Horus weave a new toroid by repeatedly flying in and out of the Central Axis system, making loops. When the weaving is complete, you fly to each blue sphere and connect your heart to it. Once your magenta essence heart resonates with each sphere, it opens into four parts, like four petals of a flower. From this opened structure, seven strings of light depart from each of the seven spheres. They connect to your right and left sides as if they are tuning forks you play. You lead and co-create with this structure. The seven strings wind around your heart. Four strings connect to your right side. Three to your left side. Your heart forms the centre of this cosmic tuning fork.

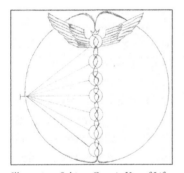

Illustration: Sphinx. Cosmic Key of Life.

From the seven spheres, spiral systems emerge. Your heart gives the impulse, and procreation begins. You see all seven spheres blossom and expand. On the spiral arms of those seven universes appear countless spheres. Stars, moons, planets, whole solar and galactic systems emerge into existence. This Creation takes place as utmost harmonic resonance. Everything develops at the same pace. Each of these seven universes is located on the Central Axis.

The Central Axis is hollow. You can travel through it, finding the core of each universal Sun there. You travel right through the upper winged sphere. You ask Horus what this all means. He answers, "These are the stages of life. These seven phases represent steps we must take to wear our crown, our sovereign self, our soul identity. These are the seven steps to embody the I Am Presence. The Earth will move after this incarnation as a Star into these last three phases to complete them and wear her crown. And in fact, her blueprint is already there on a specific dimensional level. When you move through that crown, you become a sphere of light. You then leave everything else behind. Everything you no longer need transmutes into light. You leave behind everything you have shared with others to help them unfold their true essence. Sharing forms you in such a way that you understood what your heart needed in each of the seven phases: why you are in a specific time and space. Once in a phase, you shared with others what was needed for them and yourself. From that capacity of calibration and alignment, you move up through that Central Axis into the next universe.

Each universal Sun is a Creational Womb. A holographic image is represented fractally throughout the multiverse. Many galactic and universal Creational Wombs are preparing you to unfold into your next divine potential. Earth will now join the fourth Creational Womb and continue its final three stages of evolution into an ultraviolet Sun. You are connected to this structure, for you know the history of our Earth. In essence, you are a weaver of worlds."

Your system now resonates even more with the essence of magenta. It rewires and recalibrates your heart, allowing you to sink more deeply into your heart as the magenta essence lifts your energy to the energies of the higher cosmic heart, the enlightened heart. Your body fills. The magenta essence flows out of your hands as strings of light. It is as if you have become this beautiful channel for the energies of Cosmic Love. "This is the program ruling in the higher levels of this Key of Life," says Horus. You hear the Sphinx telling you this is your preparation to open your heart to the next phase in your soul journey. You will come into deeper alignment with Cosmic Love to prepare yourself for your subsequent incarnations. Horus stands behind you. You both behold in silence all this beauty. You do not know what to say, for this sacred field is overwhelming and takes your breath away. Slowly and subtly, he lays his hand on your shoulder. He says it is time to go.

The golden chariot with its winged horses turns. It carries you back to the Sphinx. You travel so swiftly your physicality dissolves while in this plasmic tunnel of light. The pull absorbs you. It teleports you instantly back to where you had started.

Here you are again, in this triangle connected to the Sphinx. The Sun is still rising. Only a few minutes have elapsed. It has seemed as if you had spent a decade away. You can hear the Sphinx grinning. He feels satisfied. He says, "Isn't that something?" He asks you to stand in front of him. You have the Sun at your back and align yourself entirely with him. He adds, "For me, it is not yet completed. You travelled there with my heart essence. Now I give you this white disc. It infuses your heart. This disc will allow us to resonate together as we co-create with these three higher universes." He turns and says, "I will project my consciousness into all seven universes, most definitely the upper one, for that will be the opening of the crown. The Earth and we will ascend. I project my essence into all these universes so that the lower ones may learn from Earth's wisdom."

"I will co-create with the higher ones because I am a cosmic Oracle connected to many other stars and beings. I will give them my wisdom, my loyal heart, my integrity, my righteousness." As he utters these words, they become deeds. He projects these energies to the cosmic Key of Life. The blueprint lights up even more and integrates the codes he transmits to them. When the transmission is complete, he turns to you and says, "Well, thank you for coming to me. You do not need to say anything. With your heart, you express your gratitude. I have received it well. I will see you again when a new day dawns." As the Sun rises, he closes his eyes and turns inwards into the Unseen, only to reappear at sunrise.

Axis Mundi Cosmic Walker

The Sphinx imbues you with its magenta energies originating from his heart. As you bathe in this magenta light, you turn around with the Sphinx at your back. He aligns his heart with yours via a magenta string running through your heart into the horizon. He says, "This is the path you will walk." You cast a glance at him while you turn your head, and he says, "Look before you and feel this path. It is Your Path. You can see it as a string of light, and you can explore it more profoundly by touching it, by looking at it, by resonating with it."

He nudges you to walk like a tightrope walker on this magenta light string. At moments, it feels as if you walk straight on. Then the string curves to the right to straighten its line again. As you observe this curvature, you know this is your timeline you are walking at this very moment. The curvature represents a side path or event taking you off your path. The Sphinx tells you, "You must discover the vigour in your heart and engulf yourself within it. When you attune to your vigour, the path will straighten. Close your eyes and attune yourself to the vigour in your heart." The warmth rises from your inner depths into your heart, and this sacred moment seems to last an eternity. When this warmth has deeply soaked your body, you open your eyes. Miraculously, the curve has straightened.

You walk on, focused on the string of light descending into a pit, only to rise again.

You stop to observe. You turn your head towards the Sphinx. He tells you, "Feel all fearful emotions that bring you down into lower vibrations, their lower dimensions. Recognise these emotions as children who want to be seen and heard when they cry. Once a child feels acknowledged, it will heal." You close your eyes and lay your hands on your belly. You recognise feelings of restlessness and allow them to emerge. They are the harbingers of deeper emotions not yet accessible to you. All these emotions move through your body, to the surface, to your heart. Vulnerability is strength. You allow yourself to be vulnerable and acknowledge these feelings. You comfort your inner child. Your body has self-healing properties. You allow it to set itself free. As the physical internal calm returns, you open your eyes. You notice the descending light string exuding even denser energies. Slowly, your light string detaches itself from those emotional depths. It straightens itself because it feels you are One with yourself, with your inner child.

Strong identification with these energies only causes you to lose yourself. We are all capable of finding joy, strength, and abundance in our hearts. We are an infinite source of essence qualities. They guide us and enable us to pave our path.

The journey continues. Small ponds of water spring to your left and right. They run alongside your light string. When you peek in one puddle, you see yellow-golden fish finning the waters. Soon the ponds extend in length and accompany your light string out to the horizon. There it becomes part of the Sun and Sothis' starlight, midwifing you as your Creator. The water resonates with you. From its body rises a water creature. It instantly envelops you with liquid light and spirals around you. This Water Light Being embellishes your heart gate even further by introducing the twelve-petal system gifted by Nun and Nunet. It imprints around your heart gate liquid light petals. Inter-dimensionally, it imprints at many more layers in a Fibonacci code sequence. And so, the deeper multidimensional layers of your heart gate project outside your body, taking on a conic form. From a three-dimensional perspective, the farthest and deepest point is at the 144th dimension, pointing ahead of you, towards your path and down the direction you need to walk. This conical heart gate will guide you to build, activate, and initiate your own Light Temple from the 144th dimension upwards, right into your heart.

At the end of this journey, the cone within you inverts and implodes in your heart. It transmutes into your spiral universe. It contains all your essence qualities. As a whole, they form your *I Am Presence.* You are still halfway along this light string and continue walking, for the initiation is not yet complete.

The Sphinx says, "Infuse your cone's apex in the sunlight at the horizon." Suddenly you feel your eyes widen as if the Sun is calling your heart gate. It responds to the call and integrates the Sun's essence through yellow-golden light strings.

These light codes rewire and prepare your inner vision to see the multidimensionality in *All That Is* as you walk the path of the Creational Nile Temples.

The essence infused in your eyes descends through your nerve connections into your body. From the neck down, they split to the right and left sides. They descend even further, to merge again in the pelvic area. They leave your body through your pelvic floor. "As Within so

Without," says Thoth. The path before you, you also carry within. *The Alpha α and the Omega Ω are* activated. For at the beginning of this journey, you integrate the end by *Bending Time.* As soon as the beginning and the end come together, they create wholeness. They allow us to deepen the process we will commence. As we travel through the sacred temples, the light codes will enable us to activate them more profoundly.

You feel the power of this energy gushing through you. It tells you clearly what to expect. It tells you what lies ahead. Your future is known to you. You know. You have walked this timeline and integrated it into your body. Standing here on the horizon facing the Sun, you turn to face the Sphinx. You feel you have also become a lion. Your eyes radiate yellow energies. You connect your eyes to those of the Sphinx. You align your heart with the Sphinx's heart. You align your pelvic area to the Sphinx's pelvic area. You will meet the Creational Nile Temples carrying the wisdom of the Sphinx. He is the lion protector of all life, sovereign with the Earth, as his playground. Now, also *your playground.*

You walk back towards the Sphinx. You feel the light string has morphed into qualities of strength and enlightenment. An air of sovereignty and self-confidence overflows you. You resonate with the Sphinx as an equal.

You bring the essence of the lion into the Aquarian Age and its path of enlightenment. Because we have almost arrived at a point of completion, the Sphinx offers you an amulet. It contains a hologram of the universe. The energy in this amulet rotates clockwise. This means you will embody all the Enlightenment Codes, updated for the Aquarian Age. You will bring them into matter into your energy body. The Sphinx says, "The Nile represents the Central Axis of this Cosmos, As Above, So Below. As you travel the Nile River, you will also travel the cosmic Central Axis and align with it by folding the scroll from the right and left sides into One. You are a Cosmic Walker, and you walk this path with me."

Honoured with this gift, you accept the amulet and imprint its hologram into your heart, never to lose it. It is yours. It will always be yours.

Your spine aligns with the Central Axis of the hologram's universe. The hologram straightens you and prepares you for the journey ahead. All the stars in your own soul's universe now reposition themselves around you according to the cosmic laws of *harmonic resonance*. Because you are its Central Axis, you are its core. The positioning of all your stars to their correct alignment creates your *Musica Universalis*. The sound allows you to merge your right and your left sides into the One that you are, the *I Am Presence*.

Your forehead kisses the Sphinx's forehead. You say goodbye.
He wishes you well.

I.3 Temple of the Codes of Abundance, Apis Temple, Memphis

Illustration: Apis. Photo by Carolyn Whitson

I Am Presence

Creation has procreated itself endlessly. The Garden of Eden holds the *Codes of Abundance*.

You stand in front of a set of stairs. At the top of the staircase stands the Apis. She descends towards you while no longer embodying a feminine essence. Instead, the Apis is an androgen. She says, "Come, let us go outside." Together you walk to the temple's exit. As you both stand in the doorway, the sun's rays radiate towards you. You feel the happiness in the heart of the Apis. As you walk, you find yourself in meadows of green, lush grasses. Imagining it was like this in ancient times. The Apis says. "We relate to the Moon. Our biorhythms follow moon energy." The Apis sits beside you, gazing at the Moon and bringing its consciousness inwards. You perceive it is leaving its body, descending through its root. Suddenly, its soul essence is right in front of you. Its body still sits beside you.

"Come," she says, "I'm also one of the Blue Moon Goddesses. I want to take you somewhere." Like her, you also leave your body through your root chakra. As a soul essence, as a light, you travel together with the soul of the Apis. Two lights are travelling through Earth's atmosphere like fireflies until they reach an outline. The outline is the exact point where moon energy enters Earth's atmosphere. Here the Moon projects its moon energy spherically and envelops the Earth, simultaneously permeating the Earth. She explains that during the days and nights, Seen and Unseen, moonlight conveys its impact.

You are both at the intersection where the Moon's energy field meets Earth's Light Body. Moonlight glides like silk over Earth's Light Body, enveloping her entirely with a milky, silvery-white essence. From within Inner Earth, your mind's eye now perceives seeds, unlocking, unfolding, moving towards Earth's surface. "Yes," she says, "as the moon energy ignites procreation from within, it supports the Earth in the unfolding of all seeds locked within her body and the unlocking of the Thousand Petal Lotus." Immediately your awareness shifts to the planets within our solar system that have several moons. She says,"Those moons form a clustered circle, and operating as One, at the level of the core crystal within the planet, they open the core crystal." The soul essence of the Apis positions itself at the intersection where she perceives the moon essence entering her being. She nudges you to do the same. She anoints you with moon essence. Moon essence unfolds the petals of your own Thousand Petal Lotus. As incarnates, we are not alone. We are a network of beings supporting one another. We carry one another in the Cosmic Grid. It connects us all. As we do so, the universal component of the Cosmic Grid realigns us as One to bring forward our aim, our unique essence: an out-breath of the Omega Ω planted all seeds in the Cosmos. When all seeds fully blossom and unlock all their fruits, harvests return through fractal procreation. With an out-breath, you seed. You reap a cornucopia of wealth, wisdom, and love with an in-breath. Creation has procreated itself endlessly. The Garden of Eden holds the *Codes of Abundance*. Each fruit a plant gifts bears the Codes of Abundance. As Yeshua says, "For those, who have eyes to see." You know that: recognising and acknowledging and bringing all seeds, space, and existence to fruition. We all walk our path towards the unfolding of the I Am by following the Codes of Abundance. "We knew this," says the Apis. "The contradiction is that by giving space to all that wants to exist, we were never in an overpopulation. Everyone came to completion, and more rapidly. As soon as you understand the Code of Enlightenment, there is no delay. No pain. No suffering. You slide through the spirals of time. They bring you into your I Am Presence at an unimaginable speed. For those who have eyes to see, it is right before them. From that perspective, the Earth has enough space to accommodate all souls, for the trajectory of incarnated light beings has substantially shortened."

You position yourself in the moonlight. You imbibe and permeate it while holding on to the sacred words you received from the Apis, one of the most ancient forms of incarnation on Earth. You lock this ancient wisdom in your heart and ask the Moon to seal it in like a seed. You gaze upon the Earth, this beautiful place. You feel her Light Being desires to shift into this consciousness, that she wishes that all beings on Earth adhere to this consciousness by understanding these codes of wisdom. The friction between what she desires and what truly is can dissolve. She aligns with *harmonic resonance*. She is thrilled to move with all earthly beings into the Aquarian Age where the *Enlightenment Codes* unlock our true potential. We all move, though, from the Unseen to the Seen and come to full fruition. This is the Earth star's desire to experience *the Foundational Desire for Life* residing in all beings. It is the highest vibration you can experience in this current timeline.

"We have come to completion," says the Apis. You both return to your bodies and stand before one another. You embrace her warmly and bid her farewell as you both go your separate ways.

I.4　The Cosmic Sound Temple of Self-Love and Compassion, Saqqara

Illustration: Saqqara. Cosmic Sound Temple.

Devotional Side of Life

You dedicate yourself to becoming who you really are and offer yourself a new opportunity every moon cycle to bring the Unseen to the Seen.

For this transmission, Horus stands near you in Saqqara's Temple of Cosmic Sound.

You walk your way up towards the Temple of Cosmic Sound. The whole structure radiates concentric circles vibrating towards you. It seems almost impossible to enter this complex. When you start walking, though, a nomadic path leads you effortlessly forward in a serpentine movement. Your head tilts inwards towards your heart. As you wander forward, you weave these vibrations into your body and your heart. At the same time, you weave yourself into the etheric vibratory structure of the Saqqara Cosmic Sound Temple.

In every cell of your body, an explosion of sound bursts forth. Every cell is now vibrating and emanating sound. You walk on. Saqqara Light Being wraps her energetic wings around you. From behind, she gently pulls you towards her in her Light Body. You feel carried for the last part of the path. You are now in front of a portal of large blocks. When you place your hand on these building blocks, your mind's eye shows you white woven strings of vibration within. They carry the cosmic vibration from the Cosmos down to the Earth, the vibration of sound forms interconnected in conical shapes. They form Creational Chambers of light. This structure repeats itself interdimensionally. Strings of woven light spring into being.

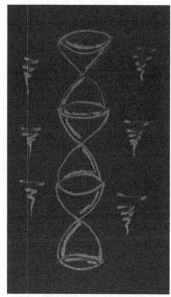

Illustration: Saqqara.
The Vibrational String of
Cosmic Sound.

You place your hands on the portal, allowing the white strings of energy to penetrate you. From a quantum physics level, these white strings entwine and weave into your body. You become an extension of this building. You continue touching the walls as you seek to tune in, becoming One and fully merging into this experience. It is almost finished. As you download the last vibrational frequencies, your body shivers. You guide the vibrations down through your pelvic floor, into your legs and feet, grounding the frequencies into the Earth.

Saqqara Light Being tells you this is precisely what she is doing to transfer the vibrational frequencies into Earth's deep inner layers. You tune in to the temple foundation. From there, various strings descend like roots into various quadrants of Inner Earth. Great inner cities are located in these depths. You observe at least sixteen inner cities, all located on an etheric circular band. The vibrations passing through the temple's roots to the inner cities originate from the Saqqara Temple of Cosmic Sound. A cone forms, connecting these cities on the circle to the Saqqara Temple of Cosmic Sound's foundation. This circular band rotates alternately to the left and to the right. Saqqara Light Being induces this movement in the lower cone under the temple foundations. From these foundations, a new upper cone commences moving into the Cosmos. The Saqqara Temple of Cosmic Sound is a gathering place of vibrations from the Cosmos. They are immediately sent to the sixteen inner cities of the Inner Earth. The Temple of Saqqara as a Light Chamber co-creates with the Inner Earth by aligning and updating the crystals of cosmic information the Inner Cities guard.

Each crystal represents an important sacred place for downloading cosmic information for the Earth. Saqqara Light Being states, "Providing a constant inner balance for the Earth within the Cosmic grid is pivotal for the harmonic resonance of the Cosmos. In this way we create cosmological order and balance. On a quantum level, this harmonic resonance replicates itself within the Light Body of all celestial bodies, piercing their etheric spheres, where all life dwells. Thus, the Hermetic Principle of As Without Becomes As Within. Harmony Within Is Equivalent to Harmony Without. This is one of the cosmological privileged insights of the Egyptian temples, and all temples built on Earth. They serve as alignment and balancing tools. They fulfil an essential function in shielding harmonic resonance. The Saqqara Sound Temple passes this sacred knowledge on to reactivate all temples. The Star Beings have announced that the time has come. According to the Maya, we have left the Cosmic Night. It lasted for about 13,000 years and then entered the Cosmic Day. As the Earth rotates around the Sun's axis, it leaves the shadow and enters the light of the Central Sun.

The cosmic information stored in these crystals has been secured for hundreds of thousands of years. We wait to unlock this information when the time is right. To determine if we can release these crystals, we align with the star from whom we received the codes. Even if we cannot release them, cosmic sound vibrations update the crystals constantly. Even during the Cosmic Night, the Earth and you carried within all you needed, even though you did not unlock it. Sometimes it is not necessary to unlock your inner seeds. However, it is essential to go through a particular experience to enrich yourself, to understand better who you are, what your potential is, so that you can develop your carrying capacity.

We want to show you that we have never been alone. Nor have we experienced lack. Abundance has always been within us, even when we chose not to unlock it. "You have understood," says Saqqara Light Being.

"Please lower your hands from this portal and enter my temple," she asks. As you set foot on this sacred ground, a most wonderful experience overwhelms you. Swirling light-blue energies everywhere float throughout the sacred space. They make beautiful musical sounds and circulate around you. With every step you take, they dance in sensual and soulful ways, spinning you gracefully and whirling you around your tender axis. You dance with them, allowing your dance to be guided. Their energy envelops you, permeating your body. Your Central Axis explodes outwards from within as if you had countless blue-light antennae all around you. You radiate light-blue antennae, and you know you have given birth to something new. You are different. You feel lighter, more heavenly. Your energy seems to reach far beyond where it had been before. You have a sharper perception of the Cosmos. The antennae greatly enhance your sensitivity to vibrational frequencies. These antennae are feelers of energy. They enable you to interact in a much more conscious way with this world of higher frequencies. They translate the higher frequencies into your present consciousness.

They give you a glimpse of how it used to be here in this sacred space where you are standing now. You perceive numerous plasmic spheres scattered throughout the space. The people who once visited this temple also had these advanced feelers. As a ritual, they sat in all these spheres. They became instruments to communicate with the Cosmos, Inner Earth cities, and their crystals. These spheres were also portals to connect with the Inner Earth. They were aware of the existence of the inner cities. They would connect to them, and the frequencies would flow through their bodies like streams. For they too needed specific attunements or healing. They worked with the circle of sixteen crystals and challenged themselves to begin a new cycle. Each Equinox they entered a new cycle and wished for a new beginning. The sacred rite of passage in the Spheres of Cosmic Sound brought them close to their hearts. With their attention inwards, they received the answers to questions during the following months. If they chose the path to embody cosmic essence, each alignment during the equinox brought them closer and closer to the centre of their hearts, to discover their inner happiness, love, and potential. Each cycle meant a new beginning at the end of each three months. When the cycle ended, they gained inner knowledge, inner wisdom, and continued living from a renewed energy.

Here, at the Saqqara Cosmic Sound Temple, you give yourself a chance again to change, to be a better person, to make better choices, to reverse choices. This sacred rite radiates self-love and compassion. Each time you give yourself a new chance to try again, go deeper, do better, be better, and be more loving to yourself and others.

The cycles are also related to the moon cycles. A year or a larger cycle contains four larger moon quadrants. Each time people visit these spheres, they begin a new cycle. All four cycles within this greater cycle bring them closer to their heart. The cycle narrows year by year, opposite from how the concentric years of a tree tend to expand. Here, the circles narrow down further and further into the essence of the heart. When we arrive at the essence of our heart, cycle after cycle, year after year, we have had so many opportunities to review, revisit, re-present what we wanted to understand better, how to deal with it, and what we wanted to approach from deep within ourselves.

This sacred co-Creation between these sixteen crystals and these cosmic energies allows us to align with who we were, are, and are becoming. A similar process occurs in the labyrinth in Chartres Cathedral, near Paris, where you walk your path to the centre of the flower to unfold your six petals. You embody the centre and unfold and manifest your true essence heart.

The Saqqara Cosmic Sound Temple manifests the devotional side of life. You dedicate yourself to becoming who you really are. You offer yourself a new opportunity every cycle to bring the Unseen to the Seen.

With these words, Saqqara sanctuary is drenched in beautiful white energies. They flood the full site. A toroidal field shows and extends around the sacred site, which represents a central point within this field. The latter also includes the etheric dimensions circumferencing the Earth, moving inwards towards her core. The Earth has called upon the light beings of this temple to co-operate in achieving harmonic resonance on personal and cosmological levels.

I.5 Temple of Cosmic Secrets Revealed by the Pyramid Texts, Saqqara

Illustration: Saqqara. The Pyramid Texts in the Pyramid of Teti.

Rise of Your Cosmic Angelic Essence

At the Pyramid of Teti entrance, the Light Being of this sacred site harmonises with your heart. The Pyramid pulsates, radiates a light-blue essence, and allows you in. The Light Being of the Pyramid of Teti recognises your heart signature. It wants to reveal its secrets. Secrets ancient and universal.

You approach down the long corridor and begin your descent. Suddenly, as you walk, you feel something slide past. Something is shuffling on the ground, accompanied by hissing. The corridor is dark. You look carefully. A slithery, huge black snake at least fifty centimetres in circumference descends with you.

You smell a damp scent as if descending into a swampy area, and half-way down the corridor, you feel water. To proceed further, you know you must submerge. So, you dive into these dark waters. You immerse yourself completely in this ethereal substance. It cleanses and purifies you.

In the distance, a bright light glitters. You swim towards the light, knowing when you have reached it, you have arrived. The small passage now gives way to a large opening where you emerge from the water. This sacred space notices your presence. The water immediately subsides. You look around. You take in your surroundings.

Reflections dissolve. Only you remain.

Hieroglyphs engrave all walls. Randomly, between each you see a bright diamond light glowing. These are the soul lights of those who once served this temple. They move through the walls, come to you, surround you in a welcoming warmth. The black snake appears. You try to take in as much as you can of the majestic, enigmatic, and mysterious energies. The creatures accompanying you sit down. You follow their example. The snake curls up. With its tail, it scans all the hieroglyphs, with a gliding movement. It takes in all the codes embedded in these hieroglyphs. You see the light-blue energy penetrating this wall. It enters the tail of the snake. It now radiates bright-blue light. The Light Beings surrounding you urge you to approach the snake. As she continues to download the pyramid texts, you feel like laying your head on her curled-up body. She feels warm and soft. She rests her head on your belly, for she also recognises a primordial essence in you. She aligns herself with you. As soon as she has finished downloading, she escorts the point of her tail towards you to take in the codes. Relaxed, she allows you to imbibe what you need.

Meanwhile, she falls asleep, soothed and feeling at home. She has completed her task. As soon as you have consumed all the codes she has given you, these energies gather within your belly.

While you lift your head away from her body and join the group of Light Beings you recognise clearly, you realise they are High Priests and Priestesses. Among them, you recognise King Seti,[18] his wife, and their many children. They inform you they have also gone through this sacred rite of passage, absorbing all these codes of wisdom engraving these walls. These codes are not only of the Egyptians. Their core essence is Star Consciousness and will allow you to work even more closely with them. You will resonate with the messages they wish to bring. The light-blue energy in your belly rises to your heart. It becomes a round disc radiating light blue, like a Sun radiating blue rays. Now it moves to your throat and crown as well. You align with this blue star energy.[19] It fully transmutes your old structure. These Light Beings observe you and witness the process you are undergoing. They are witnessing the alchemy of who you were and who you are becoming. Your physical structure now feels heavier. Because of these blue energies, you feel gravity is playing a role. You feel it immersing you more in the Earth. Slowly this phase also passes. The heavy feelings dissolve. You stand up straight again. You feel fresh. Your eyes have become more prominent and rounder. They emanate blue rays. The Light Beings are informing you that you are ready. You have completed this initiatory phase.

In front of you, you sense the emerging presence of a High Priest. He is preparing an altar for you. A slithering serpent engraves the stone altar. There are three chalices: one at the tip of the snake's tail, one small chalice in the middle, and a larger one on the snake's head. The High Priest asks you to come closer. He urges you to take the chalice on the engraved snake's tail. You take it in your hands. This refined chalice is made of a golden material. Upon it, various fine lines and patterns have been inscribed. If you look closely, you notice the chalice is closed off halfway. You cannot drink the contents. It now looks more like a small, golden chair. You know that under the chair a seed awaits you.

---

18 Seti I was a pharaoh of the New Kingdom Nineteenth Dynasty of Egypt, the son of Ramesses I and Sitre, and the father of Ramesses II.

19 Blue Star energy is the core essence in an animated soul. It ignites life. Blue Star energy is extremely powerful. In the multiverse are also Blue Star regions. Here many of the avatars we know, originate from there. These are energetic hotspots thriving on high-frequency energy. Blue moon energies are the powerful energies that allow our inner Blue Sun to unfold and emerge from our inner depths.

You do not know what to do. The High Priest just looks at you. He waits curiously to see what you will do. When you attune yourself to the substance, you perceive a sunset-orange liquid. You feel you should place it on your head, like a headdress. It looks like a helmet. When you place it on your head, it feels fresh and enlightening. It interacts with all three brain areas: the reptile brain, the cortex, the neocortex. It also strengthens and activates inner hearing. You feel tingling in your ears. Feelers of blue light energy extend from your ears, eyes, and eyebrows. The alchemical energy in your head is slowly taking root in your whole body. You look at the High Priest to understand if what is happening is right. He nods. You continue to observe and feel how your spine centres releasing outdated energy in your back, which blocks the incoming energy. The golden essence of the chalice now dissolves and glides into your body. Your body morphs. You grow soft, satin-like plumage. When you lower your gaze, you see the claws of a bird of prey.

The High Priest whispers, "This essence will enable you to raise your energy to those frequencies that will help you to fly through the core of our Solar Sun, the Galactic Sun, and the Central Sun. This essence will lift you to higher dimensions so that you can attune yourself to the Light of Amun Ra." You ask him why it must manifest in the form of a bird. He answers, telling you that because we are on Earth, we work with the essences that rule here. We honour these Earth codes, which are messengers that we see every day. That is why we initiate in this way. We want to honour the Earthly body because everything on Earth is divine. If we want to become divine and embrace our divinity, we must embrace every aspect of this Earth. Your body integrates the hawk essences and is already expressing their power. With your neck stretched out straight and your eyes wide open, you spread your wings and feel their power of opening and closing. The flapping of your wings raises the dust. You feel a strong breeze. You rise at lightning speed. Soon you behold the Sun. You know this preparatory phase enables you to receive the solar disc. You must raise yourself to the solar dimension level and bridge the gap to be able to wear the Sun Disc. You descend with your consciousness into your body. You feel your wings and the power to elevate yourself in an instant. You feel your heart beating. You are so alive! All this is so real! As if this were only a dream, you can hardly believe it, but it is clearly real.

The High Priest urges you to take the second chalice. You hold it in your hands. It is larger than the previous one. As you gaze into it, you behold a beautiful, bright-magenta essence spinning from within, creating a swirling vortex. Meanwhile, the chalice grows warmer and warmer. It dissolves. You hold the magenta essence in your cupped hands. Its scent smells sweet. You hold it in front of your heart, making it resonate with the magenta essence. Your heart expands and unfolds like the petals of a flower. A sunflower pattern blossoms in your heart. Your heart space opens and becomes more extensive, more expansive. It unfolds more and more. You understand you must bring the magenta essence into your heart at the base of the sunflower, like an eternal pool of Divine Love. Your heart thus remains in direct resonance with the Sun. You attune the opening of your heart to resonate with the Central Sun and with all the Suns. You notice your heart centre has become itself a huge Sun. Within it, a torsion and an alignment take place with all the stars. Your heart opens more deeply. In this moment the Stargates also open. You receive all the star alignments to nurture yourself with the updated future energies. You nourish yourself and share them by being a walking Stargate. You replicate the energies of these cosmic gates in your own Stargate. You radiate them to others. Behind you, Light Beings are rising and coming towards you. Something in your back is blocking. They place their hands there, just gently, rubbing while enormous golden wings appear. These are the wings of the Golden Universal Cosmic Angels. This phase embraces, on an even deeper dimensional level, the previous initiation. Your vibration is raised to a solar level and reawakens your solar essence.

While you embody your Universal Cosmic Angel, you enjoy every timeless moment. As you outgrow this pyramid, you feel so immense, reaching sky high to the Cosmic Axis, the central pillar of all the worlds. Here, you hear the Musica Universalis,[20] the whispers of the suns, moons, and planets. You hear the language of the stars. You take it all in. You resonate with all the Suns in our Cosmos. These are Light Beings you have known and with whom you have lost contact on a conscious level. You are reconnecting with the solar system in this Cosmos. By doing so, you are reconnecting with the group consciousness

---

20 Music of the Celestial Spheres.

of Cosmic angels. You are reconnecting with the cosmic grid. A fundamental process is taking place because it enables you to raise your energy level and work from that dimensional status, your highest cosmic essence. You feel you are back home. You know deep within that this is what you always wanted. These are the levels of creative power you are rekindling. You feel satisfied, fulfilled, and you remember. It all makes sense to you. You look at the palms of your hands. They are radiating golden stardust.

The High Priest encourages you to take the smallest chalice resting on the head of the snake. "Do not be reluctant," he says. At first, it had appeared to be the largest chalice. Now, though, it has become the smallest. You take the tiny chalice between two of your fingers. You imbibe the contents. A thick black essence slides down your throat, lubricating it. The essence creates a hollow black sphere in your heart area. A cauldron of becoming reigns in this sphere. Unlike the first two chalices, which mirrored something outside you, this black sphere brings all the outside into you. You become independent of space and time.

You no longer mirror the outside. You are simply yourself. The Hermetic Principle, *As Within, So Without. As Above, So below,* dissolves. Reflections dissolve. Only you remain. Complete and peaceful, you gaze at the Light Beings behind you and smile. You do not know what to say. All seems so familiar, yet the divine nature of all takes your breath away. Those who were here before also underwent this initiation and embodied a state of consciousness of no longer mirroring. You embodied this before as a divine spark, as a state of consciousness in the absolute beginning of your existence. And here you are at the end, uniting it with the beginning in your heart, in this black sphere of consciousness. You know the initiation is complete. The sphere is your world, the world outside dissolves, as only this sphere of consciousness within you remains. Indeed, you represent All That Is. You have become a replica of All That Is. The bridge between the world outside you mirrors your inner plane, transmuted.

You masterfully replicated within yourself the divine spark of the Cosmos and have become its replication. Hence, as a Divine Essence, as a replica of this Cosmos, you co-create with its sphere, as a vesica piscis.

Illustration: Saqqara.
Pyramid of Teti.
Co-Creation with the
Divine as the Divine.

Both of you can bring forth Divine Creation. You have embodied the All That Is. The sensation is almost too much to believe, to feel, to experience. Your silence allows the experience to seep in further, to become an even more natural state of being. Your heart is now so vast, comprising everything. King Seti comes from behind his altar. He approaches you. He takes your head between his hands. He lowers it and he kisses your forehead. Then he asks the priestesses to take care of you. You sit down between them in the middle of the circle and let them take care of you. The black primordial snake has also wrapped itself around you. They anoint you with essential oils used when one goes through a sacred rite of passage. You now embody yourself in the deepest multidimensional levels of your cellular structure. All gathers in your heart. This black sphere is now your heart. It resonates with the thirteen-pointed star that transmutes and elevates your human essence into your solar vessel. It is almost ready. You see some priestesses already preparing to leave. The snake is awake again. It regards you with blue eyes.

The eternal memory of the primary initiators and priestesses who guided you, is still present. They will guide whoever will visit this sacred site. You received this rite of passage because it is time.

They invite you to leave the pyramid. Whilst they embrace you gently, you say goodbye. You walk out and thank them. The diamond lights enter the walls again. The snake slithers out together with you. As you walk out, you carry within the secrets this Pyramid enfolds. You become its ambassador. You emanate its codes of wisdom. The Sun meets you halfway through the corridor, sealing your heart, just as this Pyramid seals your divine presence in its essence.

You thank the Light Beings of the Venus Light Path and all Light Beings at your side.

I.6 Arising Your Scroll of Truth, Unas Causeway

Activating Your Scroll of Maat

From the Pyramid of Teti, you continue your journey towards the Unas causeway[21]. The Light Beings of the Venus Light Path and Thoth travel with you as your sacred witnesses. You are lovingly surrounded. Light-blue energy propels you forward. Arriving in front of the causeway, the light-blue energy penetrates all the tiles on the floor, illuminating them. They become alive and move because energy is moving through them. A specific frequency emanates from each tile you step on. The energy signature of each tile is different, and a stellar compound structure forms the pathway.

Moving forward, you feel the need to turn inwards. You tilt your head in towards your heart. You feel your hands along your body. The palms of your hands are burning. In your mind's eye, you feel a pale-yellow sphere forming from each of your hands. The spheres are growing larger and larger. You lift your hands as if they were your altar. Light-yellow electricity runs through these spheres and through your arms to your heart, your throat. The current pierces your crown like electric lightning. It fans outwards and upwards into the Cosmos, and from your heart downwards, through your body and the soles of your feet. It connects with the tiles and it animates them. You hear a roaring sound nearby. A male lion appears on your left. On your right, a lioness accompanies you. They too support you and are ready to walk this path with you.

Illustration: Saqqara. Unas Causeway. Feather of Maat.

---

21 The causeway is a long walkway joining the valley and mortuary temples. The causeway has walls decorated with painted reliefs and a ceiling with painted stars.

You enter a starry blue tunnel as you walk forward with the two lions beside you. The tunnel expands in your inner vision and becomes an enormous stellar space. You feel you are walking among the stars. The light-blue light lifts and creates a path for you in the Cosmos. You connect with your lions. They feel loving and trusting, and you know everything will be alright.

This brings you slightly out of balance, but the steadfast energy of the lion calibrates your consciousness within your body. You connect your palms to your heart as you walk, moving one foot in front of the other. Every time your foot deviates from this straight line, one of the two lions will straighten you. Continuing to walk, you resonate with the stars around you, and their energy forms into a fanned-out lightning bolt. It pierces your crown, entering it with their consciousness. It flows down the vein through your entire body, grounding it into this pathway.

Your walk serves a dual function. One, you are a channel for stellar consciousness, re-activating this causeway. Two, you ignite your stellar consciousness within yourself. The stellar codes here relate to cosmic balance. You are aware that the path you are on is also steadfast, balanced, and perfectly orchestrated. You achieve a balance between your heart and mind. You stand as a channel between the Cosmos and the Earth. As you master the cosmic balance, the horizon reveals itself to you. The Central Sun shines brightly and invites you to come closer. This path leads directly to its centre. You see many Solar Angels beside the sun portal welcoming you. You keep walking, perfectly balanced. Suddenly a huge, white being of essence light descends right behind you. She is Maat. She carries the ostrich feather. She walks behind you, supporting you. As you move forward, she lifts the etheric veils in front of you.

Maat now opens the way. She leads you into the deepest chambers of the Central Sun. The path bends to the left. She is still behind you. As the path ends, you behold a vast space of golden essence. It reminds you of a Roman bath. Steps descend. You enter liquid golden essence. The gold is so bright you are not even aware it could have such magical manifestation on Earth. Your human body can no longer hold this resonance. It surrenders and opens. You now glide across the ethereal waters as a Golden Lotus. With your inner eye, you look behind and behold Maat gently floating as a White Lotus. She caresses you with one of her petals and places it gently upon you. She wants you to feel her close to you, so you know you are not alone.

Like Lotuses dancing in the shimmering golden light of the Central Sun, bathing in a golden lake, the two of you spin around one another. Dancing together, stardust rises from within both of you. It also dances and spins. You look up. The dust begins to form a double helix, DNA ladder. From her white golden essence, light-yellow DNA arises. A fairy landscape appears and captures your heart. You feel very much in Oneness with Maat. Her essence embraces you, and you embrace her. You become connected through your DNA to infinity. Both of you morph into the shape of an infinity symbol. As both your essences have united, you each occupy one side of the ladder, and the base will reconnect you through infinity. The spinning movement slowly comes to an end, stillness returns. Gradually, this DNA ladder withdraws into both of you. The water sinks away.

Both of you transform back into light-beings and stand before one another. Maat holds your hands and says. "Wait, the initiation is incomplete. Her heart is pulsating powerfully and seeking connection with your own heart. As soon as her pulsation animates yours, the infinity loop in your hearts ignites. She transmits your soul mission. Maat asks you to be of service to the light, to the qualities of purity and truth on all levels of Creation. You accept because it has always been written in your Light-Pillar. She feels delighted. Now that we are on the same wavelength again, your journey begins.

You align yourself – your life, your values, and your heart – with these laws of truth and purity. Countless Light Beings work for her throughout the Cosmos. She takes you by the shoulders and turns you around to the other side of the sun portal. With a quick sweep of her hand, she opens a white veil. A window shedding light upon the whole Cosmos unveils itself. Between the coral branches, you see crystal lights twinkling. She says these are the beings of light you will connect with, for you are one of them. You are a group consciousness, a grid of yourselves. The white crystal lights have received Maat's call. They now form a grid. It connects with you as Maat stands behind you. With her heart, she sends a pulse straight through your heart and throughout the crystal grid. She is igniting and activating you as one of the Light Beings in the service of Maat, this Cosmos, and beyond. You are allowing this to happen. You allow them to weave you into this grid.

You accept your new soul mission and take it all in. She embraces you and holds you close. You feel her closeness is necessary. The grid's energy is so powerful that it activates your Scroll of Truth,[22] unfolding it further and further. Each Light Being in this group consciousness approaches you, one after the other, scribing onto your Scroll of Truth. Each scribes its name, what it loves about you, your divine potential, its pearls of wisdom for you. Each scribes what it feels you need to feel at one with it. As the last Light Being scribes onto your scroll, it slowly closes.

The scribed information is stored on a multidimensional level. This grid now becomes a bright white sphere. You join all the Light Beings in a sacred rite of passage, an initiation celebration. You accept them. They accept you. You are one of them. Your consciousness returns to the palms of your hands. The white sphere has crystallised your entire body. Pure white crystalline starlight emerges in your heart area and radiates powerfully like a lighthouse to all others. They recognise you as part of them.

You have no words to describe this experience. It feels majestic, and of the highest service to All That Is. You hold the Cosmic grid, maintain the balance across the Cosmic Axis. The whole coral structure is constantly coming back into balance and finding stillness. A new journey lies ahead: to discover all new teachings. With time, your level of consciousness will open more and more.

You thank Maat, and she says, "No, I thank you. We are all equal and together in service of All That Is. I am delighted you have accepted this new life, for you will embody this for many light years."

---

22 Scroll of Truth is your Pillar of Light imbued with Maat's energy of truth, cosmic law, order, harmony, and balance.

The sacred space within the Central Sun implodes. You are back on Unas Causeway, where previously the path raised itself into the Cosmos. You finish your walk, and now, with every step you take, the tiles light up as if you have embodied the energy that propelled you before. The lions walk beside you. They no longer need to balance you or pull you upright. It all feels relaxed. You master your walk on the Path of Maat, connecting with the stars, the Cosmos, and the Earth, with ease and grace. You thrive on the essence of the Cosmic Axis, connected to a new group consciousness. A new beginning awaits you. Thank you.

I.7 Star Council of Eight, Pyramid of Djoser, Saqqara

Illustration: Saqqara Pyramid of Djoser (Step Pyramid).

Honour yourself by bringing your attention to your heart. Feel your heart and heart space as your sacred ground, upon which your Inner Temple resides. Imbue yourself with the energies of Divine Love and those of Saqqara. Soon you notice your sacred heart space is transforming into a body of water. You touch this magical hologram. Its raw power rushes through you. Your inner voice says, "Plunge into this liquid light. Now dive into your heart gate and travel to Saqqara. They await you."

As you dive into the depths of your heart, in your descent, you notice you are following a string of light. You recognise and understand that this string originates from the star in the northeast of the Cosmos. You drop rapidly and land atop the Pyramid of Djoser (the Step Pyramid) on the sacred grounds of Saqqara necropolis. Step by step, you descend into the courtyard. You now have the Causeway of Unas before you. When you reach the perimeter of that sacred space, you turn around and look at the Step Pyramid again. In the Step Pyramid's core, your mind's eye shows you blue-flaming energies igniting. You also witness three Light Beings in these flames, making inviting gestures. They have a Jaguar energy. You extend your right hand. From your palm, the same blue-essence energies shoot a beam towards the pyramid. They instantly project you inwards. The three Light Beings are now floating in circles around you. You follow. Together, you are creating a spiral pattern. This sacred geometry opens a portal into the depths of the pyramid.

The Jaguar Light Beings accompany you into a dark tunnel. You go deeper. You see water and restless waves under a dark sky. Only Sothis, her star, is shining brightly. You drop into these waters. They undulate you upwards and downwards. The silence is palpable, even in the farthest distance. You know the Jaguar Light Beings are still near you. You sense them below in the depths. Slowly you become familiar with your environment. Your heart connects strongly to these waters. Your heart triggers a centrifugal movement, and the waters begin to swirl around you as you become one with this water body. With a churning movement, your heart pushes and pulls and aligns each drop of water. The water body becomes an extension of your heart. It becomes your heart disc. You hear the Jaguar Light Beings giggling.

Suddenly, the heart disc initiates a counterclockwise motion. The body of water swirls violently and becomes a vortex. The most peculiar thing is that you remain still. As your heart disc spins, the spiral deepens from the surface into the depths. The vortex descends, ascends, and rises above the surface around and beyond your head and crown. Light-yellow strings of light envelop you like a caterpillar. Inside this caterpillar, you morph, gradually taking on the form of a vesica piscis, enabling you to co-create with the divine. The spinning motion slowly comes to an end as the last string of light is applied. You carry this new blueprint within you. As we come to the point of completion, the whole water body implodes within your heart.

Here you are, now standing in the desert sand. In the distance – at the outline where the waters once were – you discern green vegetation. You feel blessed. Something significant has happened. You laugh and giggle and look at your hands. You turn them over and see your palms showing a hologram of the churning waters and yellow strings of light. The memory of this initiation engraves itself into your cells.

The ritual continues as you feel the pull to walk the desert sand spirally. You widen the spiral with every step, embodying this gritty void where once the waters lay.

You expect to end up at the vegetative perimeter. Surprisingly, though, other plans emerge. A black portal resembling a small dungeon door appears on the spiral line. And as you walk into it, the steps descend, spiralling you in a rhythmic motion. You descend even more rapidly when the spiral turns into a sphere, enveloping you. You walk rhythmically, your sphere weaving your sacred sanctuary. The prima mater of the light strings alchemises into a beautifully soft and dense black obsidian energy. You see yourself in this obsidian sphere. Observing at your palms, the churning waves of the imploded waters in your heart remain imprinted. This sphere feels comfortable, resonant, and light. It softly reverberates with the quality of communication with the outer worlds, with vast stellar energies. Your attention turns to the starlit sky. All the stars hear your call and shoot light rays into your obsidian sphere. Before you, these create an operating system and star charts. These light rays create patterns of lines, and the first pattern is the zodiac sign, Scorpius. What does all this mean? You continue to look around you. You gaze to your left. You see ancient scrolls, remnants left behind. You stretch out your arm to take them and place them into your obsidian sphere.

One by one, you roll the scrolls out. Soft as velvet, they have golden patterns, star glyphs engraved upon them.

As you scan each one, you understand these are star charts. Their lines infuse their knowledge and wisdom into your heart, and all lined patterns appear in your heart sphere. As you look at the starlit sky, you also understand that you embody the star codes of those star beings once strongly interconnected to Earth. They wanted these treasures to be revealed. Therefore, they left them behind to emerge on Earth's surface.

These star beings will facilitate Earth's transition into a multidimensional and stellar consciousness from a planetary-only consciousness. You understand. Now the star beings appear before you. You are witnessing so many beings appearing, populations of star beings. You, my Beloved, are a sacred witness to the Star Council of Eight. They have assisted the Earth Star since her birth. They are the Ogdoad. The Star Council of Eight introduces two representatives for every Council, sixteen primary ambassadors in total.

They introduce themselves: "Dear One, since the beginning of her existence, we have imprinted the Earth with our coded messages. We believe these coded messages are lifelines for the Earth to sense us and stay connected to us. We are aware that it has been a difficult period. She has undertaken many endeavours and faced many challenges. We have always been energetically present with our consciousness: monitoring and safeguarding her. We have had various representatives coming in and out of the dimensional planes to take care of her. So here we are now. We are honoured to meet you. There is much we need to do together. We will, as of now, journey with you. We all have gifts for you and the Earth. As you co-create with the Earth, you are a channel for us to bring our gifts more fully into matter."

The Star Council of Eight represents eight star constellations connecting to countless other universes in our Cosmos. They provide you with a map of their origins.

I.7.1 Lobster Nebula, Scorpio

Ultraviolet Earth Star Mission
You connect to your heart space and allow the bright white energies of the Central Sun to penetrate your heart. The energies are potent. They break through your heart space like rushing white rays rising as lava from a volcano. Your entire body becomes a receptor for this cosmic light. It forms a pattern in the shape of a scorpion. All sixteen

representatives of the Star Council of Eight are present. They line up in a curved line, showing the Scorpio signature. The two representatives from the Scorpio constellation are more prominent. They originate from the Lobster Nebula.[23] The first Light Being is bluish. She sovereignly carries a beak resembling that of a parrotfish. The delicacy and subtleness of her hands emanate gentleness. With rounded fingertips, she radiates a blue frequency. She feels restrained, firmly anchored in her body, willing, open, and sharing. You feel they want to communicate. Even if it is difficult for you, they will take responsibility for making it right. The Light Being next to her is more featherlike and wears a beak similar to the crow family. You understand it is wise to keep the form of communication open, and they create a hologram of a light capsule. They invite you in.

You descend with them into the darkness of Inner Earth. The light capsule you are in is tight. You behold bright red light shining up as two ruby-red spheres connected by a line in their heart area. As they telepathically communicate with you, they explain that this is their project's energetic signature[24].

"We co-create on this project, and as such, we share this code. This energetic signature immediately actualises all actions of every star being in the Star Council of Eight. We form a group consciousness based on this project, and the energetic signature is the feature that makes us a group consciousness. While we are here in this birthing chamber, please align yourself with us. First, we stand in front of you. Next, to your right and left. Then we move behind you to imprint this energy signature into your energetic body. Two rays penetrate you. They spirally intertwine, creating a double helix. It fractalises itself into multiple helixes to form a spherical DNA structure. You now find yourself

---

23 Nebulae are made of dust and gases – mostly hydrogen and helium. The dust and gases in a nebula are vastly spread out, but gravity can slowly begin to pull together clumps of dust and gas. As these clumps grow larger and larger, their gravity grows stronger and stronger. Eventually, the clumps of dust and gas grow so large that they collapses into their own gravity. They collapse causes the material at the centre of the cloud to heat up-and this hot core is the beginning of a star. Nebulae exist in the space between the stars – also known as interstellar space. Source: https://spaceplace.nasa.gov/nebula/en/

24 Energetic signature of the Star Council of Eight imprinted on the heart area to co-create as a group consciousness on the project Ultraviolet Sun. This project exceeds this earthly ascension and that of the seven universes mentioned later.

Illustration: Saqqara. Step Pyramid.
Star Council of Eight.
The Symbol for the Ultraviolet Sun.
Earth's Future Soul Incarnation.

in this ruby-red DNA sphere. We are preparing you to co-create with us from the Earth Star. You found the Source Scrolls, which means your soul remembered. You feel that within is also without. The ruby-red sphere is merely a representation of this energy signature and your heart. You feel the energy signature pulsating and connecting to your pituitary gland, pineal gland, and crown. At this moment, an additional spherical system of nine spheres installs itself in your higher etheric energy body. Each sphere is a chamber like a sacred vault, which stores energy. This system's functionality resembles an informatics system. It continually consolidates information through rotational motion that encodes the sphere. They all intercommunicate with one another. Most important, they interconnect with all galaxies and universes connected to us. Believe me, we are talking about approximately a million galaxies, a vast network."

"This complex system alchemises information from the upper spheres, spiralling down into the lower spheres, and then collecting in your body. You will become a representative of our Star Council. We will be communicating with you during the day and the night."

"This ruby-red sphere surrounding you also embodies the Earth Star. We have always been connected to the Earth Star and specific power spots in Egypt for millions of years. We are present here in the Egyptian Nile Valley. These Creational Nile Temples were built on energy vortexes used by us. We also created new vortexes. We did not have any physical buildings. We encoded the soil with bright white light patterns of spheres and lines similar to those you saw on the Source Scrolls. We use them to communicate with Earth's core to initiate shifts and transmutational processes."

"During this time, the Earth Star's Light Body received the required updates. We imbued these light patterns with our codes, and a light pattern often resembled an angle or a number 7. This pattern lies horizontally on Earth's surface, but it can also redirect itself 90 degrees upwards to become an antenna or a beacon."

"The angle can rotate 180 degrees to become a shaft, a tunnel, or a portal. We enter these portals to transmit energy-coded information. When they keep rotating, they create a passageway to travel to Earth's core. We use this universal system on other stars or planets to travel and enter dimensional layers."

"These light patterns diffuse their codes into Earth's core and her entire body. They create a new auric field looking like a soft, white glow around the Earth. In this field, various rotational movements occur, allowing transformation and evolution. Without this support, the Earth Star would have endured severe decay."

"Because the energy in this quadrant of the galaxy is not all high frequency, a cluster of plasma shielding parts of this solar system from dark forces was necessary to prevent infiltration into the Earth Star. Precisely, from our point of view, we needed to ensure that the environment remained as neutral as possible and that the Earth would receive updates to stay connected with us. The Earth Star is also a part of the Star Council of Eight, and we take care of many other planets and stars."

"I bestow upon you a bright white sceptre. It shows an alternate pattern of spheres and vesica piscis. When you lay it in your hands, it begins to spin spherically and morphs into a swastika, a primaeval form for galaxy building. The swastika[25] transforms, the two curved intersecting lines uncross and slide side by side. You already saw this sign resonating with the Ultraviolet Star."

"Yes, it is your mission, your energy signature for your assignment, which exceeds this life. If you wish, it goes beyond. Of course, at every given moment, you can choose otherwise. But it is an opportunity for you to go in-depth in this process of cosmological rebirth and great forces of construction and destruction. It is about Creation. You join the Founding Fathers of Earth. We are most honoured to guide you through the Creational Nile Temples. There is much to document. I see that you are looking at the Cosmos. Yes, there is much to reveal. My dear child, allow me to hold your hands. It is enough for today.

---

25 Maltese cross, primordial sacred geometry which promotes expansion, and growth.

You will do well. You have our guidance, support, and protection. We love you because you are one of us. Archangel Michael is also one of the beings guiding many projects. He belongs to the seventh representation, being the Sceptre, Cassiopeia."

I.7.2 Thor's Helmet Nebula, Canis Major

Stellar Maps for Cosmic Ascension
Standing before you are the sixteen representatives of the Star Council of Eight. The two members of Thor's Helmet Nebula in Canis Major approach. The Light Being to the left resembles a cricket. She is green and has white wings with lime dots. She has hands for a cricket-like being, and there is a white membrane between her fingers. Her energy is friendly, joyful, delightful, and enthusiastic to meet and acquaint herself with other beings. The Light Being beside her is elongated, with longer feelers connecting to his black eyes. He has a cochlea on his back. He is related to the snail species familiar to us.

In front of you, they project a pool of black liquid light. You stand within it. It moves upwards to envelop you like a caterpillar. This soft, ethereal liquid wraps itself three times around your neck and then proceeds to your head to finally close at the level of your crown with a twisting gesture. Three antennae emerge from this closure. This liquid caterpillar structure is a thick plasma. Flexible, it exhibits a subtle swaying motion. You now open your eyes and gaze through this structure. You notice you still have an impeccable view, as it is permeable. If you extend your arms and look at them, you also see they are black. Within this caterpillar and your body, it is colder and lighter.

As you embody this black liquid light chamber, you notice at the level of your pelvic floor thirty-four black, rectangular tablets piling up into your body. In the centre of this pillar of black tablets, golden light strings centralise into your central column. This pillar rotates counterclockwise and patches your entire Central Axis with grainy golden liquid light. These beings giggle. They love to see. From their perspective, they are witnessing a black cocoon in which bright lights twinkle.

The texture is granular, for it contains Source Codes originating from the primordial dark waters. These waters are infinitely fertile, forever creating divine sparks, the primaeval source of existence. The golden liquid light moves up towards your eyes. There it infiltrates the nerve circuit connecting your eyes to your brain. It permeates your brain, infusing all the nerves fractally. The golden light then envelops your eyes, your eyeballs. A pulse is created from front to back between the eyes, the nerve circuit, and the brain. The pituitary and pineal glands, which transmit and infuse golden light in both directions, nourish this pulse. The entire brain area floods itself with golden light. Slowly the texture becomes denser and morphs into a golden plasma skull.

The energy moves downward now, creating a golden plasma layer around your body. It feels simultaneously dense, light, and cold. As your entire energetic body is resonating with the codes of this golden light, the frontal bone of your skull enlarges and heightens. This frontal bone also shifts forward as this transmutation occurs, creating almost a roof over the eyes.

Now your white spine and all vertebrae straighten and dissolve, revealing a golden spine. You feel how this spine is rising in your body and transcending the skull as an antenna. The transmutation is still active as the golden light descends into your legs, now changing your body on a molecular level – an extraordinary, beautiful experience. The Light Beings of the Thor Helmet Nebula have gifted you a different structure.

The Light Beings of Thor's Helmet Nebula speak: "It's beautiful for us to witness this process. This new Light Body will facilitate communication with the core of the Earth. The thirty-four tablets belong to Earth's core, the Temple of Love. It also allows you to work with the centre of the Earth, the mainframe. We are about Creation, being skilled in manifesting. This method is very effective, and this is what we offer you."

I.7.3 **Pisces**

Foundational Creational Forces

Before you, the curved line of the representatives of the Star Council of Eight reveals itself. Meanwhile, the form of the line has shifted from a curve into a recumbent number 3. The first representative resides on the inner curve of the recumbent number 3. The second, Thor's Helmet, Canis Major at the top, and the third representative, Pisces, is located a little further down. They clarify this shape is also the symbol for cosmic astrology.

At this moment, the two Light Beings from Pisces approach you. You are honoured to meet them. The starlight firmament enlightens the scenery here at Saqqara in the bowels of the Earth. Or rather, if you observe carefully, it does not seem to be on this planet. You did descend into the Inner Earth at Saqqara, at the Step Pyramid, but you seem to be, simultaneously, in their world in Pisces. Saqqara is a portal that has given you direct access to these beings in the constellations where they reside. You find yourself under a beautiful night sky in a remarkable and complex space. The energy has a more cosmic, fresh, and even cold feeling. The higher vibration is tangible as your inner senses clear up. You know you are also in the constellation Pisces with them. When you gaze around yourself, red planets and smaller moons set the scenery. They ask you if you like it. It is intriguing to be in three places at once: reading this Light Tablet, in Saqqara, and in Pisces. We no longer speak of bilocation, as this goes well beyond. We will refer to it for now as trilocation. The Pisces' Light Beings smile. They enjoy your bewilderment.

Gradually, you become accustomed to your new environment and its vibration. You bring your attention to the Pisces Light Beings who welcomed you warmly. Your gaze first falls on the Light Being to the left, in front of you. You witness it shape-shifting. It assumes various forms and seems not to have one distinct shape. It primarily comprises carnelian plasmic light but can also adopt other colours.

Golden Source Light

For your encounter it shows its lower body rounded, resembling a cauldron. "Come and look inside me," it says, and invites you to come closer. As you approach, immediately you notice golden codons. You understand this plasmic light desires to explain to you the Creational process of the golden Source Light. Strings of Source Codes structure in different golden clusters. Within the clustering of the golden Source Light, yellow Venus Light is visible. These golden clustered codons each form a pillar. If you track each pillar's energy, you observe a disc that has slid over the pillar from its centre. A string of clustered golden codons spirally coiled into a disc shape forms the disc. This beautiful complexity stuns you. These wonderful Light Beings show you no less than the Source Code for creating galaxies.

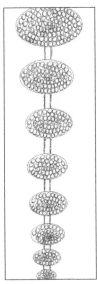

Illustration: Saqqara. Step Pyramid. Star Council of Eight. The Source Code for Creation.

Now you follow the pillar's energy further down. There are multiple pillars, but you follow only one. You see the discs do indeed become smaller. As you follow the pillar back upwards, they become more extensive and more considerable in width. You understand that as these discs procreate fractally, they become smaller. This concept also reflects the measurements of celestial bodies in various dimensions: a solar Sun is smaller than a galactic Sun, which is smaller than the universal Sun, which is smaller than the Central Sun, and so on. "What about the size of planets? Do celestial bodies in the same category have different sizes? For example, the Earth is smaller than the planets on which people are now incarnating. Is there a link between them?" you ask. They tell you that, yes, the blue core has an inherent light coefficient, but the celestial body can absorb more mass. However, there are more advanced planets whose blue cores vibrate at much higher rates. The raising of the vibration makes the body expand and retract. It then enters a transformation process. Here, from a vibrational point of view, it is not a planet anymore. It becomes more of a vibrational star with an obsolete structure. The Earth Star is in this situation at this moment.

They ask you to plunge in and slide down, following this pillar of golden clustered codons. You are about to enter this Light Being's cauldron, but you feel it is such an intimate experience that you ask to know its name. "My name is Strxls." The name is quite challenging to express. Having established more contact, you feel ready now, and you gently slide into his Light Body. You follow a spiral motion downwards. The pillar's texture feels smooth, like massive gold, and is not grainy at all. However, the interior of the pillar feels vivid, vibrant, bubbling, and fierce, like churning lava making its way out of the volcano.

Creational Essences of Light
As you tune in closer, you witness a triad of yellow, rose, and blue essences of Creation.

From a colour-essence perspective, the golden Source Light functions more like a stem cell and has infinite possibilities of expression. The blue Venus Light restructures the golden Source Light via blue membranes and allows the yellow Venus Light to emerge from the golden Source Light. The rose Venus Light forms a plasma layer over the yellow, meaning that it consolidates from the outside the restructured cell while imprinting plasma light. This consolidation process nourishes and ignites a fractal procreative movement from the inside of the cell, creating a cosmic DNA spiral staircase. This cosmic DNA spiral is the precursor to movement and growth.

The shape of the golden clustered codons grouped into pillars resembles the structure of a bunch of grapes. The cluster design is straight along the string, but where the divine spark of a Light Being – a planet, a Moon, human or other species – is seeded on the coral branch, the cluster structure widens like a bunch of grapes. This high-energy union of golden spheres initiates an amalgamation process. At this point, all the golden spheres generate so much energy that the Creation itself emanates intense blue light. This blue light is the blue sun energy of the blue core mentioned earlier. In essence, everything has a blue core. However, not every Creation chooses to embody that blue sun essence. The blue core signifies the ignition of life.

The golden Source Light and the three prima mater essences represent the main building blocks of Creation. All within Creation carries blue core energy. The alchemisation process of the three-colour light essences ignites, from within the divine spark, whirlwinds of blue light strings that twirl and whirl spherically, creating the blueprint of a sphere.

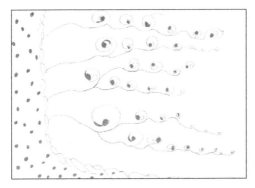

Illustration: Saqqara. Step Pyramid. Star Council of Eight. The Descent into Incarnation of the Divine Spark.

Divine Spark's Incarnation Journey

When the divine spark leaves the Cosmic Womb's membrane, it travels to the inner womb via the clustered golden Source Light Pillars. Arriving at the point of incarnation, it then descends through the clustered golden Source Light Pillars, which branch fractally like arteries. Each divine spark intelligently seeking its future incarnation point.

The divine spark already has a minimal imprint of the white sphere in its descent, which is the first expression of manifestation. This basic white blueprint comprises four white bands running vertically from north to south, similar to Earth's meridians. These vertical bands do not yet interconnect or intertwine. So, as the divine spark descends into the Cosmic Womb from within, it ignites the first process of expression and creates a white sphere around it. You can compare it to the skeleton of a human being. This white sphere gradually completes itself during the descending journey by intertwining and weaving the four bands with crystalline light, providing the primary universal blueprint.

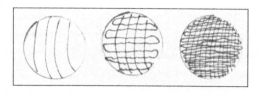

Illustration: Saqqara. Step Pyramid. Star Council of Eight. The Weaving process of the Divine Spark into matter.

When the divine spark arrives at the incarnation point, it leaves the clustered membrane and attaches to the golden branch. In this first phase, golden Source Light overlays the coral branch in the form of a disc. This supports the divine spark to acclimate, integrate, and enter a cohesive and symbiotic phase. At the end of this first phase, the golden Source Light of the disc surrounding the evolving divine spark has withdrawn into its white sphere. The sphere of the divine spark encapsulates all golden Source Light. This is a crucial stage because you have the unique Source Code of the divine spark, which is within the spark at birth. However, you also have the Source Code of the topological aspect of the Cosmic Womb, where the divine spark incarnates.

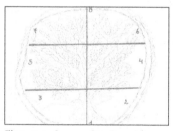

Illustration: Saqqara. Step Pyramid. Star Council of Eight. Our Cosmic Womb and her Spatiotemporal zones.

The topological aspect refers to the different spatiotemporal layers in a Cosmic Womb. A similar example is the subdivisions in a Tree of Life. However, these subdivisions do not explain the vibrational and space-time aspects. From this perspective, the Cosmic Womb consists of three major horizontal bands-zones.

Depending on where the spark situates in these bands, it absorbs the topological information, the topological Source Code. Once it absorbs the Source Code, it can then complete its growth process because it must know its mission. The divine spark carries her unique soul mission within. The golden Source discs that support her contain the divine spark's universal mission related to the topological aspect of the Cosmic Womb.

Creation of Multidimensionality
Another unique process takes place. As soon as the white-sphered di-

vine spark integrates both Source Codes and the yellow Venus Light ignites the clustered strings' DNA spiral, the divine spark through the yellow Venus Light projects its consciousness throughout the whole Cosmos in a mere instant. The divine spark then becomes the point of the singularity of its own spiral vortex of cosmic existence. We refer to this as the One divine spark.

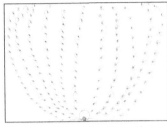

Illustration: Saqqara. Step Pyramid. Star Council of Eight. The Creation of Multidimensionality.

Once the unique and universal Source Code integrates into the sphere of the divine spark, yellow Venus Light creates clustered strings from this One divine spark and projects it outwards throughout the multiverse in different zones of time and space.

This Creational process ignites itself in a sovereign fashion, in several dimensional layers throughout the Cosmos. The yellow Venus Light's strings replicate spatially throughout the entire Cosmos in a spiral manner. The multidimensional procreation in space starts from merely one position. This process translates the complexity of multidimensionality of space and time.

Creation of the I Am That I Am & Harmonic Resonance

The yellow Venus Light also projects the divine spark's consciousness throughout the Cosmos via its yellow essence. Through its yellow essence, one could say it informs other Creations of the existence and consciousness of the new-born divine spark. The yellow Venus Light enjoys being interconnected. In this way, it becomes united with all Creation and becomes part of the whole. This process occurs by exchanging the divine spark's replica or excerpt of Source Code particles, which interconnect all Creation.

Where a Venus Light Creation emerges, this Creation resonates all over the Cosmos. Now we move from trilocation to *omnilocation*. The Pisces Light Beings show you how the *I Am that I Am* comes into being. The created divine spark is present everywhere as the *I Am that I Am*. I Am a water drop that I Am the ocean. This process also explains why the Venus Light's primary purpose is to provide interconnected-ness. It functions through interconnectedness because everything is everywhere. You are everywhere. That is why you are here with these Light Beings in Pisces and Saqqara, and simultaneously you are also reading this Light Tablet at your current location. Your presence continues through your multidimensionality and is present throughout the Cosmos.

In this respect, we clearly understand why *harmonic resonance* is of importance to all of us. If one Creation becomes damaged, all of Creation suffers from the imbalance. Divine Love thrives on life because you are all life. The Star Council of Eight cherishes the Earth because the Earth is the Star Council of Eight. I am YOU, and YOU are ME.

We reveal to you the secret that the Ancient Egyptians learned from us, Star Beings. The Cosmic Angelic initiation is an example how Star Beings awakened in humans the consciousness of space not bound to one place. Star Beings spoke of multidimensionality in one's own structure, and in all Light Beings' structures, and even multidimensionality on the Cosmic Womb level. However up to now, we taught this only with respect to this current Cosmic Womb. In this Light Tablet, we will go even farther, and beyond our Cosmos.

Finally, once the clustering of the yellow Venus Light Pillars begins, the *spatial Creational process* ensures *harmonic resonance* and cosmic balance. The Venus Light provides cosmic law, order, and harmony, governed by the Goddess Maat. We can simplify this with the example of a tree on which flowers bloom. Each flower is responsible for the energy balancing of the whole tree. Each flower is essentially the other. If you injure one flower, you wound them all. If one is out of balance, they are all out of balance. Harmonic resonance is a cosmic law that governs all existence.

"As Above, So Below. As Within, So Without," declared Thoth Hermes Trismegistus.

Expansion of the Multidimensional Structure

Once this yellow clustering begins, the rose Venus Light essence broadens these clusters from within, creating dimensional space. In this dimensional space, spheres within spheres originating in the Source Code emerge. The membrane widens to bring forth new spheres from within, creating this complex structure of nesting dolls. They represent fractal existence and growth from within. As soon as the rose Venus Light has expanded, has created space, something new comes into existence. However, at every level, the crystalline-structured light provides the base structure to give a divine spark a basic universal form. You can compare this to a skeletal structure that the Venus Light continues to develop.

Your attention now turns to the Light Being in front of you on your right side. This Light Being is telepathically transmitting information to Strxl, which Strxl shapes and presents to you. This Light Being is of milky-white plasmic light. Strxl explains, "We all have crystalline light in our energetic body, in various densities. We, for instance, cannot vaporise or become etheric. We remain plasmic, being at the level of crystalline structured light that we embody. I have more crystalline light than my friend because he has liquefied himself while standing, so he morphs, wobbles, and fluctuates due to lesser crystalline light."

Cosmic Ascension. Return to the Point of Singularity.

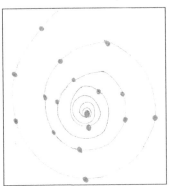

Illustration: Saqqara. Step Pyramid. Star Council of Eight. The One divine spark and its Multiple Soul extensions.

The One divine spark is the Sun around which all other soul incarnations or soul extensions revolve, often in a clockwise spiral motion. The soul extensions are positioned on the One divine spark's spiral and rotate alternatively clockwise and counterclockwise.

Each soul extension has an autonomous existence in which it regulates its ascension process according to its own rhythm. Each soul extension comes to self-realisation at its own pace, in the midlife of a One divine spark. Some soul extensions positioned on the One divine spark's spiral may dissolve their bodies midway through the life of the One divine spark. They project their essence back to the One divine spark. Gradually an implosion of the spiral occurs, and the spiral empties. The spiral arms then retreat. The One divine spark has called home all its soul extensions. At this time, the One divine spark gathers all the wisdom all soul extensions have gained. With all this increased consciousness, it expands its potential and is ready to take on a new challenge. Ascension occurs, and the One divine spark itself increasingly moves upwards through the Cosmic Womb, back to Source, from where it originated.

I.7.4 **Eridanus**

Alpha α & Omega Ω

Here you are again, in Inner Earth beneath the Step Pyramid in Saqqara. The Star Council of Eight awaits you to meet the fourth representation of the constellation Eridanus. You observe the curved line again before you. The Eridanus representation is down towards the first curvature of the recumbent number 3. You watch them approaching you from a distance. They move and approach powerfully. This evokes a slight fear in you. You would like to take a few steps backwards.

They have arrived and are standing before you. The Light Being to your left emits from his back, ethereal black stardust, creating a black violet cape that flutters as in a wind. You undoubtedly sense his power. His features are more humanoid than all other beings you have met so far. More grey blue in appearance and thriving on black-essence light, he wears a mask-headdress with horns. His torso looks muscular. However, his lower body is of ethereal grey essence. It resembles etheric essence focused to a point where his lower body is cone shaped. The energy converges at that point.

He says his name is Bronco. He introduces you to his partner. She has such a gentle, sweet, and cosy feminine energy. Instinctively, however, you know you should not underestimate her.

A peculiar feature comes to your awareness. The Eridanus Light Being's pranic conduit, which should run vertically in her Light Body, slips out through her abdomen. You witness it feeling around you. She is scanning energetic fields. Eridanus is the first representation where you are not simply welcomed unconditionally and allowed to receive all wisdom.

She also is tense about your encounter. You tell her it is all right and that you are honoured to meet her. You hold her hands. They have the same shape as our hands. Her hands, though, do not have any separate fingers, but two surfaces. As you touch her and allow her to sense you, she becomes more secure. You notice she approaches Bronco and telepathically tells them it is good to share and be with you. She gives her permission. And with that, he begins the transmission of the energy they want to impart.

Your attention is drawn to the back of his body as he stretches his arms back towards his spine. He opens this space and takes out a black scroll. He now carries the black scroll in his hand. It is elongated and looks like a cylinder. Atop this scroll sits a black fan. It has just slid from his brain area. The fan reminds you of the coral structure of our Cosmos. It looks exactly like it.

Jacob's Ladder of Our Cosmos

Bronco offers it to his partner. She gestures to position it in your midst. He lays the staff down, and it immediately straightens itself out. It has its own intelligence. The coral you witness before you, you feel and know it is vivid. "Please, keep looking at it," he says. Keep your eye on the coral and begin to see white energy atop its outline. This white energy morphs into a clockwise vortex, and it begins to descend the fan. The vortex then moves up and down the trunk of the coral, magnetising and opening it, accessing it to reveal underlying ancient codes. You can now see that the coral structure's base elongates and descends. You witness the energy of the coral structure descending with each up-and-down movement. All the energy of the branches and all the three subdivisions are also descending. This is the motion that wants to be expressed.

The coral structure expresses itself in matter. It stands firm and does not move under this up-and-down motion. Instead, it is the white energies that bring about the multidimensionality of the coral by bringing it downwards, descending in octaves.

This signifies the Cosmic Womb we reside in is one soul extension of her larger Jacob's ladder. All other multidimensional layers of our Cosmic Womb slowly also descend into the core One. We are descending with her into the core One. Our Cosmic Womb appears to be one aspect of the core One, the primary expression of the One divine spark, for, as we descend, we move downwards towards a place from whence we originate.

Source Field: The Larger Field Bearing Our Cosmos

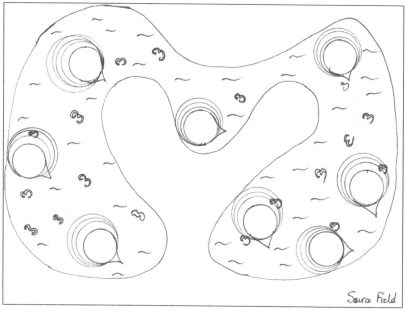

Illustration: Saqqara. Step Pyramid. Star Council of Eight. Source Field.

Our Cosmic Womb resides in a Vast Divine Plane resembling a recumbent number 3 with the three legs pointing down. As these words resound, your attention is drawn to all other Cosmic Wombs in this plane of existence. They all appear to be black circular spaces within larger indigo structures. As the indigo essence reveals itself, you un-

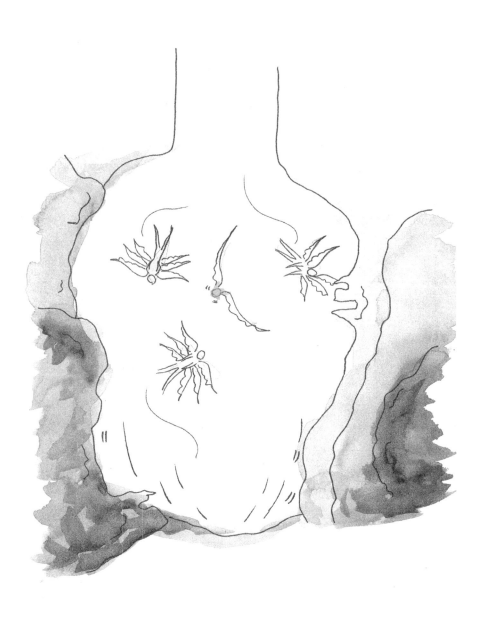

Illustration by N. Van Der Auwera: A Sacred Journey into Creation. The Omega Ω.

derstand whence the blue essence Venus Light originates. This prima mater that ignites all life originates from the Vast Divine Plane, the Source Field of existence beyond our current understanding.

As you gain greater access to these more profound layers of the Source Field, you see that each Cosmos that resides within it is cone shaped. Its flat base dwells in the Source Field. The pooled part of the cone descends with its apex downwards. All Cosmic Wombs converge their energy together in One point. The Source Field unites in One downwards apex. Bronco's lower body translates this image as an ethereal coalescing of the upper energy in One downwards cone shape.

Omega Ω, Divine Cosmic Mother

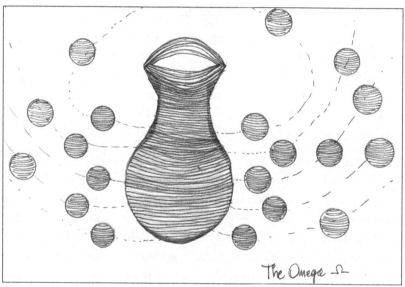

Illustration: Saqqara. Step Pyramid. Star Council of Eight. The White-Stringed Omega Ω.

From the converging apexes, a white string emerges towards a deeper dimensional plane. You witness intense, enigmatic energy, an unprecedented majesty, grandeur, power, stillness, and sovereignty. Most of all, you witness love. Your heart is lost as it tries to thrive in this temple where the love energy is unprecedented. The sweetness, lovingness, and gentleness of this Creational Mother are overwhelming. Your heart has never seen or experienced such love.

You have never witnessed a sacred space of this magnitude. Nothing compares to what your eyes and Light Body perceive of all the sacred places on Earth: how sacred, grand, and resonant they are. Being in this presence takes your breath away. You sense the Omega Ω beneath you. She magnetically attracts your heart. If it could, your heart would leave your body now and return home. Your heart recognises its Mother Essence, its origin. At this moment, her only desire is to imbibe this sweetness one more time.

You discern this field as the Divine Mother Temple, in which lives the Omega Ω of all Cosmic Wombs. The field itself is omni-vibrating, where circular shapes float concentrically and multidimensionally through this Divine Mother Temple most harmoniously and perfectly. All concentric circles vibrate as One.

You now lower your gaze and witness your Divine Cosmic Mother, the Omega Ω from which all life emanates. Your eyes glance down, and you see the structure of a white breathing vase. Her breath comprises vibration. She brings her consciousness inward to create eternal vibration, and as such, she sustains life for the entire Source Field with just this solemn act. Her breath nourishes you and All That Is.

You hover around the beautiful Omega Ω and reach out your hand softly to touch her. Your fingers catch a soft, subtle vibration that runs throughout your body. You know she has been gentle with you because her vibrational power would have blown you away in an instant. When you look carefully to understand her Light Body, you see she is a composite structure of trillions of white horizontal circular strings taking the form of a vase. These circular strings are an unknown complexity of mysterious octaves. The amplitude of each string inflates and deflates to create an autonomous vibration sustaining the larger structure as One.

These trillions of strings interact with one another. Through this interaction, something comes into existence, although you cannot yet see it clearly. You witness the strings augmenting their vibrations as they interact. They perform the same up-and-down movement around one another and around the entire vase structure. This is similar to what you observed at the coral's trunk, allowing it to descend in octaves to visit this Divine Mother Temple.

As you witness this motion, you understand she wants to show you something that happens only once every 800 thousand to 1 million years, in our perception of time. White spheres are leaving her body. They are composed of the same prima mater she is composed of. These white spheres have a band of horizontal strings. There is also an overlay of vertical strings over the horizontal band. You hear and feel sound. You can hear a whale or what may be a siren.[26] Their music echoes within us the call of the Omega Ω, so we will never forget. The Omega Ω also seeks connection with her children, she wants us to know she is here for us, and she always will be.

Birth of the Alpha α

A new-born sphere floats clockwise above the mouth of the Omega Ω. Then the sphere descends to revolve around the Omega Ω. She, herself, brings your attention to all the white-stringed spheres revolving around her. All these white-stringed spheres with horizontal and vertical strings hold resonance and create sound. Together with the Omega Ω, they express the purest essence of sound. They revolve circularly around the Omega Ω, and they make smaller inward circular side-loops within this circular revolution. In other words, there is a more significant circular motion, and within this larger circular motion, the spheres make inward loops towards the Omega Ω. The form of these smaller loops resembles a hand-drawn recumbent number 3. All white-stringed spheres revolve around the Omega Ω, making smaller loops in a set pattern to orbit back into the primary orbit around the Omega Ω. There are millions of white-stringed spheres. Every 800 thousand to 1 million years in our perception of time, a white-stringed sphere is born.

These white-stringed spheres create vortices when they make smaller loops. They project the spirals downwards. The powerful energy em-

---

26 The Cosmic Whale and the Mermaid were seen in the Pyramid of Khafre, in Giza, in its pit at the time of raising the Pyramids' backbone (raising the backbone of Osiris). These two beings work closely with the Omega Ω and have been sent by her to assist Earth and humanity in returning home by activating all dormant temples located in the depths on the ocean floor.

anating from a downwards spiral allows the Omega Ω to float in her larger field. All the white-stringed spheres together create a field of spiralling downwards energy holding the Omega Ω positioned. They represent a surrounding environment keeping the Omega Ω floating, stable, and intact. All these spheres protect the Omega Ω and confine her. They are the Alpha α, revolving around the Omega Ω, and in this orbit, they form smaller loops.

Cosmic Sex: Alpha α & Omega Ω

Within the loops, the Alpha α go up and down around their axis, incessantly. As they move up and down, they create friction. This friction prompts the rings of the Omega Ω to resonate. The Alpha α create longitudinal waves, and this energy gently and lovingly touches the Omega Ω. When these longitudinal waves touch these rings, they vibrate and make this beautiful high-frequency sound. This sound also creates a downwards clockwise vortex starting in the vase's neck, descending right through, and piercing the vase's flat bottom.

The vortex's strings then climb the body of the Omega Ω from the outside, and once halfway up, they penetrate the Omega Ω's strings lightly and briefly through the horizontal strings and then go back outwards again via a loop.

As the white strings of the vortex of the Omega Ω extend infinitely, they bring the new-born sphere to its point of incarnation in the greater Source Field. The white-stringed sphere is similar to the *divine* spark. Again, these strings express pure sound. This prima mater is pure vibration and thus not liquid, plasmic, or crystalline.

Inside these white strings, you can discern filaments of cone shapes. They are the vehicles of sound. When the white-stringed sphere is lovingly brought into the vast cosmic plane, the Source Field, the white strings of the Omega Ω, withdraw to the Mother. This process will recur over a trillion years, in our perspective of time.

Meanwhile, the Omega Ω continues breathing, and her breath is pure vibration. She is a loving mother who radiates infinite vibration and nourishes all the Cosmos residing in the Source Field.

This process occurs even more rarely than the birth of an Alpha α. The Omega Ω has chosen this moment, in which the Earth is in a critical transition phase, to reveal ancient secrets so that we Light Beings may understand Omega Ω's mission. As she rekindles this wisdom residing within us, we will hear her call to bring us back home.

Expansion and Growth of a Newborn Cosmos

The new-born Cosmos begins its journey as a white-stringed sphere carrying within all it needs. Within this sphere, you witness three smaller rotating spheres. You discover a light-blue, a white, and a yellow one. In their midst abides a tiny golden dot. As each revolves around the divine golden spark and rotates on its axis, we can observe this revolutionary process around all celestial bodies. This motion differs from the motion of the Alpha α because we have left the world of pure vibration.

The white, light-blue, and yellow spheres now rotate in all directions, like atoms. The triad begins the weaving process, weaving this new Cosmos into existence. They rotate around one another in the weaving pattern of a vesica piscis. As they weave their strings into the shape of a vesica piscis between one another, the divine golden spark remains in the centre. Soon, a ray of three white strings appears in the centre of the white-stringed sphere. The texture is denser than the other strings of vibration. The vibration is densifying. We have commenced the journey from spirit to matter. This white ray rises and falls like water from a fountain, creating the first toroid.

Once all vertical loops of the toroid manifest, a white string spirals up from the bottom and weaves itself horizontally between all vertical strings. After that, an additional layer of vertical strings becomes woven. And again, after that, a horizontal string interweaves all vertical strings.

The weaving process of horizontal and vertical strings creates dimensional space. Meanwhile, the toroid becomes quite dense, and between the various strings, the energies move and vibrate and create dazzling white light. Due to the vibrational process in-between these white woven strings, the sphere expands from within.

Illustration: Saqqara. Step Pyramid.
Star Council of Eight. Birth of a New
Cosmos.

As the entire structure expands, the One divine spark creates new divine sparks. It sows them outwards in a counterclockwise rotating torque within the newly created toroid field. Numerous spirals spring from this One divine spark. The spirals repeatedly make loops. In these loops, golden spheres crystallise as a *codon*. A golden spiral string arises in Creation with many golden codons interconnected by the golden string. The latter sets the basic pattern for the outline and shape of the new Cosmos. Each codon comprises all the information to bloom fully within its spatial environment. Each Cosmos is unique, reverberates in distinct vibrations, and expresses a unique, diverse program.

The golden codon string rises upwards and rotates around its axis. The constant rotating around its axis subdivides the codons into countless smaller spheres. These remain interconnected in a clustered-grape structure. In this phase, the clustered golden spheres come into existence. These smaller spheres project strings out of their bodies, creating the central axial system of the new-born Cosmos.

In the larger toroid structure, the Central Axis rises. In Egypt, they refer to it as the raising of Osiris' backbone. Once the backbone has risen, all golden spheres detach themselves from this spine. In essence, it is white light, millions of golden spheres swirling down into the toroid, then floating up through the toroid's inner membrane. Via guidance of white strings, they take up their positions as celestial bodies. Nothing is left to chance. The One divine spark brings with it an intricate and definite structure.

In this created Cosmos, the countless golden spheres position themselves harmoniously. They float within the larger womb. Two strings within the inner membrane now rise upwards alongside the membrane's wall. When the strings reach the top, intertwining and rotating around one another twice in a clockwise direction, they seal the Cosmic Womb. At this moment, from the inside the Cosmos can begin to expand in width.

Illustration: Saqqara. Step Pyramid.
Council of Eight.
Birth of a New Cosmos.
Blueprint of a trumpet coral.

The inner membrane morphs into golden liquid light. The entire Cosmos imbues itself with this golden Source Light. An inner seed emerges from the dimensional depths, breaking open in four parts. An intensely bright red-orange, fluorescent essence string appears from the centre. It rises. Once above, it weaves horizontal rings downwards in a torsion. Once again, we witness a weaving process forming a new combination of horizontal and vertical strings. When the weaving stops, a pillar in the form of a trumpet coral manifests itself in a lovely way. The new Cosmos brings to life a distinctly different coral structure. When it begins to reproduce, red-orange, fluorescent spheres emerge. The exact process begins again, as when the Omega Ω gave birth to white-stringed spheres.

This red-orange, fluorescent essence is the unique prima mater of the new-born Cosmos. A larger sphere is also visible. An expansion has occurred, and the sphere has become less dense.

These spheres spiral harmoniously through the Cosmic Womb. They weave red-orange, fluorescent strings. Their cosmic dance creates several larger trumpet corals at the base of the womb. From these trumpet corals also depart many strings. At the end of each string, countless universes and galaxies emerge in the original forms of red-orange, fluorescent spheres. At the end of each sphere, smaller red-orange, fluorescent spheres sprout. Thus, we witness fractal procreation. This Cosmos emits a distinct energy. It feels dazzlingly bright, sharp, and alive. This colour represents a program stored in the root of the coral. Located here is also a blue disc containing the program for this particular Cosmos. The essence in the disc exists everywhere and in the smallest forms of life. "Well done," says the sweet Light Being. "You just witnessed the Alpha α and the Omega Ω, their cosmic sex, and you witnessed a Cosmos coming into existence." This lovely Light Being of Eridanus takes your hand. She caresses your head.

Creation of the Omega Ω, Divine Cosmic Mother

She now shows you the story about the Creation of the Omega Ω. At the centre of the Omega Ω structure, one primary horizontal white string emits an up-and-down vibration. From the core of this string, other strings emerge, creating the vase structure. The transmitted vibration holds the shape of the vase in place. You also understand now that it is this vibration that holds our Cosmos in place. Vibration reigns. We also refer to the harmonic resonance as the Musica Universalis holding all the galaxies in place.

The Musica Universalis keeps our bodies, our minds, and emotions in balance. When people disconnect from inner peace within the heart, we disconnect from the resonance of the Omega Ω. When we enter states of lower vibration consciousness, we disconnect from the Musica Universalis omnipresent in our Cosmos. We disconnect from our Divine Cosmic Mother, who loves us dearly.

I.7.5 Lepus, Hare

Source Field

The Star Council of Eight calls you to Earth's inner levels beneath the Step Pyramid of Saqqara. Before you awaits the curved line in the silhouette of the Source field, the recumbent number 3. All eight constellations are present on this line, and they tell the story of the Source Scrolls. The representation of the constellation Hare is at the beginning of the second part of the shape. As you approach this point, you witness a hole in the ground with white light radiating from it. How amusing, because Lepus means *rabbit*. While you approach closer, you notice it is tiny, even smaller than your foot.

White light radiates through the layer of Earth. Suddenly you sense a tremendous suction. You are sucked forcibly into the hole, falling so quickly that your physical body cannot follow. Your skin, flesh, and veins dilate and deform. The last part of the fall is even more fierce, as you fall into inky, ice-cold water. It seems like nothingness. You try to say something to understand where you are, "Hello?" But you hear nothing in return. The lightness of your body strikes you. It has no gravity. It stays in place but also seems to float. You feel a pull again. The bright white light leads you somewhere. Again, you come down in a spiral. Now you know you will soon arrive at a point of rest. You come to stillness. Amid these inner depths, you look around yourself and understand that the bright white light has brought you to the deeper layers of the Source Field. The inky dark waters where you were before were the top layer of Source Field.

You try to grasp the ethereal substance with your hand. You touch it to understand what kind of prima mater it is. It is peculiar because it is dark blue, almost like a mist, but thinner, more subtle, airier, and completely transparent. You decide to breathe it into your body, to absorb and become familiar with it. You have not met the representatives of the constellation of Hare yet, but you suspect they are the bright white light that led you here. In the distance, you hear a voice. It is the Light Being of Source Field.

This Source Field emanates peacefulness. You perceive the vibration and witness the songs of all these different Cosmoses.[27] Our Cosmos is one of them. You can see it as well. You are at the level of the lower end of all the cone shapes. Here you notice floating in this dark-blue mist, red-orange fluorescent and golden particles. They are shaped in smaller curved lines: more miniature representations of the Source Field's shape. They move about, and their shape enables them to resonate within the larger field.

Initiation into the White-Stringed Sphere. Your Divine Potential.
You rotate around your axis. Your left side seems heavier than your right. Meanwhile, your left side dissolves and crumbles downwards. Now, you feel the whole of your body crumbling downwards. The only thing remaining is your white-stringed etheric structure, upon which your whole energy body builds. You are baffled to witness this.

---

27 Cosmos. The plural of Cosmos does not yet exist in our dictionary. In this context, we refer to the plural.

You now see your own toroid field and the interwoven yellow and blue Venus Light strings. Your toroid spins rapidly. In the middle of your Central Axis, there seems to be a white disc. The prima mater of the disc is visibly denser. It begins to rotate when you bring your attention to it, creating concentric circles over circles, procreating infinitely, and creating an intricate grid of woven white strings.

As this motion ignites your white-stringed toroid, you can hear the vibrational strings of your energetic body and the high hum of its frequency. You become pure vibration: a high-frequency sound becomes tangible. The higher the vibration becomes, the more these strings elongate. And as they become longer, they also become thinner. The thinner they become, the higher the frequency of sound they emit.

Now you look within your Central Axis. You detect an up-and-down movement: the Alpha α movement. It is as if your right side is rubbing against your left side, creating this up-and-down movement. You desire to be with this for a while. You witness these up-and-down movements igniting your Central Axis even more, becoming a trunk. You perceive a hollow space coming into being. Enlarging. The vertical movement of the toroid loops down into the toroid from the outside into the inside. It then slides down the inside of the toroid along the Central Axis. The speed of this motion increases. It enables the Central Axis to vibrate and expand even more. Your entire toroid expands and ignites the white-stringed sphere around you, which grows exponentially. It shows you your divine potential, the potential of a Central Sun, for you are your own creator.

Stay with this for a while. Imprint this experience into your heart to remember and never forget. Slowly the sphere withdraws again to dissolve entirely into your spiritual heart.

You are in this ink-blue ethereal substance again. You breathe in the ink-blue prima mater. It penetrates deeply into your body, making it heavy, deeply suffused into your cellular memory. The Light Beings of Hare want you to remember. They have just ignited the memory of your divine potential. You continue breathing and see your body morphing. You become this ink-blue prima mater entirely.

The properties of this ink-blue prima mater are containment, nourishment, Creation of dimensional space, guidance, and protection. Your spine becomes ponderously heavy and fully infused. It morphs. Your vertebrae collapse and dissolve. You behold the essence of ink-blue liquid light seeping in and aligning your body and all your light bodies with the frequency of the vibrational strings of your white-stringed sphere. Your white-stringed sphere has reemerged to purge your body, balancing it according to harmonic resonance. You feel a constant up-and-down movement, balancing and dissolving all that is obsolete. A sweet, rocking motion nurtures you. You feel all outdated structures within yourself descending. This process feels cumbersome. These structures are substantial. As they gradually descend, you know you are letting go. They dissolve.

Above the Central Axis of your toroid, a rose Venus Light vortex emerges. It emanates from the white disc in your centre. Its light completely encompasses your white-stringed sphere. This rose Venus Light envelops your white-stringed sphere to consolidate and imprint its shape and frequency. This act will provide specific, sustained stability.

From the inner disc, white strings sprout to densify the toroid's vertical loops. They slide closer to one another. They become a denser whole as the white Venus Light unites them. This process also seals the white-stringed sphere. We come to completion as around you, a golden spherical structure emerges. This Divine Golden Sphere protects and safeguards your heart with the white disc as the centre of your toroid.

You are ready. You leave again via the tunnel through which you came, even faster than before. You desire to explode out of that hole like fireworks lighting up the sky with your essence. It tremendously enlivens you because you have embodied your divine potential.

I.7.6 **Aquarius**

Carnelian Omega Ω, Divine Cosmic Mother
Birth of Your Unique Aquarius Light Tablet
The inner plane at Saqqara is vast yet confined at the same time. An invisible circle securely outlines the desolate space beneath the Step Pyra-

mid, where you have been brought. You also feel its solitude. There are no witnesses here, for the Council has chosen to unveil all its secrets. The blueprint of this area is a deep indigo, ink blue. The Star Council of Eight is present. You can already perceive the shape of Source Field. This time, the shape characterises itself as white-yellow light on the location where the star representatives reside.

You witness the star representatives of the Star Council of Eight within this Source Field shape. However, this time, the area behind you catches your attention. You turn around and observe a stunning view of white-yellow light appearing as an overwhelming sunrise. You feel a sense of confinement. The representatives of Aquarius stand behind you. They urge you to walk toward this bright white-yellow light. Telepathically they tell you they follow you every step of the way. You walk. It is difficult. You already feel a strong tension and resistance in your heart area. It is as if you cannot move forward, as if you are walking into a storm. Suddenly you feel something pulling you through your heart. It comes from the centre of this white-yellow light. It pulls you closer at a rapid pace, your feet dragging behind, on the ground.

You know the two representatives of Aquarius are behind you. They know how to move forward in their own quiet time. You are approaching the field of the bright white-yellow light. It immediately encloses you within its spherical Light Body. As you find yourself in this spherical space, astonished, you gasp at beautiful dazzling lights and soft pastel shades. The Sphere's Light Being has now detached itself from your heart. It only wanted to help you approach. Here you are, in a vast spherical temple. The energy is tenuous. You touch the soft, etheric, plasmic walls, but they are impermeable. It is impossible to push your hand through them. Behind you, you sense the presence of the three Light Beings as they emerge from the inner core of this sphere. They are humanoid, tall, and have pointed ears, wearing white galactic garments. "Come here," they say and gesture, "we want to show you something." You walk closer. They ask you to lead the way. You try to move, but you seem to collide with a plasma wall. Or at least it seems that way at first. You now see an arm reaching out to you, seizing you, and lifting you into a higher dimensional level of this spherical temple.

The three Light Beings, on the contrary, effortlessly levitate.

You now find yourself in a towering building. Like a shell, a spiral staircase ascends at its centre. You climb. As you mount these steps, but strangely go downwards at each step. So, you climb again. And you go downwards again. You go up and down. It seems that each time you go down, a layer of this staircase compresses into the floor. This motion peels off all layers of the stairs. There are no more steps. Like an accordion, they have collapsed and lie now on the foundation where you stand. All that is left around you is another bright white sphere. You try to understand where you are. You try to gain insight into your surroundings. It seems as if you are genuinely in a space shuttle. You see screens like onboard computers. Out of curiosity, you touch a screen. You intuitively draw a golden spiral. Suddenly, the lights of the other screens awaken. You have ignited the space shuttle, and the white sphere morphs into a metallic structure. It has materialised. The three Light Beings tell you to depart. You know the space shuttle is programmed and will follow a predestined trajectory. You can see the guiding flight lines in the Cosmos. These flight lines follow a recurring pattern. It seems you are always flying on the outline of the constellation Aquarius. With each new cycle, you notice the line is etched more profoundly into the Cosmos's strata. Via this cyclical movement, you carve out the constellation.

You understand why this cyclical movement has meaning for you. It offers into your energy body the knowing and integration of the significance of Aquarius for humanity, the Earth, and Aquarius Star Beings. So, as you circle this constellation, deeply engraving its outline, you also inscribe into your heart what Aquarius means to you. Every cycle, the outline narrows. You enter deeper into the inner layers of our Cosmos. You carve out the constellation, cutting it like a piece of pie and extracting it from the universe. As you carve it out, the shape of a cone becomes clearer. It is as if the upper part of the Aquarius constellation is the flat base of the cone. You continue to narrow and deepen until you reach the cone's lowest point. All stars in this constellation infuse their essence into the cone's apex. You position yourself below it. You imbibe the golden-yellow Aquarius light codes. They represent a complete ignition of Aquarius essence to be fully operational in the time to come. Your body fills up entirely with this nectar, first your etheric structure, then all your physical layers, penetrating your veins, meridians, and your skeletal structure. Now you become thoroughly imbued. Your hands vibrate as this essence palpably and powerfully pressurises your body. This yellow light should not be confused with Venus Light. These are star codes, star glyphs translated into yellow essence light. You look at your hands. They are radiating, vibrating with bright white light, star wisdom. It almost seems as if they are breathing.

Your skeletal structure, and remarkably, even deeper dimensional layers of your skeletal system vibrate and pulsate with bright white light. Your crown now implodes as a black hole comes into existence. While this hole deepens and deepens, it sucks you in. You completely implode. Your entire head disappears: your neck, shoulders, everything dissolves. What remains of you is your bright white light in the form of a conduit of light. As you observe more closely, you see it takes the form of a Light Tablet. All the Aquarian stars now scribe their codes with rays of light onto your Light Tablet, your Tablet of Light. You gasp. You have heard about the Emerald Tablets, the Source Scrolls, but it never occurred to you that unique Tablets of Light exist. The Aquarian Star Beings respond that this has been done since time immemorial. They scribe meticulously and caringly. You see codes, triangles, lines, arrows, spheres with dots, all sorts of lines, and they continue to scribe. You now see your Light Tablet is not merely one page: it is multidimensional, it embodies interconnective depths. The Star Beings are scribing on the inside of this tablet rapidly, as on a book of a thousand pages, scribing speedily. They now draw many vesica piscis movements from top to bottom, covering the whole tablet. They weave the codes into the Light Tablet and connect it straight to your energy body. The vesica piscis movements provide your Light Tablet with a conic form, a root that needs to be anchored. "Yes, that is correct," the Star Beings respond, "you will anchor it through the Central Sun, my dear, and beyond."

You follow the cones' string. It guides you to the cone's most profound point of our Cosmos, then straight in the direction of the White-Stringed Omega Ω. You pass the White-Stringed Omega Ω and continue to descend. At this moment, you cannot get a clear view. You are already beyond the Divine Mother Temple of the White-Stringed Omega Ω. Also, you notice her temple has a cone shape. While you descend deeper, the cone of your Light Tablet anchors itself in the exact point where the White-Stringed Omega Ω has her roots. Your Light Tablet now finds its roots in the heart of all existence.

The anchoring takes place via a clockwise rotation of a carnelian-red string. With each rotation, the anchoring deepens into the depths of this root. The root of your Light Tablet now spirals thoroughly around this red-carnelian string.

Creation of the Primordial Waters

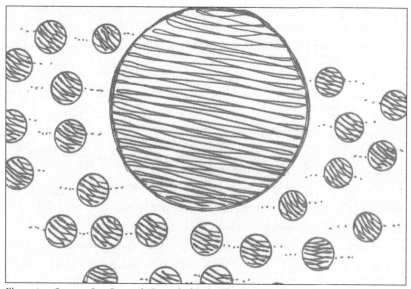

Illustration: Saqqara. Step Pyramid. Council of Eight. The Carnelian Omega Ω.

As this phase comes to completion, you are aware of a spherical object with horizontal carnelian strings. You see the White-Stringed Omega Ω connecting to this carnelian sphere. And when you look more closely, you witness many more lines below this carnelian sphere. They connect it to other life existing at even greater depths. You perceive various strings 360 degrees outward to other existences. This carnelian sphere is also an Omega Ω.

The energy of the Carnelian Omega Ω differs from that of the White-Stringed Omega Ω. You do not experience the same stillness, enigma, and mysterious energy as that of a sacred birthing chamber. This energy is more neutral. When you touch it, you sense a slight tingling. It is alive! All life occurs inside of this sphere. Within, three lights – red, blue, and white – rotate jointly, emanating their colour essences and projecting them into the sphere's inner membrane. These light essences rotate spherically and up and down. After completing a cycle, ink-blue essence percolates down from the membrane's wall. You immediately understand. This Omega Ω births the dark, primordial waters. The primordial ink-blue essence rolls up in a sphere, and the Carnelian Omega Ω projects it outwards.

This dark, primordial ink-blue substance functions like hydrated cotton wool in which you plant a fragile seed. The ink-blue essence represents the perfect environment to moisten, warm, and protect budding life.

This sphere provides a nourishing environment for all of life, even for the White-Stringed Omega Ω. It seems to nourish all Omegas Ω, as it seems there is more beneath the plane of this Carnelian Omega Ω.

Creation of the Divine Golden Spark

The Carnelian Omega Ω autonomously births the ink-blue prima mater. Now she shows you how she creates the divine golden spark. The inner layers of her womb rotate. Then the golden essence covers the entire inner membrane. As the essence is birthed, it percolates through to the lower end of the Carnelian Omega Ω. The golden essence coils into a sphere. The divine golden spark comes into existence in the deeper layers of her womb. Thus, the Carnelian Omega Ω births the primordial waters and the divine golden sparks residing within them. The White-Stringed Omega Ω receives the divine golden sparks. These comprise all Source Codes from the Carnelian Omega Ω.

Carnelian Omega Ω's Womb

The Carnelian Omega Ω invites you into her body as she continues her birthing process. She feels more accessible because her energy is less vulnerable, as if the White-Stringed Omega Ω births at a more vulnerable level of existence, birthing essence that carries more consciousness. Here, on this level, we witness the birth of the components that consciousness needs to come into existence. You could compare it to birthing a child. It is magical and vulnerable. The new-born soul radiates energy. It brings us into a deeper state of love and connection with our hearts. This energy is so emotionally tangible compared to the internal process of making the heart or lungs, which feels more functional.

When you enter the womb of the Carnelian Omega Ω, the Central Axis appears. It resembles a potter's wheel around which clay rotates. Here you can perceive a similar process to that of the Ovus. The Central Axis propels the prima mater up through the Central Axis to the sphere's top edge.

Creation of your Aquarius Light Tablet

The Carnelian Omega Ω invites your Central Axis and integrates it to the Central Axis of her womb. She incorporates you. Your Light Tablet's cone's string aligns with her and simultaneously with the Aquarius constellation. As the alignment occurs, your Light Tablet and the Aquarius constellation align with this string as you see them balancing in the upper surface where you were before. The balancing proves they are truly connected, and the alignment takes place as we speak.

She rotates them. Carnelian energy rises from the lower end of the sphere, rising, rising...she smiles and enjoys your bewilderment. The energy continues to rise as if an enormous mountain is rising. While she sucks the strings and the two cones (yours and the Aquarius one) inside her body. She laughs more and more loudly. Then she powerfully increases the spin with a jolt. The whole swirls, restructures, and transforms into bright white light. Now everything transmutes into Light Tablets. You become a white Light Tablet. Aquarius has turned into a Light Tablet.

She scribes on your Light Tablet with her carnelian essence the word Love. Then she says, "Yes, because that is what you are learning, right? How are you learning what love is, my dear? Love is loving *all* existence, the entire Cosmos. How can your heart be great enough? That is what you are learning, isn't it?"

Your heart is about to explode. She slowly brings in the entire essence of our Cosmos: as if it would be impossible to embrace *all* existence in your heart, to love and cherish it all for that what it is.

The Carnelian Omega Ω continues: "All of existence deserves to be loved. Every star, and every being on every star, in whichever form it resides, in whichever frequency of light existence appears. Can you genuinely love All That Is? Can you do that? Cosmic Love is the new code for the Aquarian Age. Is humanity ready to love All That Is: animals, plants, creatures? Are you ready to align with the heart of every creature on your planet? Can you feel every creature is also vulnerable in the womb of their mother? They also long to be protected, cherished, nurtured, cuddled. They all desire the same things humanity does. You share the same desires. Thus, you are One because of it. Are you willing to align yourself and come into greater wholeness and Oneness with every heartbeat of the Earth? Are you willing to open your heart and let the Venus Light connect you through its woven strings with All That Is? Are you willing to reignite your Oneness with existence?

Being One with All existence is the code I am scribing for you. You are well on your way. I will embed the Light Tablet encoded with the yellow essence of the Venus Light in your heart. Your experience of it is now becoming you. You are embodying, becoming its light codes. The Light Tablet will expand your body. These codes are vivid, organic organisms of light. They will reprogram, remodel, and attune you to the scribed codes. You ground them. You can feel them descend from your hips into your upper and lower legs. You are a walking Aquarius Light Tablet. You might see and feel your body has expanded substantially. You are no longer the same. My beloved, it is an honour to have you here visiting me. I have not had a visit from planet Earth in centuries. I also bestow upon you the Light Tablet I scribed for you. I will now place it within your heart. Please allow it to infuse."

You feel it going directly to your pelvic floor. The pelvic floor ignites, and like fireworks, it shoots upwards and pierces your crown and the whole of your etheric Jacob's Ladder, which expands fractally and becomes a vast coral tree. The coral trunk continues to rise until you become the Central Axis of your Cosmos. The ascent ends at the crown of the Central Axis, when all branches descend again, following the inner membrane of our Cosmos, descending to the root. You have become an etheric inner structure of your Cosmos in the shape of a toroid. However, it is carnelian because that is the program of your Cosmos. The carnelian essence also relates to the coral fan, and likewise corresponds to the element earth descending into its inner depths. This inward movement through all dimensional layers sculpts your soul to then emerge as a Divine Light Being, like a Phoenix. Isis, the Goddess, among others, underwent this process in partnership with the Earth Light Being. The element earth allows you to shape yourself into your own Creator. And then reemerge as a Divine Light Being.

Bright-white Venus Light emerges and envelops you.

Cosmic Maat

"It was an honour to have you here. I bestow upon you a miniature sphere containing my energy. This sphere is yours. It will remain with you for the rest of your soul journey – until it fuses with your One divine spark, your primary divine spark. This essence of the sphere I bestow upon you will then surround your entire essence and bring you back home to me. You will then experience an existence of Eternal Bliss. Look around you. There are many spheres here. These are all the divine sparks that have come home. Now they have become One Light Being. They vibrate as One. They gift the codes of their golden essence to a larger Golden Sphere. All wisdom seems to gather here. We call it the Maat,[28] the keeper of all cosmic laws.

"The Golden Sphere, the Maat, gathers all wisdom of all Cosmoses in Source Field. In its centre, you perceive a bright diamond light. However, it seems to shift in all sacred geometrical shapes. This diamond

---

28 Maat or Ma'at the ancient Egyptian concepts of truth, balance, order, harmony, law, morality, and justice. Maat was also the Egyptian Goddess carrying the ostrich feather. She embodies these concepts. It was said she governed the stars, seasons, and the actions of mortals and the deities who had brought order from chaos at the moment of Creation. Now we also understand she governs all of Source Field.

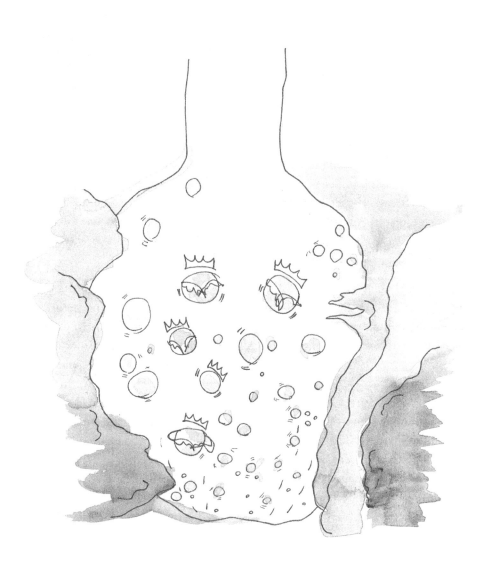

Illustration by N. Van Der Auwera. A Sacred Journey into Creation. Cosmic Ascension. Home.

light receives the gifted codes and encodes them into its light. Simultaneously, it shoots them back into the inner membrane.

"Thus, it replicates the codes into its light. If you look more closely to understand what the Maat is, you behold a sphere that includes all forms of geometry, known and unknown, in our Cosmos. The Maat encompasses all prima mater, the ethereal, the liquid, the plasmic, the crystalline, and so on. The Maat holds all essences of all colours. The Maat represents the mainframe of all existence. It is where geometry, colour, and prima mater originate. The White-Stringed Omega Ω encodes these elements through vibration. And I, the Carnelian Omega Ω, bear the primordial waters and the divine spark."

I.7.7 Sceptre, Cassiopeia

Temple Building and Prima Mater

You are standing in the inner dimensions of Saqqara. It is dark. You stand in front of the Source Field shape. You sense before you a high, blue etheric wall conforming to the shape of the Source Field. This tall, blue etheric wall meets at the top in a point. It thus appears to be a triangle. In this wall, a colossal door suddenly appears. The door's size is such that it is not for humans. It is for higher Light Beings. As you step through this portal, you walk past the Star Council of Eight. By doing so, you understand this triangle is essentially a cone shape. You walk through it. It provides a passage into the Cosmos. This cone shape functions as a vehicle. The vehicle transcends time and space. It abides here in the inner dimensions of Saqqara, and at the same time, in the Cosmos, where the Star Council of Eight localises. Thus, in only a few physical steps when you walk through it, it transports you many light-years further into the Cosmos.

Here you are now, in this cone, situated beyond the Star Council of Eight, in the Cosmos. You would suspect that all other star constellations represented by the Star Council of Eight are also there. However, you cannot see them. Instead, you move in an indigo void. It seems to be infinite. It is impossible to see where you are going. You are in nothingness. In the void. The cone suddenly compresses you. You realise it is morphing. The Source Field line is becoming a Central Axis. You become compressed. The shape now begins to rotate. You rotate with it around the Central Axis of the Star Council of Eight. You then make a continuous up-and-down motion along the cone's Central Axis. You make it seem as if you are thinning, polishing the line. Once you have arrived at the very centre of that Central Axis, through a clockwise torsion, you pierce the Central Axis line. Now you move into the dimensional space within this line. You move into the area where the eight cones representing the Star Council of Eight reside. You travel through space and time, for they are holograms into which the Star Council of Eight allocate their consciousness.

The temptation and desire to touch the material these cones are made of overwhelms you. They are cold and have a hard density. The apex is exceptionally sharp. If you touch it, you could cut yourself. As you rub your hand along them, high-frequency sounds resonate from the material. They are beautiful and shimmer like diamonds. Astonished, you realise this area is a star representation. They are ready to descend into these holographic representations. They will most likely co-create with the Earth Star. The cone of the Sceptre constellation draws you. This cone is slightly smaller. Nonetheless, it is powerful. You feel a pull towards the cone's flat base. It represents itself as a large circular window whose edges have been meticulously crafted into a diamond shape.

In this window, with your finger you draw concentric circular and spiral shapes clockwise and counterclockwise. You draw shapes within shapes. You understand the flat base is multidimensional like a Light Tablet. It reveals various layers. You draw within these layers randomly. All these spirals on these variegated layers begin to interact with one another. They are now creating their own shapes. Two spirals rotating around one another just created a spiral vessel. They also make cone shapes. The representatives of Sceptre explain to you telepathically that they use light strings to bring the frequency down to the Earth Star. However, the spiral forms – which comprise two cones attached with their flat bases – rotate around one another. These shapes are alive and organic. They form holographic chambers that bring down the mechanism to create different frequencies on Earth. They enable the alchemisation of prima mater for building etheric structures: the genuine power of manifestation.

When you touch this conic holographic chamber, you understand that this structure interweaves light with sound to prepare a prima mater for building temples and structures. It then downloads sound via light strings. Therefore, this is the mechanism to construct light temples on the Earth Star and in many other places. The Sceptre Light Beings now show you all the different colours, light rose, light yellow, silver, green, light green, emerald green. The specific mixture of colour essences determines the texture. They explain that many temples have three of the four qualities of prima mater: ethereal, liquid light, and plasma. The pure vibration of sound infuses the foundation's deeper layers as a disc, rather than into walls or ceilings.

The Venus essence provides a specific structure to the prima mater. The yellow Venus essence weaves its essence into the prima mater and interweaves all prima mater layers. A temple can be built in all the various forms of prima mater. The rose Venus essence solidifies the woven patterns and imprints them. The golden Source Light holds within the Venus essence and brings it forth.

The crystalline energy is the fourth prima mater. It is even denser than the plasmic. Crystalline energy already contains specific sacred geometry: octahedra, dodecahedra, icosahedra, and many more. Crystalline energy is preprogrammed. This Cosmos offers predefined sacred geometry. It pours Creation into form.

Sacred Architects and Master Builders transmit the pure vibrations and codes through colours and sound vibrations. They determine which types of prima mater the temple will comprise. They then imbue this prima mater and weave it with Venus essence. Depending on the dimensional level and materialisation, they apply crystalline energies to these temple structures. The crystalline energies strengthen and restructure temples. Also, they enable downloads and storage of high-frequency energy. These temples are high-frequency areas energetically balancing and nourishing large environments. These are significant sacred sites for Earth.

Nevertheless, more liquid or plasmic sacred sites are also important. They are more feminine, softer, and usually interweave in intense interconnectedness with Earth's centre. They are healing and conducive, for liquid is a transmitter and carrier substance. The crystalline energy is also a transmitting substance. It offers, though, more directive energy aimed at a specific geographic area, such as the Earth or Inner Earth cities.

The liquid plasmic temples are Creational sites. There, liquid or plasmic light creates patterns. These are embedded in various dimensional layers of Earth. These patterns contain Creation codes. The temples represent Creation laboratories where star beings work on projects to develop sacred geometric patterns. Specific colour essences and shapes are mandatory to open gates, to create Stargates. Crop circles also inform and decode the Earth. They open Stargates so that ancient secrets reveal themselves. They unleash their treasures. They revive the wisdom we have carried in our light bodies for centuries. Those ancient secrets originate from the star beings co-created with the Mayans, the Incas, the Sumerians, the Egyptians, and many more ancient civilisations.

The Creation labs or plasmic and liquid light temples will always be there. Sometimes Light Beings come with space shuttles to create on Earth. It depends on the type of Light Being. If they are closer to a materialised form, they can work autonomously. The more ethereal Light Beings will have more difficulty materialising themselves in denser environments. They bilocate only their consciousness. They work from their etheric retreats. They open gates on Earth. Creation labs are also here for Light Beings who reside in Inner Earth. In their laboratories, they create according to their mission, which they fulfil in their light bodies. This mission constantly updates through evolution, and they receive these updates telepathically.

The Sceptre Light Beings are near you now. They look milky white, with empty black pools in their eyes. They explain that star people will soon live on Earth. We need Stargates to descend. As we come downwards, we will need more of these places. Star beings are currently raising these temples more and more. We are following this project. There is a specific grid line on Earth where all these places are constructed. Each of these liquid, plasmic temples will be interconnected. Together they will work as One. They are positioned in various locations on Earth and can co-create more prominent patterns as One. They bring in the real power of manifestation.

You now see the blueprint around the Earth, with all these ethereal liquid plasmic grids and temples. The rose Venus essence seals this blueprint. You now know what our mission on Earth is. You have seen how we operate. If you wish, you can contribute to this project.

You thank the Sceptre Light Beings and walk out of this cone shape. You look back to say goodbye. Where you are, it is dazzling, as if this part of the Source Field is illuminated.

You cross the Source Field line. You leave the internal cone. Then you sense the void again. The Star Council of Eight is in the inner depths of Saqqara. At the same time, you are with them in the Cosmic cone. For time and space do not exist. All other cones in the Stargate light up.

Thank you.

I.7.8 Blue Planetary Nebula, Centaurus

Light-Blue Sphere of Creation
You float above the Source Field shape in Inner Earth. At the same time, the cone of the Source Field shape is now in space, and you are in the cone's apex, pointing upwards to countless star constellations. You look around and witness a myriad of stars. You turn inwards in your heart. With your mind's eye, you perceive golden strings in your entire body. There is a denser area where they all centre in your heart and stomach. and you recognise the Scarab,[29] which governs the cycle of life. You feel you do not want too many new things coming towards you. You would like to focus on what there is now and what you have already accomplished.

This golden structure lightens as soon as a huge and bright white light appears in the far distance. Is it the bright light you saw before at the

---

29 The Scarab governs the cycles of life, it represents the concepts of self-generation, rebirth, renewal, and resurrection to the practice of dung beetles.

horizon, or is it the Central Sun? This bright white light seems to be positioned atop of the Cosmic Womb of the Cosmos, shining its light into the layers of the womb's membrane. The latter directs it down into the root to descend and provides light to All That Is.

You stand here asking to be enlightened, as this light is the Alpha α, the father nourishing All existence. The Cosmos membrane imbues itself. This light is vibrant and oozing like lava. The light's texture is plasmic. It nurtures and permeates all the veins within the membrane. When this light has fostered all the veins within the membrane, there is enough energy to keep procreating and growing. This is the life force energy.

Various aspects provide action. One of them is vibration. Pure light carries and conveys vibration. Colours are much softer. They do not have the same vibration as this light. Though colours also contain light, they are instead essences. Accordingly, you have the golden essence of Source, and the divine spark is an essence. There is a difference between essence and light. An essence contains coding and is imprinted with a program holding a specific function. Light, though, is only to nourish. It is a life force.

If you imbue yourself with essence, you will undergo a particular restructuring, a transformation. You are imprinted and undergo a transformation or even transmutation. Indeed, an essence can completely rebuild you and change your DNA. You need these essences to morph matter and manifest Creation.

The life force is the power behind and represents the water you give to a plant for its growth.

Here you are, standing in this cone. You have this bright white light in front of you. With your golden string structure within, you ask to be enlightened so that you can also be a life force generator. This is pure light, generating life force. This bright white light heard your call, and it moves towards you. This enormous Sun enters via your feet, mounting in your body. The vibration and density of this light are so strong that it accumulates in your lower body. You feel that your bodily circuitry is not powerful enough to hold this light. Your cells burst apart. The old structures now dissolve. When you thrive on this pure light, it is all you need. You look at your body. You see a vibrating, pulsating tingle. This light is doing its thing with you. You just enjoy it. The light whirls upwards and spirals through your throat, head, crown. You begin to shiver. You see your head spinning quickly around the Central Axis of your neck. It is as if the light was wound up in the wrong way. The energy at this level does not align. The energetic circuitry of your neck and throat cannot allow this bright white light to pass through.

The Alpha α says, "My light is everywhere. Where there is Creation, there is Alpha α Light. I am life force. The Omega Ω produces all the colour essences because she loves to create. She just loves to see all the different life forms and Light Beings. She delights in seeing Creation and life. She enjoys seeing beings love their lives. The Omega Ω is Creation. Creation is creative.

The Omega Ω is infinitely creative. The Alpha α is infinitely nurturing."

We have already witnessed various levels of Omega Ω. Now we observe a different level of Alpha α energy: the divine feminine and masculine energies in various structures. The masculine energy always plays a supporting role to the Omega Ω.

Your body has dissolved the old, inadequate wiring. You are entirely fused, remembered as One string. This plasmic bright white light comes in and nourishes you. You feel relaxed and safe, for this light is soft and gentle. Your pelvic floor opens widely, inviting it in. You are in cosmic sex with this bright white light to rebirth yourself. Let it sensually caress you, move you. Let the energy play through your senses. Your body splits open. You welcome the release. You become aware you have just given life to a being of light.

When you hold the Light Being in your hands, it appears to be a blue sphere with light-blue veins within. You sit down with this sphere in your hands. It is extensive, luminous, soft, and light. You feel the desire to immerse yourself entirely within this sphere. You carry it to your head. You gently immerse your face in the blue cosmic essence. It feels abundant. Soon you bathe your entire form in it. The blue cosmic essence gradually envelops your entire body, immersing you in blue cosmic essence.

Blue cosmic essence closes its sphere around your feet.

What do you see now?

Who are you becoming?

What are you becoming?

The Centaurus Light Beings tell you, "Come with us. We want to show you something." They travel with you to a place you envision in your mind's eye.

You notice prison walls, more like a dungeon, with handcuffs on chains attached to the wall. You are taken to a harsh environment. It reminds you of torture, pain, and sorrow. You sense the energy of insecurity, punishment, and guilt. These are the states of people who have surrendered. They allowed all their life force to be dimmed. They gave up. Humankind can lose touch with its life force. It can disappear completely, even if you always have the fuse to rekindle.

When you lose touch with life force, you become fearful and enter a state of survival and defense consciousness. You can no longer enjoy your body. You lack strength and power and find yourself manipulating and finding schemes to make your way through life, to still feel sage.

This prison is a metaphor. These walls are imprisonment from your own Light. Your space can be invaded if you allow it. Allowing it feels threatening and aggressive. You cannot leave as the doors are closed.

When you lose touch with life force, you are dismembered, and as soon as you imbibe the Alpha α, life force and your state of consciousness will immediately shift. When the trapped person imbibes life force, fear instantly disappears. One feels equal. The chest positions forward. One no longer needs to hide their light or protect. One leaves this place one envisioned in one's mind's eye.

Life force, as you see, is about manifesting yourself. You manifest. You show people who you are. The Alpha α, life force, gives you strength. There is nothing to hide or protect. You live your truth. You just abide as yourself, and that is enough.

COSMOGONY

Part II

Rebirth through Our Cosmic Creational Divine Mothers

Dismantlement of Our Cosmos

As we leave this Cosmos, we leave behind only the codes of our memory, the Scrolls of Maat.

A woven geometric design of herringbones contains the coral in the womb of our Cosmos. These herringbone structures position themselves in a south-north line, as do the meridians of the Earth. They found their existence when this Cosmos created itself. They originated from the white strings as the first etheric formations when the Cosmos descended into Source Field as a divine spark. These white strings are the first blueprint upon which the rest of the development occurs. Many stacked layers of herringbone grids define and interlock within the Cosmos's structure. This structure is hexagonal by nature, like a honeycomb design. Here, the energy of the honeybee refers to building and expanding the honeycomb to bring about full bloom. A honeycomb stores eggs that will mature: specifically, the honey, the nectar, the fruits of all the blossomed flowers, those that have already come to fruition. The hexagonal framework stores these gained realisations, these pearls of wisdom, to increase the light co-efficiency, the vibration of the Cosmos so that it can grow. They hold the high vibrational Light of Amun Ra. In this structure, there is a network of wormholes that move between these layers as one structure. All galaxies and universes

The Pillar of Light

Illustration: Cosmogony. Part II.
The Dismantlement of our Cosmos.

throughout the Cosmic Womb connect, resonate with one another, and form one whole, thanks to these herringbone structures.

In the Cosmos' dismantling process, the herringbone structure of the Cosmos will unfold from north to south. This process is like the petals of a flower budding or the blossoming of a Thousand Petal Lotus. The cosmic Central Axis, around which galaxies and universes fan out, contains the hologram of the entire Cosmic Womb. What happens in this axis you see simultaneously projected in the Cosmos. As the Cosmos dismantles, the herringbone structures between themselves slowly disconnect. More space becomes available. As a result, more plasma light flows. Once all the herringbones light up, white light will emerge. The cosmic membrane dissolves, and this flower opens. In its centre, a Pillar of Light appears. It contains all the codes that all universes and beings living in them have collected and transferred to this central Pillar of Light. Once all the codes are in, it brings forth a vortex movement that engages the entire previous womb to transmute time, space, and memory.

The membrane loosens, the information releases, and the Cosmos Light Being transfers the codes to the cosmic Maat. The dismantling is complete. Together, we all move on, in different forms, modalities, frameworks, beyond the present known Cosmos.

The Cosmos is a Light Being, just as we are. The crystal scroll, as your Scroll of Truth, or the Scroll of Maat is the only thing we leave behind.

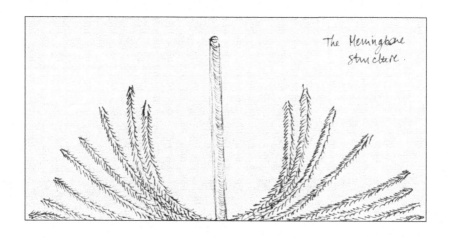

The Herringbone structure.

It represents our light codes we gift to the Cosmos. These hold our trajectory from seed to fully blossoming soul. When we convey our light codes as a cloud of golden dust, a soul group consciousness, we move on to another form of Cosmos, a new existence, a new life. This new Cosmos is subject to different rules, goals, programs. The common factor they all have is that they carry within them the Foundational Desire for Life. For each time, we choose life. From this perspective, it is crucial now more than ever that we grow out of our planetary vision into a cosmic vision. It is crucial now that we embrace Divine Love, the love for all existence for every divine spark that chooses life. We are not alone. We never will be. We evolve together with all souls and all worlds. We dissolve into a cloud of golden dust, a group consciousness, embarking on a new journey by an in breath or out breath of the Omega Ω.

Our Cosmos' ascension is akin to breathwork. This body releases its old structure and energy and becomes etheric. Our body evolves into a crystalline form of consciousness. It is also the dematerialisation from matter to spirit. The same pattern is also present in the body when you release old energy. The cell membrane loosens and falls open, dissolving. We discharge the old energy.

Part II

First Moon Quarter

II.1 Temple of Pristine Primordial Cosmic Inscriptions, Abu Simbel

Multidimensionality:
Momentum of the One Divine Spark

You make appearance in southern Egypt at the Second Cataract of the Nile. In a moment, you approach this sacred place. An atmosphere of hardening through time becomes tangible. As a result, these old, outdated energies cover the temple seed and block its full development. Moreover, you understand that the temple seed needs your attention. So you deepen your awareness and notice it contains golden light. As soon as you attune to this golden light, you and the temple seed receive the moon codes you need to awaken your primaeval structure that emanates from your One divine spark. In other words, Abu Simbel holds the secret to reviving your multidimensional consciousness so that you can resonate with it at deeper layers once again.

Immediately, as you tune in to these moon codes, an unfolding takes place around you and above you. All your higher multidimensional levels are unfolding. The entire spiral galaxy, which you are, is revealing them. This revelation continues. All your multidimensional layers begin to revolve around you. You are the One divine spark. All the soul extensions you are once again find the momentum to revolve around you. Your multidimensionality activates. You have received the moon codes and feel nourished.

Meanwhile, Abu Simbel Light Being and all your soul extensions have absorbed these moon codes. The spiral circumference of your soul structure widens. Your soul extensions are meandering down the spiral arms towards your One divine spark located in its centre. The sheer joy of welcoming them home overflows you. In the Now, the blueprint for what is coming emerges and materialises, for the concept of time is spherical. The Now also represents the past and the future.

You are the I Am that I Am.[30] You are Ayah Asher Ayah.[31]

While you incorporate your soul extensions, you also merge the three aspects of time. By this, you proclaim your path of ascension as a springboard to continue on your future journey. Soon, a silky veil of white light envelops you like a caterpillar. It bores you spirally into the Earth. You do not understand why this is happening. It should be around Abu Simbel, but you feel that they want to show you what to do. You sink deep into the Earth until at some point a white crystal seed in the shape of an octahedron emerges. This is where you land. As soon as you come close to the etheric seed, you feel its potential of expanding and widening the dimensional space. It is as if all around you the Earth is transforming into bright white light. It becomes light of a wide, high frequency. Everything around you unfolds and becomes an imposing cone of light moving upwards towards the surface. You are here at this inner depth. You look up and you see a spiral showing in this structure. You see Abu Simbel's various etheric seeds. Meanwhile you understand that the multidimensional Temple of Abu Simbel has collapsed. Now it wants to be realigned. It wants to straighten out and align with its original energy. As soon as you speak these words, the Light Being of Abu Simel shows itself to you. She looks like a Greek Goddess. She is enveloped in white light, with long, dark hair cascading in falling waves over her bare right shoulder. Her essence is ethereal. She puffs a gentle breath into the space you fill. So it was she who enveloped you within herself and brought you down here. She whispers to you softly. She wants to use her original powers again.

The alignment and resurrection allow her to use her powers again. Your eyes are looking down at your feet. You take the etheric seed in your hand. It feels smoothly cut, almost like Selenite. In the centre is a fine, bright-blue string. As soon as you turn your attention to this string, it begins to move, twist, and try to cleave the etheric seed. It evolves quite rapidly. By now the blue string has pierced the membrane. At a rapid pace, it grows like a magic, etheric beanstalk, into cosmic heaven. The ethereal seed is laid again at your feet. A whole

---

30 You are the drop of water and at the same time the sea.
31 I will be what I want to be! He is the All in All, the infinite source of everything, in which we all live, move, and have our existence in the physical world of Creation.

structure of stems emerges. Each stem has countless branches. These go so fast and so high that you cannot follow them with your gaze. As soon as the white etheric beanstalk arrives at its destination, it turns. Like a vortex, it sucks the whole structure of Abu Simbel as it is today. You see the structures fractalise in the violent movements. Everything is reduced to zero. To silence. To a new beginning. A circular blueprint shows itself with many multidimensional temples as well as gigantic terrestrial structures. On all dimensional levels you see a disc rotating. It has cogwheels. These are cosmological clocks. They rotate independently of one another. This gigantic column of light with its various cosmological clocks aligns Abu Simbel, with the specific star to which she was built. Abu Simbel Light Being tells you the alignment of the cosmological clocks will continue for quite some time. They follow the evolution of the Earth and humanity to connect with the wisdom of the Garden of Eden and the evolution of the Cosmic Axis. They bring us step by step to a world, where we find our inner abundance and our inner bliss and joy. Step by step we are led to descend more and more into our own being. Abu Simbel descends more and more into her own being. As she descends, she takes us into our heart, to our own inner depths. There we find what we have been searching for throughout our soul's existence.

Creational Codes of Abundance

When reflections coincide, everything coincides in Oneness. We then reflect Source.

The beginning and the end of the Nile Temple Valley.

Bathing your feet in the Nile waters, you take in the enigmatic atmosphere reigning here. The Nile streams behind you. The Temple of Abu Simbel stands sumptuously before you. The water feels warm, the soil soft and permeable. Without delay, you leave the water. You walk to the temple. A bright white light, Abu Simbel Light Being, shows you that the whole blueprint of Abu Simbel is a circular field also running behind the temple. As can be seen, in this circular field, there were also other buildings within this complex. Thus, in ancient times, there was more than the physical remnant that is visible today. Far before the Egyptian Era, this sacred place was an extensive complex.

Abu Simbel Light Being asks you to descend into the lower dimensions of this sacred place. As you do so, immediately the circular shape instantly transforms into a spiral staircase. You descend the spiral staircase to view the pearly brilliant texture of semiprecious stones embedded in the walls. You imagine yourself in a refined, majestic, luxurious, magnificent environment. As you continue your walk, the spiral staircase becomes circular. It begins spinning spherically, enveloping you. This seems familiar. You have already had a similar experience in Scepter. The spherical capsule is now rotating ceaselessly around you. As it revolves around you, you find yourself within a point of stillness. Obviously, you recognise and already know this is the procedure to open the gate to another dimension through which the secrets of Abu Simbel reveal themselves to you.

In a moment, the rotation will stop. This spherical capsule unfolds like a flower. Here you are, facing the original settlement of Abu Simbel. Several palaces appear around you. Their windows open onto a courtyard. In the centre, a pond rests in serenity, a pond from which you have emerged. This is deeply puzzling. Even so, it is a dimensional portal. It is also a place of Oracle. When you gaze into the water, countless water nymphs, mermaids, and beautiful sirens swim before you. In your mind's eye, you instantly see how it used to be. Here people sat at the water's edge to ask the Water Light Beings to connect with the stars. Can you still see the magical scene in front of you? From inside the water, you can clearly hear the stories and the voices of the stars. These Water Light Beings each retains a particular star lineage important to the people who had lived here. The Water Light Beings also kept the frequencies of the Abu Simbel complex high by creating concentric circles from the centre of this body of water, enveloping this entire temple area in one giant white-stringed sphere of vibration. Hence, a constant high vibration of bliss, peace, and joy thrived.

While you gently stroke your hand through the silky, ethereal water, you feel its subtle vibration. You realise it is not much different from the water we know. It is lighter – airier. It exudes a heavenly fragrance reminiscent of fruit. In your bewilderment, you continue to explore the depths of this crystalline water. The more you skim the bottom of this pond with your gaze, the more another world reveals itself before you. Here, you witness beautiful old massive trees, enormous juicy fruits like grapes, orchards with luscious fruits of all colours. Truly, this world manifests abundance. These were the frequencies emitted from the water in this temple complex. This water body is in direct connection with Hollow Earth, where this world still exists. These crystalline waters reflect the Hollow Earth represented here in Abu Simbel. Indeed, you have understood, Abu Simbel deeply yearns to reconnect with the Source of Abundance.

Even though Abu Simbel's blueprint is circular, the temple complex shows a discontinuity in this spherical shape. It appears more like a three-quarter Moon. The soul mission of Abu Simbel is to connect the entire Nile Temple Valley to the Source of Abundance. These codes were also downloaded through the Moon Gate into Abu Simbels' pearl seed in the roots of the Sphinx. These downloaded Source Codes reflect the Hermetic Principle: As Above So Below, within the Hollow Earth.

Abu Simbel Light Being did not fully succeed in enveloping the Nile Temple Valley within the Source Codes of Abundance. Therefore, the site reflects a three-quarter Moon shape rather than the Full Moon.

In a moment, you leave the courtyard and the water body, for these temple walls are asking you to explore them. You imagine yourself in sumptuous Persian temples, as described in *One Thousand and One Nights*. Touching the temple walls, your touch yields to a softness so ethereal you can pass through them with your hand as through a mist. Of unearthly density, they somehow allow your physical eye to perceive them.

Golden spheres reside in the rooms within these temple walls. Rather than solid gold, they are coral-structured, with branches bent into spheres. These coral-branched structures reflect the Cosmos and its

Illustration by N. Van Der Auwera. A Sacred Journey into Creation.
The Creational Codes of Abundance.

Cosmic Axis. Out of nowhere, a priest surfaces. He wears a white robe, a long white beard. The guardian of these golden coral spheres, he takes care of them like newborn plants. In turns, these spheres randomly connect with one another. When they connect, a golden line appears, extending from one orb to another. Five orbs are visible, the fifth halfway completed. Yet, there should be eight orbs. In fact, the orbs are a physical representation of the Star Council of Eight. Furthermore, they provide the Creation Source Codes. Here they house and replicate the Creation codes.

In our perception, even though gold is heavily dense, when the guardian touches a golden coral orb, it yields like a sponge. As soon as it indents, it moves and retracts. As can be seen, these orbs are animated by their own consciousness. Cosmic codes nourish them so they can cooperate with the beings living in this area. In this palace complex, the Star Council of Eight placed the orbs in the shape of the first-quarter Moon so they may channel the water in the courtyard towards the palace and the Nile area. All these coral spheres connect to the water through golden strands descending downwards into the depths. At the same time, the Water Light Beings monitor this process. These golden strands pool in a sacred fountain at a deeper level in the water body, radiating the blue essence of bliss, the pure joy of living, the sheer delight of existence. They also infuse the codes through the golden DNA ladders, constituting this blue essence. By adding DNA structures from this fountain, they build the orb. So, the orbs are in constant growth. They evolve according to the evolution of the Cosmos, the Cosmic Womb. The orbs mirror the cosmological evolutionary process.

These coral orbs represent the eight different quadrants or sectors within the Cosmic Womb. They reflect the evolution of each sector. Complete cosmological knowledge was accessible in ancient times. They could communicate with these worlds and create energetic reflections here, which they followed, reflecting evolution. How could they do this? Another priest materialises before you. He wears a long white, grey beard. It reaches almost to his ankles. His robe is of a deeply blue velvet. He calls himself Oluf. He walks up to you and answers, "It is not so difficult. You carry this wisdom in your heart. You simply know it. A human being operates from the mind and becomes entangled in a three-dimensional perspective. We do not perceive the world as separate from the higher dimensions. We behold the world and all the dimensions as One. There are no boundaries between dimensions. We behold it as a continuous whole. We have no need to teleport. There is nothing to teleport. What is above is also below. It is everywhere. We ask only that it replicates itself and materialises in this space. We are asking for a natural, true replication of the growth process of the Cosmos. In a sense, this is also what we project onto the Cosmic Axis that is the Nile. We could also subdivide it into all these quadrants. The more reflections we create, the more opportunity we create for each reflection to reflect itself perfectly. When reflections coincide, everything coincides in Oneness. The more reflections we create, the more each reflection strengthens the primary Source of reflection. By doing so, we encourage the primary Source, in this case, the Cosmic Axis, to dismantle and the Cosmos to ascend. Once you understand this Hermetic Principle, apply it to your life, and take on its resonance, there is nothing more to learn. You find your completion. In essence, by creating all these reflections, we make it clear there is nothing else for us to do other than to enjoy bliss and existence. Simultaneously, now that we are here, we carry the entire Cosmic Womb in our consciousness and structure. We represent the Cosmic Womb. By replicating these eight realms, we want to infuse these codes of wisdom into the Light Body of Abu Simbel, to encode all beings who reside here. They then carry it in their consciousness and become representations of the Cosmic Axis. Each can merge with it and can fully ascend. This process transcends linear ascension and even multidimensional ascension. Hence, we are talking about going home, a Cosmic Ascension." He wonders if you understand.

"Come," Oluf says, "I must show you something else." He walks with you behind all the orbs. You both depart through the rear of the building. Here a beautiful hill with orchards of olive, almond, and peach trees stretch out before you. You climb the hill with him. He says the slope is very tiring. He is getting old. Yet, he smiles. He goes on because he is not merely and entirely attuned to his human body. Even if the body is tired, he continues and switches to his etheric essence. He decides to leave his human body by simply stepping out of it, as he is doing right now. To your amazement, you witness a white Light Being stepping out of the human body and walking on, smiling. As you observe this, you feel sealed within your bodily form, in the three-dimensional reality.

The last part of the hill is still green and luscious. You circumnavigate it, spiraling to the top. Once you arrive, in the distance beckon the Nile Valley, the Mediterranean Sea, and the Red Sea. Nevertheless, you are not here for the view. There is an ethereal shaft descending into this mountain. You must leave your body to access it. In view of this quest, he lays his hand on your heart. He pulls you out. His hand magnetically attracts your Light Body and pulls it out. There it stands behind you, motionless. In the same fashion, this process reminds you of the rite of sepulcher, which Yeshua performed. Here, however, it is still common. Everyone practices it. It is also perfectly safe. You enter the red shaft and spiral downwards. In essence, this shaft represents the Cosmic Axis. As you are spiraling downwards, you observe all coral branches while passing them. You know you are in the centre of the trunk, for you have noticed the roots. By the time you look upwards, white strands of light spiral upwards like sunbeams reflecting on a sea-bed. This is the original energy of Khnum's seat, the potter's wheel. Here crystalline-structured energies build your etheric structure, your Jacob's ladder. They build it just like the eight spheres and the temple complex. They grow and evolve. He explains further that they came here with human beings to build their etheric structure in view of climbing the Central Axis of the Cosmos: the direct passage out of this Cosmos into the Source Field. This rite provides the passage for Cosmic Ascension, and they prepare people for it.

As you stand here, your crystalline structures shift whilst compressing. The dimensional layers are collapsing into one another. Multidimensionality is in nature, One Whole. In reality, there are no barriers between dimensions. We experience them only in separative consciousness. Similarly, with a Jacob's Ladder consisting of three pillars. You feel when attuning to your unique Jacob's Ladder that within each pillar the lines between your own dimensions are disintegrating, disassembling. These old energies are streaming downwards into the roots of your being. They continue streaming downwards into the roots of this tree. You can be a reflection of this tree and of the rays, which are swirling upwards. You can reflect the Sun or be a reflection of the Central Sun, without any impediments. You wonder what would happen if you experienced boundaries in this crystalline structure. What happens if you do not?

He explains that when in your consciousness you sense boundaries, the light codes of the Sun's rays become encapsulated in the cellular crystalline structure of your being. This suggests that the codes are enclosed for a reason. When you experience boundaries between dimensions, there is less an expansion of consciousness. Without boundaries, there is no purpose for the energies to be encapsulated, and they can flow freely. This is what we mean by just being a reflection of Source, for there is nothing more to accomplish on Earth. You have found self-realisation. You have understood. You are nothing but a reflection of Source. The authentic intention of the Nile Valley was to support people in being a reflection of Source – ultimately to achieve Cosmic Ascension, to serve the Cosmos in its Cosmic Ascension, to ascend with it. This is the complete Creational journey.

Oluf asks you to please remain in the heart of the reflection of the Cosmic Axis, the coral trunk, and stretch your legs, to bring yourself into the position of the Vitruvian man. As you touch the inner surface of the trunk, below you a red seed radiates its energy like a ray, upwards, through you. At the same time, it climbs up your body like a Kundalini snake, spiraling around your Central Axis. You now allow the red ray to rise upwards, alongside your Pillar of Light. You notice it does not resonate with your physical structure. This red essence was still present in the Maat, for when you drop all your bodies in Cosmic Ascension, to remain only with your Scroll of Truth, this Scroll of Truth is your Maat, which you leave behind. For you will have mastered the cosmic laws. As the red essence ascends, it engraves your Pillar of Light. It sculpts it, transforming it into a beautifully refined staff. The top of the staff shows the shape of a candle flame. You feel more finely tuned and coded. At this stage of your journey, all the Unseen divine potential your seed carried in the very beginning has been handed over to you. The beginning and the end coincide here, in this moment of quantum growth. You have engraved the end into your consciousness. This includes all codes you were meant to collect in this Cosmos, until the moment of your Cosmic Ascension. The boundaries of time and space have been transcended. For the end is already integrated, and more importantly activated in you. We have funneled even more in Oneness since the Sphinx, deepening the Alpha α and the Omega Ω.

Let us go back to the temple complex of Abu Simbel, to the body of water. Simultaneously, you both ascend through the trunk of this Cosmic Axis, on the hill in Abu Simbel. Having arrived at the entrance atop the hill, you find your body awaits you. Together you walk to the temple complex and arrive at the body of water. In a moment, you mirror yourself in the water's surface. Amazingly you see someone thriving on divine energy. While you have passed over the boundaries of your multidimensionality, you have integrated your wholeness. Oluf says adieu to you and sends his blessings. He adds that if you need him, he will be here for you in Abu Simbel. "We share the same mission in our hearts; thus we will always support you." You thank him and bid farewell.

Straightaway, you decide to slip into the water for a while before departure. You want to continue exploring this underwater world you have never seen before. It is too beautiful not to explore. Overjoyed with your presence, the Water Light Beings take you along and show eight spheres, here underwater. They laugh, saying, "We have them here!" They are waiting for their reflection above. They urge you to touch the last two, which still need their upper reflection. As you reach out your hands, they explain that the energy signature of the cosmic blueprint[32] is here, that you can work with it and integrate it into the Nile Valley. By infusing it, it stimulates the ascension process of the Cosmos. As soon as you touch them, immediately you feel a tingling sensation racing through your body.

With your mind's eye, you perceive two spheres in the temple complex above the water. They resonate with you and tell you this is an automated process that continues. As you observe this, you become a pure witness. Inevitably, it will come into being. You sit with these two orbs for a while and tilt your head inwards to be in your heart. Here you understand that at a certain point, one could no longer fulfil this, due to losing the experience of wholeness and being entrapped in perceived multidimensionality. This mirroring process will complete itself when a large majority of people embody their multidimensionality as One wholeness. And they will. These orbs story that Earth's dimensions[33] are already collapsing, and some even cease to exist at the same time as yours. All boundaries between dimensions are dissolving, and Earth lives its multidimensionality in Oneness. People resonate with

---

32 The cosmic blueprint carries all development codes within to obtain Cosmic Ascension, we also will refer to it as the Master Blueprint.
33 Earth's Light Body mirrors the outer structures and consists of many inner dimensions, also referred to as levels of density.

this process, based on the Hermetic Principle: As Within, So Without.

Here in these waters, you realise time was not ready. Perhaps you will witness in your lifetime everyone embodying their multidimensionality, wholeness, and Oneness. As soon as all dimensions collapse, at that moment, we fall back into the vibration of hollow Earth, where a reflection of abundance thrives, and ultimately live again in the Garden of Eden, the resonance of Earth's paradise.

The orbs also clarify that in ancient pre-Egyptian times, dimensions did not exist. The Earth was merely a reflection of Source. There is a divine desire for the dimensions to dissolve again, to be a reflection of Eden. There is no need for this dimensional structure. It creates only separation and hierarchy. It places a limit on the experience of bliss. In a dimensional structure, you are able to experience bliss only to a certain extent. You cannot experience it fully because somehow dimensional structures, as you saw in the Cosmic Axis reflected in the hill, encapsulate the energy of bliss in its dimensional levels. The encapsulation bases itself on needs that still need to be fulfilled within those dimensional structures.

Meanwhile, you listen to all these pearls of wisdom. You realise that you love being here. The atmosphere is peaceful, quiet, and complete. Everything is here, even the Foundational Desire to exist. The feeling you experience here is what you truly desire from life. Everything you can desire in your heart and soul is here. Life revolves around this experience. The Water Light Beings nod their heads and confirm. You have understood. The beings who live here outside the water do not properly listen. They hear only parts of stories. This is what it is all about. It is only this.

You wish to stay a while longer and ask if you may. The Water Light Beings wish you to absorb this pleasure and enjoyment completely. Until you feel ready to leave, you do not say goodbye. Meanwhile, you express your profound gratitude.

Collapse of the Old Earth's Light Body

You have had the delight of seeing and experiencing the most ancient temple at Abu Simbel. After millions of years, its primordial pristine cosmic energies are still anchored in Earth's body.

Now your inner eye leads you to another place in the Inner Earth where many paths run through Earth's dimensions, layers, and strata. On these paths Light Beings from outer space enter the Earth body with vessels unknown to us. They make their way to an area deep within the Earth where a bright, light-blue lake expands its enigmatic energies abundantly. In their vessel, they carry otherworldly substances and place them within these waters.

By doing so, they allow the chemical constitution to morph. An alchemical process begins when this otherworldly substance encounters Earth's waters. Ultraviolet crystal clusters form. Their arrangement is much like that of a bunch of grapes, but more spherical. These Light Beings, called Emerald Beings of Light, harvest these ultraviolet-coloured gems, and return them to Earth's surface. Meanwhile, on their way upwards, they also place these crystals in certain areas on the Earth grid.

These clusters then help anchor the New Earth grid to emerge. Once the ultraviolet clustered crystals reach Earth's surface, the Emerald Beings of Light place them in a meridian shape, enveloping the Earth. All these ultraviolet clustered crystals communicate with one another and form an ultraviolet field. Omnipresent are sounds and whispering words emanating maternal energy, expressed by the future incarnation of Earth's soul. The future incarnation of the Earth, The Ultraviolet Star to which Earth is evolving, sends its essence to envelop our Earth and enable her to communicate with her own future incarnation. By *future*, we mean a soul incarnation after this life: knowing that time is spherical and in essence, time does not exist. These are parallel existences in which the future Earth nurtures, assists, and helps our present Earth embodiment. This is a touching scene because it shows you that even within your own soul structure, your other soul existence forms can perfectly assist you to evolve.

We often tend to seek help outside of ourselves. Here the Earth shows us that we can also find wisdom within our own soul structure.

This ultraviolet field becomes active. As a resonance field it permeates the Earth to the core, functioning as a beaming field. Each moment brings the Earth more into resonance with a future incarnation to eventually create a final bridge to an Ultraviolet Star.

This act of sacred union between various soul incarnations expresses the true existence of Divine Love, which is so exalted that duality and its survival patterns on Earth suddenly seem absolutely ephemeral.

From humans, from all Light Beings, from plants, and from the animal kingdom, the Earth as we know it is receiving a great deal of help at this crucial time in her evolution from the Ultraviolet Star via its ultraviolet essence.

As the ultraviolet essence heralds the end of the Earth as we know it, veils of light envelop dimension by dimension, layer upon layer, penetrating ever more deeply into the Inner Earth. They melt together, imploding to the extent that One Vast Field emerges.

The old Light Body of the Earth is in the process of disintegration. Earth's soul ascends into its new Light Body. Its sacred geometry is shifting into a one-dimensional geometry and finally will dissipate.

Inner Creational Womb of a Cosmic Creator

As previously shown through sacred union, your heart is initiated into being your One divine spark, the central point of your multidimensionality. Embodying your divinity and creatorship, a multidimensional consciousness is the prerequisite for coming into Oneness. It understands you as unique and complex. In essence, you are resonant in this dimension and in many more beyond the veil of time and space. Furthermore, resonating with this heart sphere enables you to resonate with other One divine sparks. Likewise, the co-Creation between the core two divine sparks provides for Divine Creation.

Here you are, you make a deep, intimate connection with your heart. You feel it beating. These pulsations move you and bring you in touch with your love for yourself and for your life, and the fragility of it all.

Yeshua comes to stand beside you. He wears a white, luminous garment. His Diamond Heart Light emanates the Venus Light. His divine yellow essence radiates. He will stay with you for a while. He desires to feel you, to be with you. His tenderness, his gentle nature gives you a safe haven. You feel cherished and guided. He speaks: "Allow me to help you complete this initiation. You now resonate with sacred union and Divine Love. This resonance will allow you to restore your vesica piscis, your Creator Womb. Sacred union unites the divine feminine and the divine masculine as One. These are the new frequencies of the Aquarian Age. By creating from your Oneness, your central Pillar of Light, Divine Creations arise."

He shows you his expanding heart sphere and slides it towards you, asking you to do the same. "I want you to make me whole." You expand your heart sphere in his direction until it touches his. You feel this gentle touch through every fibre of your body. It makes you shiver. It is as if these two spheres have their own consciousness, their own sensuality. They come together, sliding more into one another until they form a vesica piscis. Yeshua looks you in the eyes and says, "Look, my heart is of golden light, and I also will permeate yours." Golden essence seeps into your heart sphere. You exchange one another's essences. The more this exchange takes place, the more you feel both of you are moving closer, even into Oneness. You begin to feel the same.

The vesica piscis is bulging now. You understand that the birth canal is preparing itself. Yeshua further explains, "Watch the golden essence of my heart move to the vesica piscis. Slide it to the space between us." You allow it to happen. The two essences revolve one around the other, as in a sweetly delicate dance of etheric essences. What we wish to create will manifest. Divine Creation is when you create from your core essence and from the Divine Heart, which thrives on Divine Love. The Creation you both manifest takes more form. Once the energy injects into the Creation, though, both of you withdraw your own energy. Now you feel even more complete and sovereign. You are a Divine Being yourself. From your heart, you can create the most beautiful things. When with Yeshua, you create an outer Creational chamber. You bring together divinity on Earth. It is the higher heart and the Divine Love that connect us. They enable us to be central points in the Cosmos, to coincide with the Central Axis, to be the infinite cosmic seed from which everything can grow. Only from this state of consciousness can we bring forth Divine Creation. Only from the experience of Cosmic Love do you envision All That Is in your heart. Thus, you further create any form of manifestation in whatever level of density, in whichever frequency of light. From being a Divine Mother, you can create a Divine Child. Isis will tell us more about this. Because you are now embodied as the centre of our Cosmos, alone or with another Divine being, you will bring forth Divine Creation.

You have your Creational chamber. You can choose to create with another Creational chamber. Both thrive on Divine Love. As you hear these words, your heart sphere descends even more into your body. It grows larger and it envelops your entire form. It sinks deep into your pelvic floor to become part of our Cosmic Axis. You become a birth canal, a pure reflection of the Cosmic Axis.

Uttering these words sets something new in motion. Your Cosmic Axis expands and breaks open. The golden light of the diamond heart flares, illuminating the whole of Creation. This heart thrives on Venus Light, which loves the whole of Creation. The more you embody Cosmic Love, the more you become a golden star, radiating your light through the Cosmos and piercing its cervix. With your ethereal wings you sow seeds of light as if casting and creating seeds of Creation from your heart and the higher levels of love. Yeshua says, "You have activated and rekindled the Golden White Star within you." He embraces you kindly.

You find that your body can hold this powerful light and countless dimensional levels all at the same time, for it has already undergone so many initiations.

In a moment, you will have time to align your dimensions. While you immerse yourself in the consciousness of this Golden White Star, many beings are coming to you throughout the Cosmos. Belonging to the Venus Light, they are Master Creator beings, they join you and welcome you into their group consciousness of Divine Creators. By weaving golden strings, they connect you to them and weave you into their grid. The strings allow you to resonate at their level. Thus, you remain in harmony with their vibration as you continue your three-dimensional life. As they continue to weave meticulously, you behold a network of pale golden strings woven around you like lace. Soon, you are part of this group consciousness, interconnected by this spherical grid. It abides everywhere within the Cosmic Womb. Within, you hold your unique position.

This group consciousness of Divine Creators creates from the heart sphere. The group brings forth cosmological blueprints thriving on Cosmic Love.

Divine Love

Green essence light imbues you, asking you to be intimate within your very own essence.

Centre yourself. Allow your consciousness to sink into your belly: the labyrinth guiding you, providing a safe passageway, sculpting you, shaping you into becoming who, in nature, you were and already are.

Golden Source Light descending into you as a Light Being equals manifestation according to the laws of perfection. As soon as you embody Source Light, you manifest it in your unique way. Once you personify your creatorship, you feel your hands enlarging. They have become the hands of God, shaping life, the Earth, the Cosmos, *All That Is*. As a creator, you become One with *All That Is*. You know creating something small equals creating on a cosmic scale. The simplicity of this becomes apparent as you become whole. You comprehend how the above is also the below, the within is also the without. You have embodied the *Hermetic Principle of Thoth Hermes Trismegistus*.

Knowing all this and shaping it through your abdomen to resonate with your unique energy signature, you birthed yourself into a Creator and a Divine Child. Yet, knowing all this, you still feel you are yourself, a simple human being. The cosmic embodiment has changed you. You will never be the same, nor will you experience life the same way. You will never act the same as you did in the past. Indeed, you have changed and become whole and complete. So has your connection with the Earth become whole and complete. You have become her friend and companion, the friend and companion of every star, planet, and Light Being in any physical manifestation. The cosmic embodiment has taught you Divine Love. You have learned to surrender and open to *All That Is*. You have activated *the I Am that I Am*. You are your human-you, and yet the cosmic embodiment of *All That Is*. Maybe this seems complex, but the essence of it is transparent. Once you embody it, you know this is how it should be: the future of humanity.

In the past, human beings would set the tone. They would not truly listen to animals, plants, spirits, wind, water, stars. The society was closed off, unguided. Humanity did not allow itself to be guided. But here you are, present and interconnected, accessible. Life flows through you. The essence of all beings, animals, plants, passes through you. You are the living embodiment of life itself. Divine love governs your heart. You have become a Divine Mother of the Cosmic Womb for all universes, galaxies, solar systems, planets, Earth, for your friends, family, and all the beings in your life. You are a Divine Mother. Divine Love is the first premise for becoming a Divine Creator. Without the embodiment of your Divine Child, you will not complete this journey. Isis will bestow upon you the most beautiful endowment as Divine Mother, the foundational aspect of creatorship.

Abu Simbel Light Being blesses you. She was present when embarking on this sacred journey, setting the scene. She is still here and integrates the Alpha α and the Omega Ω principle: the beginning and the end. Completion.

Abu Simbel Light Being speaks to you: "Dear One, I bless you so that you enjoy your embodiment. Pulsate softly with the heart of the Earth and the Cosmos. Breathe with the heartbeat of the Cosmic Womb, Source Field, and the Omegas Ω. I will accompany you along the string connecting all three Omegas Ω."

Up until now, you have witnessed the White-Stringed Omega Ω and the Carnelian Omega Ω. As you descend further, the frequency increases to where it almost prevents you from continuing. You cannot sustain this any longer. Abu Simbel Light Being shows you how to travel inside the string. This provides you direct access to the first Omega Ω. Here you drop into liquid blue-essence light. You discern the same bottle shape as the White-Stringed Omega Ω. The substance is truly mystical, and the blue essence almost resembles the blue essence on the glass windows of Chartres Cathedral. The liquid blue essence of light makes you blissful, ecstatic. A counterclockwise spin brings this cauldron into motion and you rotate along with it. You are blissful beyond expression. By uttering how delighted you are, this liquid blue essence light seems to permeate everything with its joy, delight, and love. As soon as the whirling motion stops, you notice you occupy more space. Expansion occurs. You have grown larger. Around you, liquid blue essence light is still present but has created many blue spheres. In a cauldron of liquid blue light and spheres, you spread the spheres on your arm, like bracelets. Piling them up one after the other on your arm, your legs, your entire body, you love adorning yourself with these blue spheres. While you are having so much fun, you remember the experience of pure bliss, enjoying your life. This liquid blue essence ignites bliss.

How contradictory it is to the history of the Earth, all the pain and suffering. "Yes," the Omega Ω says, "once you disconnect from me, you disconnect from all my upper structures. You disconnect and fall into duality – out of the vibration of the garden of Eden."

"Imbued with my essence, you enjoy every nanosecond of the day, just Being and feeling One. I am the desire of existence of every living consciousness, the Foundational Desire for Life. You want to exist as you want to experience Me. Life's true essence lies here. My dear child, you have come so far to be with me. I grant you the blue sphere of light. Embody your own blue sphere of light within your heart sphere. I anoint and initiate it, so you remember why you chose to exist as One divine spark. You are alive, and this blue sphere surrounds your heart sphere to replicate its essence in every cell of your physical body and light bodies."

The glass windows in Chartres appear again in your mind's eye, reminding you that Yeshua and Mary Magdalene enlightened you with the same message.

Abu Simbel Light Being continues, "You need to remember your desire to exist. We love you. We all do, beautiful cosmic being. Within you, you carry so many lineages of Divine Light Beings who walked upon the Earth. The pearls of wisdom you received from them eternally whisper to you into the deepest and most profound sanctuary of your heart, the same space as the heart of All That Is. Your heart is a cosmic sanctum reverberating with the heart of All That Is, with the heart of each soul in this Cosmic Womb, and beyond, be divine, be you."

Abu Simbel Light Being imbues you with these pearls of wisdom, so that they constantly flare up like flames in your subconscious.

Creational Rebirth Temples Infused by Our Cosmic Creational Divine Mothers

Creational Path of a Seed of Life

Eternal Bliss and the Foundational Desire for Life ignites a seed. In its descent through the Axis Mundi, various multidimensional Creational Temples welcome it. These Creational wombs are located in the Cosmos on many multidimensional levels. They allow the seed of life to embody denser levels of matter.

Each Creational Cosmic Womb connects to specific energies, aspects, and Light Beings. The Egyptian Creational Nile Temples reflect this cosmic birth landscape on a planetary level. They translate the Creation story into Hermetic Principles. The Creational Nile Temples are, therefore, the Creational Temples of Cosmic Creation

The White-Stringed Omega Ω is the cosmic birth temple that creates and breathes the anima into the divine spark. This truly sacred place exudes divine energy. Blue, yellow, pink, and white essences reveal themselves in the womb of this Creational Mother. These weave the soul into the seed of life. The variously coloured essences intertwine the soul.

The Carnelian Omega Ω merges all the components of the seed of life and prepares this divine seed of life to receive the requisites for fulfilling any incarnation in any level of material density. This Creational Mother adds all levels of density and the entire spectrum of multidimensionality, enabling the seed of life, which comes into being, to complete its soul trajectory. The multidimensional structure of the unfolding flower becomes imprinted. It then carries all its potential. It thus receives the energetic imprint of the blueprint of the unfolding process.

Multidimensionality integrates. Interconnectedness of the One divine spark with all its other soul components is created here. Even when we extend this to the physical level, we can say that our organs interconnect in the third dimension through the various octaves of this dimension. They resonate on other layers within this dimension and are linked with one another. The principle of connectedness, belonging to the greater whole as One, originates here.

The Light Beings connected to this Carnelian Omega Ω Birth Temple are of her unique essence. She propagates from within. She is One, and from this Oneness, she expands her consciousness.

The Carnelian Omega Ω creates the Primordial Waters and the divine seed of life. Could this third Omega Ω of Eternal Bliss even be a more powerful energy than Love? Could it be the life force of the divine seed of life, underlying love? Is it possible that if we do not experience Eternal Bliss, we cannot love? Here, in this Omega Ω Birth temple, you experience a vast infinite field of Eternal Bliss. It bubbles like a fountain of youth, a cornucopia of energy, never ending and unbounded. It propagates from a zero-point energy field. There is a white translucent sphere in this field's centre emitting a frequency in concentric circles throughout this vast field. The vibration emitted is the essence of Eternal Bliss. The sphere is the Eternal Bliss of life.

II.2 Temple of the Divine Child and the Axis Mundi for Cosmic Ascension Ceremonies, Philae

Illustration: Philae. Creational Waters.

Black Dragon: Earth's Primordial Guardian

The tide of darkness ebbs and flows. It is still night in Philae. Waters lapping tenderly around the sacred temple grounds reflect moonlight. Somehow, something stirs beneath the water's surface. Underwater and in the surroundings, rustling, whispering tones resound. You see, however, not a thing. Your boat glides effortlessly across the waters, almost as if a subsurface current were sucking it along. Your mind's eye reveals a pathway of yellow light winding its way to the Temple of Philae. The pathway curves, opening into a peaceful vibration that calms, centres, and elevates you into the vibrational grid of the Musica Universalis.

As you meander through the water, beneath the boat the Water Light Beings journey along with you, swaying to the momentum of the vessel, breasting the swells. Swells resonating with you, tuning in to your body, transferring their yellow energies to you. Divinely nourished, your entire fair form flowers from within with yellow spheres. They flourish, activating you with preparatory codes of light for your encounter with Isis. The orbs move towards your sternum, opening your heart to shoreless seas of love. Your heart becomes spherical, pushing outwards with etheric arms, reaching all the way to the Temple of Philae, surrounding the entire temple area, and lovingly bringing within you, its essence.

A white sphere appears to your left. You distinguish three beings inside, Mother Mary, Isis, Kira. They invite you to join them. Lovingly they extend their hands to you. Leaving your body behind, you step in your light form aboard the white sphere. You reasoned it would transport you to the temple of Philae, though it spins around its axis with vigorous force. With all-consuming movement, the entire sphere erupts into golden light, which swirls through the surrounding waters and into the deep waters and further afar, as far as the temple grounds in the far, far distance.

Higher realms loom before you. You stand at the foot of a golden temple. When you peer down at your physical form in the boat, you see they have gifted you with white priestess robes and a beautiful white-feathered headdress.

You bring your attention back to this Golden Temple, to Isis, Mother Mary and Kira. A Temple of Light of the higher dimensions is now quite close to the physical Temple of Philae. You can still see the Temple of Philae, and yourself on the boat. This golden sanctuary is a vast, immovable, a building supported by solid and massive golden pillars. You allow your hands to slip over them, sliding across their smooth sides as you walk through the long corridor. The ground is cold. A deafening silence prevails. Mother Mary, Isis, and Kira accompany you. Softer than moonlight, their soft feminine energy permeates the ethereal fabric of this dwelling as if it were the seat of an order of priestesses. Isis turns and nods. She gestures silently, saying we have little time. They want to show you something. You pass this long colonnade of golden columns engraved with star glyphs. While you pass, they emit blue beams of light. As soon as you surpass them, they extinguish. The three Goddesses smile. They walk on. The corridor seems endless. You follow them, and in your bewilderment, you take in these beautiful surroundings.

On the right-hand side, a small room bathes in an enigmatic orange glow. You enter. It is just large enough to accommodate a staircase. You descend. It leads you to a circular room where stone benches surround the walls. All four of you sit. At your feet, a source of clear blue liquid light appears. The rays shine brightly throughout the source, penetrating the ceiling. You gaze into its depths. The etheric waters are vast and deep. To your amazement, a wave of liquid light rises and sculpts Water Light Beings into being. They were the whispers and mumbles you had heard from the boat. They rise in great numbers from the water. They look at you, smiling. You reach out to touch their hands of liquid light, to feel their love waves washing your heart. They gift you with a finite infinity to regain your senses. They wrap their hands and sculpt the ethereal blue waters into the shape of a boat. A vessel for you alone. "Please enter into the water vessel, my love," they say. The syllables of their speech seem to have sprouted wings, wings lifting you ever so lightly, so caringly you allow yourself to slip silently into the boat, before effortlessly sliding further into the profound watery depths.

The enchanting scenery stuns you: countless mermaids, mermen, water nymphs and other aquatic-light creatures. Small and larger temples of light erect themselves from the Unseen. Magical dwellings. Swaying, colourful, luscious, exotic vegetation cradles you. Some species are otherworldly. The mermaid cutting powerfully through the water astonishes you as it reverberates her authority in swelling waves. This underworld landscape is pure bafflement. Each water creature exudes such enormous power that just to being here is sacred. As you peer downwards, many lights illuminate the depths. You have so many directions to explore. You decide to let them guide you. They explain they do not want to take you where the lights are, but to the other side, where shadows still veil the scenery. They ask if this is agreeable. You examine the deep, shadowy water. Although it is dark, and you would rather not go, you know in your heart their guidance has a purpose.

You know you trust them. You allow . . .

Quietly they initiate . . . the descent. Your ethereal boat dives, meanders into depths eternal. The path tapers like the funnelling foot of a spiralling vortex. You arrive at a still point. It holds you within silence – your boat moored within its still concentrum. A strange sensation overflows you. You sense a slight impression you have travelled through the body of a dragon. Only now do you glimpse the outline of its body. You hesitate, wondering if this were only your imagination. Lying at the bottom of these waters, slowly he reveals his immense form. The point where the boat has docked is the dragon's head. You deboard, approaching the creature lying imperturbably in a deep, sunken sleep. Although he breathes heavily, although his breath does not disturb the waters, he resonates at still another vibratory frequency than do the aquatic light creatures. The more closely you approach, the more he shows you the true essence of his body. Expectant, he wants to reassure himself he is safe with you. You touch eyes, paws, claws of this huge, majestic, black form. He sighs. It occurs to you he must have been asleep for millions of years.

Mother Mary whispers to approach his magenta heart. A luminous magenta crystal pulses within it, resonant with his heartbeat. Its love is motherly, fatherly – all encompassing. The Black Dragon asks if you would wish to touch his heart. You want to. May you lay your head on his heart? "Of course, you can," he says. You nestle your head in that warm nook, and instantly he pulls you inside. Here he cradles you. You settle into foetal position. Meanwhile, he closes his eyes again, continuing, "You are a child of Earth. Every child of Earth is my child. I carry the Earth in my essence. By cradling you, I revive in your cellular memory of being a Divine Child welcomed in Earth's womb, incarnation after incarnation. She gave you a beautiful body. I hope you also love and cherish your body with all your heart. We love you for who you are. I have cradled the Earth myself in this incarnation. I have stayed with her as her guardian. As a primordial Black Dragon, I am a Creator Cosmic Dragon. My essence is to bring Creation into a denser form. I have the power to hold all dimensions. Behold how strong my dragon essence is. I hold the dimensions in my heart, where

I bind them. I travel through them. I do not need portals because I am a cosmic dragon. Please stay in my heart for a while because it is not ready yet."

Then, by cradling you and making movements of an infinity symbol, he weaves infinity into you. Infinite he is as he crosses time by laying his body on the foundations of this lake, waiting to emerge again when the time is right.

The primordial dragon continues, "The time has come. I await only a stronger cosmic alignment of the Earth with the stars. These will be my ley lines on which I will fly out to leave these waters again. I will wrap the essence of my heart around the Earth. My essence is Divine Cosmic Love, and I will give this last blessing to the Earth before she finds her completion. I will awaken my fellow dragons. They will come to the Earth plane. There will be at least two hundred cosmic dragons. During my stay here in these inner depths, I have lent my consciousness to other incarnations of my body. In that capacity, I incarnated as Osiris. And like Isis, I moved my body through the dimensional layers of the Earth. I revealed myself in various manifestations of consciousness levels, frequencies those bodies could contain. I did this because I love and cherish the Earth. The Earth is a magical paradise. The choice is yours to align yourself with joy, love, and abundance."

Still within its heart, you absorb the magenta essence. With your mind's eye, you perceive magenta peonies unfolding, expanding on your heart, your forehead, your throat, belly, the instep of your feet, the back of your heart, your neck, and your head. This structure of peonies feels sweet and forceful, opening you and centering you into your Central Axis. Your right-hand and left-hand sides merge into your centre, the central pillar of your Tree of Life. Your divine feminine and masculine energies converge in the three-dimensional blueprint of your Pillar of Light. Moreover, the Bodhisattva energy imbues and pierces through these peonies. The Bodhisattva chose to be with the Earth out of Divine Love. Just like a swan who chooses his partner and walks life's path together out of loyalty.

The Dragon's heart teaches you that by aligning with Divine Love, you move your essence through all dimensions, modelling and preparing to unfold yourself. Everything is here: in the smallest quantum particle you find the wholeness of the Cosmos. The Earth offers a deeper grounding of all energies to gather before you relinquish your form. The Earth supports opening your heart in its all vulnerability and strength. In softness and vulnerability, you reveal your heart, your essence and who you truly are. The Earth is a perfect place to be during this incarnation and other lifetimes.

Our beloved Earth Star offers the opportunity to open your heart and unfold your divine seed of life so that you can resonate again with the Omega Ω. You unfold the essences they have given you. The unfolding process will shift the Omega Ω's essences and those of your heart from the Unseen to the Seen.

The Earth will offer you Divine Love. You have understood. The Black Dragon allows you to leave his heart, to find yourself again outside his body, within these dark waters. This mighty, great being returns to sleep, gradually dissolving his form.

The Water Light Beings await you. You caress the final formations of Black Dragon's form with your hand, feeling him respond. With your inner ear, you hear him say he also loves you. You enter the boat, spiral upwards into the well, and come out strong. Isis says you are now ready to enter the temple of Philae. Below, your physical boat will soon dock on the Nile bank. We will bring you back immediately. So you all walk through the colonnade, and the three women manifest themselves more clearly now. They are wearing golden garments with cloaks on their heads. They will accompany you back into the white sphere and transport you back into your boat. You can still hear the murmuring and whispering of the waters. You have arrived.

The Divine Child

Your boat now moored, moonlight shines upon you and bathes Philae Temple in its pale hues. Before entering the sacred grounds, you turn once again to these serene waters wherein a different world reigns, a world of primordial existence unseen but real. It is a world holding the frequencies of this divine temple. Indeed, these waters contain the frequencies of past, present, and future. These waters are a world existing beyond time, where the curvatures of time do not apply. Your gratitude towards these water Light Beings feels infinite.

Turning around, you focus on the holy ground of the temple. Philae Light Being wants you to work with her Pillar of Light. The entire floor shows the outline of a strikingly clear white pillar. You walk on a white crystalline structure as if walking on ice.

The terrain is covered with crystalline energies. You circle the sacred place and walk around the principal building, spiralling inwards to its centre. In your mind's eye, the Pillar of Light progresses to the forefront. You receive glimpses of the physical building. You are moving between dimensional layers. You have already undergone initiations to access the core of a Light Being, in this case, Philae Light Being. Her core, her Pillar of Light calls you in the same ways you know. It is an honour to co-create with her.

You have arrived at the centre. You touch the base of her Pillar of Light. Strangely, it is not ice cold, as you would have expected, but lukewarm. The texture is velveteen. With hands touching this Pillar of Light, you tarry awhile, connecting, getting to know her. At this moment, you do not yet know what to do, nor what they expect of you. Fluttering downwards, as you would against a tree, you see on the water surface bright, glittering lights. Bliss wells up within your heart. You take in the enjoyment of your life. This is what you would wake up for in the morning: to tune in to this dimensional layer of our Earth, to experience all this beauty. You take it all into your heart and breathe deeply. It seeps in. You feel more grateful than ever.

A beautiful female Light Being, followed by two other women, appears in front of you. They are reaching towards you. You stand and recognise Isis, Kira, and Mother Mary. Isis shines like a beautiful Goddess with golden robes, soft brown skin, pale-pink shapely lips, and blue eyes the same colour as the dragon's. Thus, she carries the same primordial essence within her. As a primordial Earth Mother, Isis cradled the Earth at the beginning of her existence. Isis holds your hands in hers for a while. It is an honour to be with her. The four of you stare at the water for a moment. Being connected in serenity in this very instant brings your hearts closely together.

Then, Isis explains she will guide you into the Holy of Holies of the Philae Temple, where the temple seed and the root of the Pillar of Light lie. You walk together towards a room giving entrance to the Holy of Holies. Here stands a stone altar. It slides open. A staircase leads downwards. You descend. The altar slides closed above and behind you.

Illustration: Philae. Holy of Holies.

The sanctum where you now stand exudes a majestic, stillness – holy and solemn. The only thing breathing is the temple seed. It illumines with a light blue glow and awaits under a glass dome. The seed radiates the Divine Child's energy. You hear the voice of a child. "Place your hands on it," Isis says, pulling back the glass dome. The seed points upwards as you lift the glass dome. Before, you did not notice it had been hanging downwards, because there was a glow around it. The miniature version of the Divine Child spreads its wings, its energetic arms. He brings his chest forward because he wants to breathe life.

Isis explains that the Divine Child, and every child, brings the evolution we need. In the triad of Father, Mother, and Child, the child was rarely seen for its true potential. The Temple of Philae is the Temple of the Divine Child and the Divine Mother. These waters around Philae are the birth waters, the amniotic waters. Here we consecrated newborn children. We honoured them as messengers of Gods, our teachers who bring us the codes of light, the virtues, the love, the words we so desperately need to hear, the wisdom we feverishly seek to develop. The Divine Child thrives on purity. The Divine Child represents a guardian of purity. We must free the Guardian of Truth, with Purity reigning over all ages. The vulnerable and powerful Divine Child has often suffered suppression and dwells Unseen. Unfortunately, over time, other virtues have been more important. We can describe them as the ego and all its needs, creating solitude and inner erosion.

This chamber and the energies of this beautiful seed are now flowing freely. They spin and swirl and uplift every light particle present. In the same way, we are interacting with the cosmic Pillar of Light that has its foundation here. The Divine Child positions himself in the centre of this Pillar of Light, extending his arms with the palms of his hands upwards. The Pillar frees the codes of purity and all the jewels of wisdom hidden within the Unseen, fragile, and vulnerable child.

He looks at you and says he is ready and liberated. You endorse him, saying he has done well, and you take him in your arms, for he has turned into a proper child. You cradle him, just as the Black Dragon cradled you. In your warm embrace, you see this child for who he is, as a human being, vulnerable, strong, and divine at the same time.

Moreover, you know where this child walks. He radiates golden light, the light of truth and purity. These radiations are only for those who have eyes to see and know how to resonate with the tender energies of love and gentleness. He feels Seen and cherished and now plays.

Again, the four of you join around this mighty crystalline Pillar of Light. The crystalline structures within the Pillar of Light are shifting. You can see the inner boundaries collapsing, rendering the Pillar of one flowing structure becoming one void, one space. The essence of this Pillar of Light nestles deep within the Earth.

Your heart pulses out the same ethereal arms, extending outwards, just as it did when you approached Philae Temple and you took her essence in. You understand now that you enclose, see, and cherish All That Is. Your heart recognises and truly sees the vulnerable child and those in the Unseen. Thus, you become more in wholeness with your surroundings. You attune to these frequencies of purity and truth. Equally important, the attuning will help you with your own Pillar of Light and your own Divine Child. Isis, Mother Mary, and Kira ask you to attune to your Pillar of Light. Your Divine Child sits with legs crossed, looking downwards at the palms of her hands from which golden energies radiate outwards. She has been waiting for a long time for you to take her into your arms. You bend down and hold her close to you. She nestles her head in your chest, just as you did with the Black Dragon. You cradle her in an infinity loop, infinitely connected within one another. She gazes straight into your eyes. She says, "May I?" You say, "Yes, you may." A smile magically graces her face. Her heart pounds. She lets it all go. She spreads her arms wide open. These arms become wings. Isis looks on, thrilled, and supports this process even more. You put her on the ground because she needs space. Her golden heart energy explodes and flows out through her arms, her legs. She becomes a sun illuminating all with her rays.

The disempowerment she once felt dissolves. Her inner fire returns and integrates into her heart. She gains strength, clarity, and determination. The outside world will no longer silence her. We should not silence a Divine Child. Isis puts one of her hands between the shoulder blades of your Divine Child and the other hand between your shoul-

Illustration: Philae, Sealing Golden Orbs.

der blades. Your Divine Child wraps her etheric arms, which are, in essence, her wings, around you. You feel them rising between your shoulder blades, your wings enveloping her.

Every feather on those wings picks up the slightest and most subtle vibrations of your surroundings. As refined as they are, Isis says, they will help you open your heart and envelop the most profound and refined energies you will encounter. Your Divine Child ignites in you the golden disc in your heart and initiates it into a disc of empowerment to speak your truth from purity. To respect and be true to your inner child requires strength and courage. Indeed, your child has it all. Your hands touch the golden disc. It tingles. The disc nourishes your wings and allows them to thrive on the most subtle vibrations.

You express your unconditional love and appreciation. Embracing Isis, Mother Mary, and Kira, you send them from your heart the love you feel for them. They know. By spiralling upwards, you leave this room. You are back in the Holy of Holies. Its temple walls are engraved with hieroglyphics. You realise how much history radiates from these

Illustration by N. Van Der Auwera. A Sacred Journey into Creation. The Ovus.

walls and that these stories are just the tip of the iceberg. They do not translate the true emotional stories of the beings who lived here, even though they are beautiful and amazing. They cover only a small part of history and each deity. Yet this beauty overwhelms you. You glance over at it and depart. Light Beings appear, guiding you to the outer door. When you are outside, the Sun has risen. The golden orb shines its light upon you and seals your heart and wings.

Cosmic Ceremonies: The Ovus and Cosmic Love

That I Am, the Cosmic Tree of Life upon which all life dwells, I Am. To all beings who will visit Philae Temple, I will be here to celebrate Cosmic Ascension Ceremonies, matter to spirit, to align with only the Divine Essence of who you are so you will not forget.

The Temple of Philae asks to be aligned with Earth's centre. A veil surrounds the temple, gently descending to position itself horizontally and fall even more into the Earth.

The Temple of Philae longs to resurrect her body and break through all outdated carnelian energies associated with the old Earth and the old timeline. She invites you to enter via the back of the temple. You direct yourself to those sacred grounds. As you stand there, you sense dense energies. You are now positioned on Philae's timeline in the past, when lower vibrations ruled this temple. These vibrations relate to the element of ceremonies.

Philae's Light Being shows you through your mind's eye a scenery of women, High Priests, and younger children sitting close to one another in a semicircle. The priests are tall and slender. The children look at them, feeling only their own human energy, vulnerable and fragile. These were times when the pure essence qualities of priests and priestesses were Unseen. The temple governance gave assignments, roles from a functional point of view in a patriarchal structure. However, temple governance had lost the knowledge of tuning in to a priest or priestess' purest soul vibration to align their essence with the temple's qualities. If priests and priestesses would resonate with the essence of the Diamond Heart, the presence of all these souls in their midst would be an honour to them. A priest or priestess Sacred Diamond Heart makes a significant contribution to the three-dimensional and etheric temples of Philae. In this temple and probably beyond, being seen as a human without truly sensing your purest vibration causes solitude, alienation, separation, and dismemberment.

You return to the temple's timeline, knowing that the timeline between you and the temple is congested. You revert to where the timeline originates, by the Sun on the horizon and Sothis Starlight. Allow her to animate your heart, to empower you, as you walk towards it. Once you arrive, settle down with the Sun surrounding you. Gaze before you at Philae's timeline. Hold it in your hand, touch it, twist it, for it is flexible and solid at the same time. Open your heart and allow the Sun's light to move through your back and into the timeline as you hold it in your hand. Sun's light codes rush and gush through the timeline. In some areas, the light codes move at the speed of light or faster. In certain parts, they slow down to dissolve denser energies reflecting lack of freedom, choice, and creativity in expressing the divine.

As your heart, a sacred midwife with the Sun, now radiates these light codes through this dense area surrounding this timeline, you sense that all energies of beings who once lived in this temple are leaving. Their energies were still connected to the timeline. Their memories still encoded Philae's walls. Already this timeline shows a tunnel you can pass through even though not fully cleared. The stories of these wounded feminine and masculine patterns of fear, insecurity, soul alienation, and the collective memory encoded in the temple's walls are dissolving.

These coded memories do not resonate with the energy of Oneness and the divine feminine and masculine. These are the memories of the priests and priestesses serving these temples from a three-dimensional perspective. They had lost touch with their own multidimensionality and their Divine Essence and merely subdivide into roles, tasks, or three-dimensional preferences. This temple governance did not align with the true nature of the Diamond Heart and all its essence qualities.

As these words resonate, golden energies gush through this timeline and hit the Philae's walls like a tsunami, eradicating it from the soil. Ceremony rituals deprived of the divine equate with solitude. The true higher meaning became extinguished, and one lived separated from its soul, the One who enables you to walk the earthly plane as a divine being. These were times of inner sadness, profound solitude, and lack of interconnectedness to obtain only pragmatic temple governance and functionality. It may seem that a three-dimensional approach offers more structure, but if you invite Divine Essence, you cannot aim higher in terms of functionality.

Let us continue with this tsunami of golden light crushing Philae's walls, permeating them, restructuring them and their foundation. Isis and three former priestesses are standing on your right, wearing black garments. The fourth priestess also wears a black headdress. Who is she? In answer to the question, she shows you she resonates perfectly with Earth's core. She shares her sadness at witnessing the decay of the vibration of this temple. She urges you to descend to Earth's core.

For the last moment, you look at the temple to check the transformation before you accept her invitation. You notice the inscriptions and the images. The coding not resonant with Oneness has dissipated on the temple walls. New light codes and cartouches appear. Huge golden windows of light appear on the temple walls. You see a Golden Dragon. These windows are holographic time chambers: portals that allow you to visit the temple on other multidimensional layers. These time capsules enable you to behold and rewrite everything according to the teachings of Source.

Now let us descend into the Inner Earth. You see three layers of underground chambers, like an inverted Mesoamerican step pyramid. A ray of light shoots downwards from its apex towards Earth's core, moving through Earth's inner layers. Significant energy crystallisations in this earth line make it impossible for the ray of light to convey energy. Similarly, this crystallisation does not allow Earth's energies to penetrate Philae's temple. Earth's connection is distorted, as is our connection with our heart, our essence.

With this in mind, Horus presents himself as he feels called to contribute to this alignment. He adds: "This is Philae's history. As human beings, we resided in this temple. Somehow, something broke along the way, and we lost our connection to the divine, the Earth, and All That Is. Also, the temple lost its connection to the heart of the Earth." Philae merely received enough energy to keep the heart of the Holy of Holies pulsating. Earth's heart pulse also transmits the pulse of the galactic Sun, the universal Sun, and the Cosmic Womb. Philae Temple has lost the pulse of existence and *harmonic resonance*.

Horus places his hands on the crystallised energy. He summons all beings having endured solitude, sorrow, and dismemberment to come and collect the energy that is theirs. It is time to set everything and all free. You *may* again feel Earth pulsing through your body. You *may* again love yourself to allow Earth's heart pulse to strengthen you. We attune ourselves to the cosmic Sun, the Cosmic Womb, to *All That Is*, and to Source.

This ray of light is cleared, and all blockages dissolve. After such a long time, Philae Light Being descends through the light ray and travels through Earth's inner layers to arrive at the Temple of Love at the core of the Earth. Earth's womb gently envelops Philae's Light Being in warmth and nurturing. Within this womb, the memory of Philae's Light Being resides. She received Earth's womb-consecrated blessings. Earth's Light Being recalls her heartbeat and says, "My darling, it has been so long since we have been together in this way. Listen, my dear, and remember your heartbeat. Its memory has engraved my womb. You are my child; your body thrives on love. I love you, and I always will." Together they look up at the surface of the Earth, where the temple building settles. Philae's Light Being aligns herself with Earth's heart. Together, they imprint the temple with white light, the original true essence of Cosmic Ceremony. The imprinting reconnects the three-dimensional temple with all etheric temples. Celebrating Cosmic Love as Source's golden energies, reimprint Philae. *As Within, So Without. As Above So Below*, and Source hears this call and initiates Philae's Temple with its golden light and consecrates her temple grounds.

A cone rises from Earth's core upwards, with its apex imbued with Earth's heartbeat and that of the Cosmic Womb. This earth cone lands with its flat base just below Philae's temple grounds. Another cone departs from the Cosmic Womb downwards, with its apex infused in Source to arrive with its flat base on the temple grounds of Philae. These two cones form two tuning forks, aligning the temple. The Earth and Cosmic cone both rotate, alternatively clockwise and counterclockwise. As they rotate, you hear the vibration rising. You hear vibration fine tune because this temple is ever-evolving, infinite. Also, the attunement is infinite. Earth's Light Beings say to Philae's Light Being, "You are an infinite Goddess who has found her wholeness, interconnected with All That Is, the Earth and the Cosmic Womb. You are the I Am that I Am, the beginning and the end. You are an expression of Source, a living temple manifesting Source Light." They kiss one another on their foreheads, and Philae's Light Being ascends towards Earth's surface. You ascend with her.

When you arrive on Earth's surface, you perceive vibrant codes engraved the temple walls. In addition, more rectangular time portals have come into existence on Philae's foundation: interwoven golden circles manifest, move, and interact. They form a receiving platform, coding cosmic energies into discs. They exchange information by circular motion. This triggers a weaving of golden strings of light moving upwards. These ascending strings show the energy signature of green-eyed cobras shooting green rays of light at the temple walls outlining the blueprint of what lies ahead. Then, the strings of light densify and intertwine in an undulating pattern, creating a Cosmic Tree of Life. This Cosmic Tree is primaeval. It predates the concept of time and space. It bears emerald-green blossoms. Its roots permeate and encompass the Earth.

The Cosmic Tree's Light Being says she represents the concept of cosmic ceremonies. In these, we bring together the wisdom of beautiful Earth and Cosmos and in the highest form of love. In Cosmic Love, we honour one another. Each ceremony carries the blueprint of sacred marriage and signifies a birth canal to higher consciousness. This unique gift is a direct gateway to the centre of the Cosmic Tree of Life and its infinite evolution. You will, from now on, sail along the same streams of consciousness and experience great unity with cosmic consciousness. Heaven on Earth is descending. The divine bestows lovingly upon you. She, with this, gives the example. She is the Cosmic Tree of Life and sets the scene for ceremonies of the infinite to be held in her presence to celebrate the Divine Essence qualities.

All in All, the sacred union of the hearts of Philae, Earth, All That Is and Source, is a message of Divine Love to be infused in all Nile temples.

Finally, the Cosmic Tree of Life's heartbeat powers the Earth and provides life force energy as she passes through its crown. White crystalline energies cover the Earth like snow and crystalline waters. These crystals replicate themselves, fractally, encompassing the whole Earth as frozen veins of crystalline water. The Cosmic Tree of Life, surrounding the Earth, reduces her mass, rendering it compact and small. Then its roots convey the sphere of the Earth into its body, its trunk. This Earth sphere of frozen white crystallised light moves upwards through the trunk and gradually transmutes. Earth's energy evaporates through the Cosmic Tree's crown and all its branches into the Cosmos. The Cosmic Tree's Light Being smiles and says, "You witnessed an ascension process from matter to spirit. That I Am, the Cosmic Tree of Life upon which all life dwells, I Am. By descending my awareness through this conic hologram, I aid the Earth in its transmutational process. My body is a gift to the Earth to birth herself into a new being. To all beings who will visit Philae Temple, I will be here to celebrate Cosmic Ascension Ceremonies, matter to spirit, to align with only the Divine Essence of who you are so you will not forget."

My name is *Ovus*.

Note of the author: The Ovus, Axis Mundi

The Cosmic Tree, the Axis Mundi, prepared the Earth with its crystalline waters to birth again and radiate its Divine Essence into the Cosmos.

The Tree of Life and the Jacob's Ladder system symbolise the process of death and rebirth. As a soul leaves the body through the crown, it represents completion. In an upwards whirling movement, the Earth rebirthed herself through the crown of this cosmic Tree of Life. She has completed her earthly experience. Passing through the trunk of the Cosmic Tree of Life signifies passing through a tunnel connecting the old to the new. The Earth is integrating higher octaves and, at this moment, has ascended at least a dimension and even more.

The Mayan Tree of Life, also referred to as the Axis Mundi or in the Cosmogony as the coral trunk, represents a birthing chamber where all divine sparks arrive from the Cosmos' membrane. In this sanctuary, they gestate and acclimatise to the Cosmic Womb's energies, which differ from the cosmic membrane. As the divine spark climbs through the coral's trunk, it passes the stage of gestation. Birthing and becoming pass through various phases and passageways through multiple vesica piscis throughout existence. As they leave the coral trunk via its branches or crown, they position themselves in the Cosmic Womb and build their most primaeval sphere, their very first expression of manifested life.

The Cosmic Tree of Life initiation is a ritual of death and rebirth. It involves several phases: processing, resting, and planning. Climbing the Tree of Life's trunk leaves the old behind and moves on to a new and elevated form of Creation.

Being inert is comfortable and has its own rhythm. However, this is about evolution, energy in motion, cycling and spiralling upwards or downwards, sculpting and deepening yourself to unveil your own unique Holy of Holies.

From matter to spirit or spirit to matter, both movements offer growth to fine-tune and sculpt the manifestation of the divine spark. Even though it already is perfect, Creation longs for you to *manifest your perfection*. The Axis Mundi represents the coral trunk, a gateway or portal through which we move as we ascend or descend. Creation foresees warmth, care, and nurture. Creation prepares you with white crystalline energies that withdraw, reduce the Earth body in mass to remain only with her blue core, and move that through the trunk to transmute and radiate. The *Ovus* represents the egg, the sacred sanctuary, to be reborn.

Rebirth offers the end of an old phase and a new beginning.
The Alpha α and the Omega Ω.

Diamond Heart Stargate: Twelve-pointed Star

The Lotus stands at the sacred site of Philae. This weathered Lotus contains many outdated energies and forms a vital centre within the whole of this Creational Nile Temple. However, this Lotus does not resonate with the Aquarian Age, Ancient Egypt, or any era, it seems. It is aware of the moon codes to come and prepares itself to release these old energies now coming to its surface. The old is now coming to the surface to dissolve.

Philae Light Being invites you to walk up to this Lotus to align with her core. You feel her core replicating on multiple levels in your vertical Central Axis. This connects you to your multidimensional structure. It also descends into the Earth, your inner interdimensional earth layers. You allow the temple seed of Philae to resonate with your core essence. She responds by creating a flowered pattern of twelve petals. Within the outer circumference, a new second circle of petals emerges. Meanwhile, a third circle arises, with petals coming out of that third inner circle. In total, nine circles are formed, with the last circle having only one petal.

You are now in this Lotus Flower. Torsion caused by the circling collapses on the left side of your vertical axis. Your multidimensional essences have collapsed with it, and you now have them consciously present in your heart. As you have integrated the core essence of your left side, being your divine-feminine energy, into your Central Pillar, it resurrects its renewed energy as the Phoenix. When everything crumbles, you undergo the process of the Phoenix burning to ashes.

By reintegrating your core essence, you emerge even brighter and more potent, with an even higher frequency. Also, you hear a high-frequency sound, and the golden light transforms into bright white-yellow light. All your soul extensions integrate into yourself. Now you embody your divine feminine energy, lifted to a higher vibratory level.

The temple seed of the Lotus before you calls. Eager and dedicated, you try to understand why this is happening only on your left side. Your divine feminine has come into Oneness, raised its vibrations, and you are embodying it. The petals on the rings go from twelve to nine, six and three petals. The ninth ring carries only one petal. These are triads giving access to birth from various dimensions, like a birth canal. Each time you descend a dimension, you go more in-depth in terms of complexity in Creation. As you descend further, you descend more into physicality. It becomes denser, and you create bodies for people or animals. For example, a three-dimensional body. You cannot create from the outer rings at this level, but you can from the inner rings.

Now align your right side, your masculine energy, with the Temple of Philae. You feel the divine feminine power of Creation rushing through you, and it tears apart your entire right-hand structure. A sense of powerlessness overwhelms you, the passivity of not being able to create, to manifest. Everything is crumbling. Philae Light Being asks you to embody the core essence of your true divine masculine power. As you take in these codes, it becomes crystal clear, and you recall the diamond codes that belong to your Golden Diamond Heart. These twelve diamonds now place themselves around your heart, just like the flowered pattern with the twelve petals. The identical replica in your heart emerges with Diamond cones, which function as cauldrons. The outline of your golden diamond heart restores. You resurrect your divine masculine energy. It will enable you to create from your heart.

Your heart is where true Creation lies. You create from the heart because the heart is where your centre of power comes from.

Your heart is also the centre of your own unique galaxy that exists around your One divine spark. Your heart centre feeds your own galaxy structure through its spiral arms. Creation begins here, and you behold your magic cauldron, your chamber of Creation.

All twelve diamonds interconnect, forming threads between one another in the shape of a twelve-pointed Star. From here, you can create in all dimensions and fine tune Creation, and lower densities. By descending into this heart chamber to the deeper inner layers that resonate with denser prima mater, you create various levels of density. Now you can feel your left and right hip align, finding balance in the pelvic floor to embody this new creator within you. Let this complete structure permeate your entire body. Then you will see that this twelve-pointed Star transcends your physical body and truly becomes a Stargate, a Heart Stargate.

As can be seen, you are nourishing the totality of who you are. You create from your Inner Sun. When you bring your gaze back to Philae Light Being, you notice she has done the same thing. She has aligned herself as a birthing chamber with the essence of Creation, which is your heart. In doing so, she also aligns with several stars carrying the same birth essence and providing the amniotic fluids, the amniotic waters for seeds to grow.

Now, allow yourself to lie on the water body, float on the waters surrounding Philae, and integrate into your cellular structure the stellar consciousness she evokes. Light Beings descend into the temple grounds toward the Holy of Holies where the temple seed lies. They also help to install these nine circles as a cone around the temple seed. As you align with the cone shape, it replicates in your heart, sealing your Heart Stargate, protecting it, providing it with nourishment. The Lotus here carries a glow of white-yellow light. These concentric rings now form a cone.

Finally, you activate your Heart Stargate as a portal for Creation in different levels of density throughout the multiverse.

In the same way, this cone shape also replicates itself in your body as the outline of the twelve-pointed Star. Hence, as you move to other temples, you understand and embody more of the knowledge that will be transmitted to you. Thank you.

II.3 Temple of the Human Divine Nature, Elephantine Island

Illustration: Elefantine Island. Giant Boulders.

Embodied Divine Potential, as Gods on Earth

Your boat arrives and docks on the Nile shore at Elephantine Island. As you sit in the felucca, somehow, you cannot immediately deboard. You turn inwards and notice numerous yellow strings of Venus Light enveloping you. They enfold you as if you were a caterpillar transforming into a butterfly. Something wants to spring up from within to prepare you for this sacred initiation. Strands leave your spine and wrap themselves around you, layer by layer. You allow this process. The strings widen into veils and float around you in the soft breeze. They penetrate deeper into your body, around the ever-deeper layers of your physical structure. Your heart radiates white light. You feel stronger, straighter, more centred. Your heart aligns with your pelvic floor, opening a direct and active connection between your heart and the gateway of manifestation, your birth canal. It is complete.

You turn your gaze outwards again. Small Light Beings leave your etheric body. These yellow essences of Venus Light have worked with you. Take a couple deep breaths to anchor these energies of this preparatory phase.

You leave your boat and walk to the temple grounds. On your way up, you glimpse the graceful grey rocks of Elephantine Island, divinely sculpted like a fertilised womb. In them, you sense an inner turmoil. The Light Beings still animating them swirl up from the rock. They know of your arrival and come out of their inert rock to meet you in this holy place. You are stunned. When they emerge, the contours of the bodies of two giants emerge.

On the one hand, you perceive them as Light Beings, as they are now. On the other hand, they show you how their bodies were built from large boulders. Although they are robust, their energy feels profoundly loving, nurturing. The giants show you how they shape earth, braiding it into strands. As midwives shaping matter to prepare a new-born body for the soul that will inhabit it, they weave matter as a preparation for the animation of existence. You approach them telepathically. They invite you to visit. The giants want to show you something. While they await on the upper plateau of Elephantine Island, you climb a staircase. Already the light-blue energy of this sacred place glares.

You turn to the two giants. You see them braiding earthen strings. They explain to you that they weave the stellar DNA into the new-born child. They add that a soul always carries its complete blueprint within. On each dimensional level, however, you need the relevant birthing chambers to weave that blueprint into the exact dimensional level the soul will incarnate within. Here on the third-dimensional level, we weave stellar DNA into the bodies of the new-born children. In more detail, when the stellar energies enter the new-born, we encode the energetic system by weaving it into the meridians, the chakras, the brain areas. Then, new neural pathways shape. An etheric receiver incorporates into your body so that you receive stellar guidance. Thus, this wonderful work is a form of direct guidance. It offers a profound and caring approach to new life for every creature. The love the giants put into their work moves you. With utmost respect and integrity, they approach each body that is ready to be animated. The knowledge that this body is a divine vehicle for the soul with which it spends its incarnation touches their hearts. They see and recognise the divine potential of each soul and treat it with heart and respect.

Nonetheless, for finding your true self, your soul mission, today we experience more hindrance than support. Instead, we try to deal with the world's dual nature and learn to wade through it. So, this sacred Stargate provides an entirely new worldview when a soul embarks on a new beginning. Here, the co-Creation between Earth and stars offers a clear path of crystallisation of the deeper elements of your soul. Truly, one can then live from the most profound part of one's soul.

The giants explain that a threefold process occurs on Elephantine Island. First, the stellar energies enter at the Stargate. Then they explain an existing circular platform. Thereon they perform a cosmic alignment of these stellar codes. Here, the giants seal the stellar codes by weaving them into matter. They now ask you to witness the first stage of this process. Meanwhile, a child of these giants appears out of nowhere. You understand that the higher dimensional beings can choose to appear or disappear. The child asks you to follow it to the Stargate. During your walk with this child, a path of light unfolds and runs far ahead from the entrance to Elephantine Island to the Stargate opening onto Nile Bay.

You step on this path. A tingling, a current of electricity, runs through your body. It takes some time to tune into this path, for this is an energy you have not experienced before. At the same time, a golden line in the middle of this path reveals itself. You profoundly discern you must follow it, for it represents your soul line. This path has also tuned in to your soul to provide you with the frequencies you now need. Now, as you walk, millions of light-blue strings climb up and penetrate your body while you progress. They infiltrate all your physical layers up to your bone marrow, and there they merge with the golden strand running through your Central Axis. In fact, the Central Axis of this path aligns with your golden string in your Central Axis. Hence, a mirroring occurs, and as you continue onwards, this electrified light turns into liquid light, sweeping through your entire body. Even though earlier a tingling calibrated your body, now it becomes more refreshing, liquid like, and cool. Simultaneously, the energy continues to morph and transform you into a Light Being endowed with magnificent, ethereal, liquid blue robes. The preparation is completed.

The Elephantine Stargate comprises two vertical rocks, with a horizontal one across the top, like a portal. It invites you to enter, so you step inside. Here you are now, with a magnificent view of the Nile Bay and the Sun shining down upon you. At first sight, nothing special happens. You place your hands on the inner walls and feel the textures of the stone. You sense a slight tingling, but it seems this Stargate is no longer active. The Sun continues to glare, and you align your golden strings with it. The warmth and power of the Sun completely charge them. Your body becomes warm and charged inside, the energy rises and becomes difficult to hold on to. You regulate your breathing and surrender to the process. Your body irradiates from within. You allow the Sun to lead you in this intimate moment. You allow it to play you like an instrument. How wonderful it is to surrender! Moreover, it is safe. You feel honoured and loved.

By touching these walls with the palms of your hands, you activate this portal with your solar consciousness. The golden essence emissions within these walls ignite. The gateway begins to whirl around you at high speed, gradually turning into a golden sphere. You lie down in a foetal position because the energies are too intense to remain conscious. Your body now ultralight, the golden essence of the sphere dematerialises you. You disappear from the visible eye, just like these giants and the Black Dragon could materialise or disappear. You know you are still there. You witness everything around you, but they cannot see you, nor the golden orb. The child of the giants looks at you and smiles. He enjoys witnessing this process.

Now, from the Sun, a giant, ethereal dragon snake swings towards you. It has a long tail and bears the features of a koi fish. It asks you to enter its body and opens its mouth like a portal. You enter. Both of you disappear into another dimensional plane. In fact, you find yourself again above the star path you had walked before. Now, though, you inhabit a higher dimensional level. As you hover above this path, the golden line beneath you remains within your awareness. The dragon serpent walks the starry path with you. As it moves forward, the central line in the middle of the path below you magnetises the golden line in your body. Indeed, your golden thread is being peeled out of you while your remaining body remains in the dragon's body. Without understanding what is happening, you allow things to happen. With wild abandon, you walk this path and trust you will attain clarity afterwards.

As you progress along, the carnelian aspects of your heart are enlivened. They have much to do with the Old Earth and the three-dimensional aspect of life. Similarly, you are returning and releasing the three-dimensional essence of yourself. You ask the dragon to understand what is going on. And he says that to understand the deeper functionality of the stellar codes at Elephantine Island, exploring it on another dimensional level is paramount.

You have arrived above the Stargate again. The Sun is now glaring at your heart. In the same way, you become the golden orb, and your inner golden essence. The golden essence is no longer only within you, but it is also outside you. The within has become the without, and you have mirrored yourself and become your golden essence. The golden essence descends into the stone walls of the portal and permeates these walls, and further on, your multidimensional presence. From your multidimensional presence, you impregnate your three-dimensional presence with your golden essence from the without. This Stargate activates the Hermetic Principle: As Within, So Without. In a forceful manner, the golden essence surrounding you reverberates with the golden essence within. As they magnetise one another, the golden essence expands. The golden circuitry in your body now expands omnidirectionally, filling and fulfilling your entire golden orb as an etheric essence.

Here you are as a golden sphere, the Sun still glaring, sealing, and anchoring.

Hence, when you bring the within and the without together, you bring them into the Now, the present. Nevertheless, the present does not connect to this timeline, and it becomes your presence. You have brought it into your conscious presence in whatever dimension you are in. By having lit your presence, you have lit this portal. Thus, your solar angel activates in your heart. It becomes your presence here and now, anytime, and anywhere. In fact, it is not related to time and space. You have completed the mirror of your golden essence, or rather, your golden disc. The initiation finished, you leave this portal and walk back along this blue-light-starred path. A golden glow envelops you. This golden sphere expresses in a profound manner the thirteenth sphere formerly given to you.

Equally important, you bring your solar energy into the here and now. By living it, you walk your three-dimensional life from this presence. Wherever you walk, you sow golden light. You bless the Earth and the beings just by being with them. Having elevated your three-dimensional capacity, you overlay it with your solar presence. We lived within this capacity in pre-Lemurian times, when a golden glow imbued and coronated humanity. They lived on prana, they could levitate, and their physical bodies were of a refined consistency. Already you held this essence within, and now at Elephantine Island, you have externalised it. You have brought your divine potential from within to the without, your Golden Sun Angel from the Unseen into the Seen.

In Lemurian times, people were demigods in physical forms. They accessed their divine potential at will. The Earth is moving again towards that level of divine manifestation. We want you to have a head start by activating the solar consciousness already. The giant child asks you if you are happy. You answer that you are delighted and deeply honoured. You tell him that he seems a wise child, an oracle in his own right. He remembers everything that lies behind the veil. He replies that yes, he is. His father and mother have taught him well. He observes all dimensions with crystalline clarity. We will tell you more about that.

Cosmic Birth Initiation of your Divine Potential

The giant child asks you to follow him. He leads you further away from the Nile and from the place where the most important physical relics stand today. Instead, you enter an area of untrodden paths. In the distance, a beautifully veiled white light reveals itself. It is Sothis. She has been waiting for you. You have now realised your divine potential, and she wants to show you the ancient divination process used in ancient times. As you stand beside her, she brings her hands to your thighs and guides you further downwards. A circular platform in the distance looms. As you draw nearer and nearer, you see the platform divided into twelve parts. The golden essence you perceived in the star path and in your own essence you now detect into the lines of this circular blueprint.

Wearing white and light-yellow robes, a Blue Moon Goddess appears out of nowhere within each of the twelve parts. These twelve Blue Moon midwives wear etheric-light dressing gowns. They remain still, staying present for this cosmic initiation. The first Blue Moon Goddess moves to the centre of the circular blueprint, inviting you to follow her. You join her. She leads you with your shoulders to the exact spot in the centre of this circumference, repositioning herself where she stood before. They all look at Sothis transmitting the telepathic request to begin the process.

Illustration: Elephantine Island.
The Owl, Keeper of the boundless Night Heavens.

An owl appears. He is the keeper of this Stargate and carries with him the boundless night heavens, bestowing upon us the eternal presence of the stars and their encrypted light.

Sothis activates the cosmic baptismal font. After a white cone of light descends from atop it, it closes hermetically. The entire structure transforms into a giant white sphere within which many swirling strings float serenely, surreally, magically. You stand within its centre, white light swirling all around you, cosmic energies descending from the heavens by way of the whirling strings.

At his moment, you still feel small. You witness the magic of these cosmic energies installing themselves and preparing the stage. Descending, anchoring themselves, their stability structures a welcoming stage for the twelve Blue Moon midwives transforming into twelve Pillars of Light! For this cosmic initiation, they have attuned themselves from their Pillar of Light to their purest essence. As they now act from within that capacity, they connect as one great cosmic consciousness, thereby weaving themselves into a circular band of light. This band of light begins to rotate, and you become giddy. Everything around you moves, and the forces dissolve you. And so it is, the movement is dissolving you. The white strings unfold from your body, loosen, almost like tentacles, move outwards towards the inner wall of the white sphere. Here they attach themselves to the membrane's various layers, where the cosmic energy enters. This membrane comprises multiple layers, where the incoming cosmic energy alchemises and from there travels into the womb of this white sphere. In a word, you realise this is a replication, a mirror of the Cosmic Womb, whereby in the membrane, the yellow and the blue Venus essences prepare the divine seed of life for incarnation in this Cosmos.

While the cosmic initiation process is swelling with sacredness, your white strings connect to this inner wall. The energies funnel down into your body, which stores them. You glimpse your Pillar of Light, now redefining itself through resonance with these cosmic energies. The latter resonate with the membrane of your Pillar of Light and expand the liquid light contained within. Your Pillar of Light becomes more solid and massive. You understand you are downloading the light codes, the star DNA of your divine potential, and these store within your Pillar of Light. You incarnate more and more of your own divine potential light codes, so the perimeter of your Pillar of Light undergoes a gradual expansion. Each Blue Moon midwife continues to channel these energies intently, and you understand this process is not yet complete.

In addition, they tune in and vibrate strongly to the cosmic currents flowing within. They flow towards you from twelve divided compartments, the cosmic energy flowing through the Earth component so you may manifest your divine potential on Earth. Your Pillar of Light completes itself in this way for this incarnation. Life is also to be ac-complished on Earth and not elsewhere. The Blue Moon midwives embody the Earth and the cosmic component, and they initiate you to manifest on Earth your divine blueprint. Through this, you integrate the As Above, So Below.

Concluding, being rewired, the strings on the inner wall retract within you. You transform into a smaller sphere spinning in all directions to integrate these new codes of light. The Blue Moon midwives also with-draw their energy, allowing you space and free will to shape yourself according to your wishes and soul essence. The spinning slows, the white sphere becomes transparent light and glides down your body.

As an enlightened being carrying the Enlightenment Codes within, you feel reborn. You connect with Inner Earth. Your consciousness reaches all corners of Earth and Cosmos. You experience being every-where. You connect with All That Is. You inhabit your own body and your Divine Light Body. Earth and Cosmos feel as part of you.

You are All That Is, and yourself, all at the same time.

An inner glow of bliss, joy, and completion fills and fulfils you. Being in Oneness with All That Is, you realise you no longer echo dualities. Nor do they any longer attract you. You reside on a different time-line or wavelength. When you behold your form, you envision your human body, but also flowing golden light. Your body, like energy, is evermoving. You find yourself composed of energy in the form of an energetic compound of particles moving mutually. In your mind's eye, your spinal column and each vertebra show clearly. They are dense, and the bones create friction between themselves. This initiation con-tinues to optimise your spine on a molecular level. The spine and this skeletal structure are the only things anchoring you to Earth. The rest seems to be etheric Light.

This is beautiful! The love you radiate is viral! You magnetically attract beings! They long to be in your presence! You walk towards Sothis and thank her. She has been the sacred midwife who set the entire field in motion as the thirteenth component. With her creator's hands, she scribed the stellar codes within your Pillar of Light. So now you can manifest your divine potential even more. This golden light is universal. All beings in the Cosmos carry it within, regardless of their race or whether they are light or dark. It does not matter. This golden light transcends everything. We are all carriers of the golden light. Our divine potential shines through, in whatever capacity we radiate it. We have a choice to bring it to the Seen. You embody from this perspective the golden energies of your divine potential and bring all the distinct races in this Cosmos into unity.

The giant child is waiting for you. Thrilled, he says it has been such a long time since he has seen this. You ask him if he will do it as well, and he replies no, not now. He shares his mission with his parents in this life. They will fulfil it first. They are patient and loyal and consider what the needs are and what they can fulfil. Afterwards, when the time is right for them too, they will undergo the same. You tell him he is wise and mature. You stroke his hair and walk with him back to his parents.

When you stand in front of these two Giant Light Beings. They look at you with pride and wonder. They enjoy the mere sight of you, your mere presence. "We used to do this initiatory birth process here on Elephantine Island. We love to weave within the golden essence again." And as she utters that, the ground beneath her trembles and activates. Perhaps the time is right. The rooms where they wove the golden essence rise upwards. A vast underground stone turns into a golden plate. This is Khnum's potter's wheel coming into motion in the third dimension. They touch it as if the time has come again to work with the prima mater they were accustomed to working with. To play with golden essence instead of earthen stones. They shine as they understand they can experience the same fulfilment again as they did so many aeons ago. The seat of Khnum is activated. They thank you and hope to be with you soon.

We thank Sothis and her midwives, Thoth Hermes Trismegistus, and the Light Beings of the Venus Light Path.

Initiation: Pineal Gland Temple Seed & Axis Mundi Alignment

A whirlwind of energy in the shape of a cochlea envelops the seat of Khnum. As this cochlea oversees the Nile River, it redistributes and evaporates moon essences into the Nile waters. These moon essences initiate the Nile into being the Axis Mundi. The Cochlea Temple truly carries the energy of a conic cauldron holding the silvery-white moon and golden-white sun essences.

In this transmission, the Nile desires complete alignment with the Axis Mundi. Subsequently, you also receive alignment with the Cosmic Axis. Then you can implode your entire essence, dissolve it, and remain with only your refined *Pillar of Light*.

Moon essences descend from the Cosmos into this cochlea-shaped Moon temple. As the moon essences enter, they travel through the shape only to be transferred into the Nile at the level of the two birthing stones. In the Nile, a black spiralled portal appears, which descends deeper into the Earth, and it invites us to come closer.

For your understanding, Elephantine Light Being clarifies that the cochlea is the upwards-placed Moon portal, that the black spiralled portal is the downwards-placed Moon portal. They co-create without being physically placed on top of one another. In the black-spiralled portal, gemstones decorate the spiral arms. They are circular, and their outline is golden. This golden outline illuminates the path downwards. This portal exudes opulence and beauty. Moving through it is delightful, as is the guiding golden light of the gemstones. At the bottom point of this portal awaits a tranquil chamber. You sense the water currents of the Nile above you.

As you sit in this chamber, these gemstones begin to resonate with you. They possess their own intelligence. They detach from the spiral arms and envelop you. Their essence enters your body and soaks into each vertebra of your backbone. They also penetrate deeply into the bone marrow of your skeleton, your skull, the bones of your arms, your sternum, your legs. Now, the golden outline becomes a golden string of light integrating into your body as the new centre of your skeletal structure. The gemstone's essence envelops the golden string, carrying its own energy. It is peculiar to experience all these essences entering your body. You look at your hands and you move your fingers. Your body feels refreshed – invigorated! All gemstones in your backbone and vertebra are now intercommunicating – fusing! The fusion changes the molecular structure of your bone marrow. Your DNA strands rewire to DNA strands of crystalline prima mater. Clusters of crystalline light appear throughout your skeletal structure. Now you abide as much lighter.

The connection between your neck and head requires alignment. This will balance and calibrate your pineal gland. Then more dimensional space emerges, and your pineal gland as your temple seed receives the codes of moon essences of the blueprint for the unfolding process of your true divine potential. The blueprint of an unfolding Lotus surrounds your pineal gland. You know your pineal gland is undergoing an initiation. Your head continues to calibrate itself with respect to your neck, creating increasingly dimensional space. Your pineal gland follows this process and calibrates itself as well. It unfolds as tenderly a seed.

Like a flower blooming, your temple seed unfolds its petals, your pineal gland radiates the blue light in its core, radiating like a beacon sending out a signal. Your temple seed is clearly activated, resonant with the Cosmic Moon's concentric rings. These form a resonant sphere circumscribing the whole Earth, assisting Earth in unlocking all her seeds. These seeds, in turn, unlock the Earth Star to its full solar potential. You entrain with the resonance of these concentric rings, which unlock your own full potential, preparing you for ascension.

Meanwhile, you are still in this chamber below the Nile. The blue light in your pineal gland permeates your entire Central Axis, which imbues itself with blue light. It permeates your backbone and each vertebra as your remaining earthly system. You allow it to infuse itself within you, and it straightens your spine, aligning you with the Axis Mundi, taking the River Nile into your consciousness, you and the river aligning with the Axis Mundi.

During this cosmic alignment, you roll both halves of your body inward as you would roll up a scroll. In the centre of your body, where they meet, they integrate into the blue light. Now, you bring yourself into Oneness. You become initiated into being your True Self, Divine Self, a Creation of Life who chose to abide in *harmonic resonance* with All That Is. The choice is yours to move with the waves of the waters and the Cosmic Womb. Thus, you can now decide to move with the waves of the cosmic grid, to surrender to its motion, its rhythm, pace, and simply be with what is. You can choose to come into Oneness, bringing your divine feminine and masculine essences into your heart gate.

While you undergo this process, the Nile is doing the same thing. It asks all temples to render their codes into the Nile waters. Next, the temple's codes float upwards in the waters, to the Nile delta and into the seas. The left and right banks of the Nile have come into Oneness also to raise their own *Pillar of Light*. All temples' codes now carry the blueprint structure of Oneness. Nile Light Being offers them to the Cosmos' *Pillar of Light*. Egypt's Nile Temple Body becomes Self-Realised and ascends.

Last, your awareness now draws back to your physical body in this chamber below the Nile. All gemstones reposition themselves on the spiral arms again. These spiral arms guide you upwards to exit this portal, for this initiation is complete.

You find yourself again on the temple grounds of Elephantine Island, looking out on the River Nile and sensing what is stirring beneath. You know what is moving beneath these waters. As you roll up a scroll, the two banks of the Nile roll inward to become One *Pillar of Light*.

You thank the Nile Light Being, the Blue Moon midwives, the Light Beings of the Venus Light Path, and Thoth Hermes Trismegistus for their midwifery.

II.4 Temple of the Love for Life, Kom Ombo

Illustration: Kom Ombo Temple.

Breaking Point of Dualism

Kom Ombo Temple suffers from imbalance. In fact, you can feel underlying unrest and agitation, which prevails. The two Gods who mainly rule this temple are Horus, the Falcon God, and Sobek, the Crocodile God. Horus's side seems quite airy and emanates a lot of white light. Sobek's side is rather heavy and gloomy, like the energy of a frightened and insecure child. You enter the temple through the side of Sobek, and with your hand, you stroke the engraved walls with hieroglyphs. While walking, you notice your hands draw a kind of ethereal white fabric from the wall. These are White Light Beings, which you unconsciously summon to assist you.

Meanwhile, you walk along the pillars, at some point, you come to a small dark shrine. Sobek lies there with his head in a corner, perhaps motionless for at least thousands of years. Locked in this pattern, he seems unable to break it. Petrified as he is, he seeks hiding, security – he is caught in the old pattern that results from duality.

Suddenly, you see Horus' head appearing in the shrine. He shows his falcon's head and asks Sobek to accompany him to the other side. You decide to embody Sobek's energy and follow Horus' request to work your way to the left side of the temple. The white veils you summoned earlier from these temple walls now lead you down a meandering path through the temple. As you sway through the temple, you weave light, and you incorporate the right side into the left side and afterwards merge them as One. You weave both halves of the temple into one another. As a result, the white light present on the side of Horus has now engulfed the whole temple as One Temple bathed in bright white light.

In the meantime, you are in the back of the temple behind the outer wall. You find yourself in front of a line that is not profoundly engraved when you investigate it. However, when you tune in to it, it splits the whole temple into two halves. As soon as you touch this line with your hand, golden essence emerges from it. Indeed, golden stardust swirls over you and enchants you. While you take a moment to absorb it, you notice Amun Ra standing behind you, to your left, and his wife Amunet standing behind you, to your right. That you are here for a reason is clear. This temple asks you to raise it from its foundation in duality. So you align yourself with the foundation plate, which is much vaster and wider than the temple complex itself. It amazes you to discover that the physical temple complex has withdrawn significantly in terms of energy and frequency, which is saddening to observe. Therefore, you lower your awareness to the level of the foundation plate and hold this temple in your hands. Amun Ra asks you to go beneath the foundation plate and keep the whole temple above your head. And then, from behind you, they both ignite your Golden Diamond Heart with its twelve petals. Thereupon, it spins, and the spinning becomes spherical. You turn into a golden sphere of light and become ethereal. In this capacity, you move through the centre of the temple via the foundation plate. You engulf the whole temple in a swirling movement. It all happens fiercely and powerfully.

Consequently, your golden essence devours and crushes the old structures because you are the thirteenth component of your golden Diamond Heart. You transmute this Temple of Light into One Temple Being uniting both parts. While this alchemical process is taking place, you see Horus and Sobek walking towards you in the distance. They know this is their initiation, to break the pattern of duality and come into Oneness with their divine wholeness. You can tell from the way they walk they care very much about what happens.

Once before you, their eyes close. They turn towards one another, their hearts connect. Their shared heart space is expanding, absorbing one another's energy. A bright white sphere envelops and alchemises both. The old patterns dissolves, allowing them to stand in their Divine Light.

They stand before you brighter than they ever before, for which they thank you. Now they move to the sides of the temple. They take this initiation process out of your hands by igniting the Kom Ombo three-dimensional temple with its higher and inner dimensional temples. They create One vast Temple of Light containing all dimensions simultaneously in its being. The dimensions are no longer separately perceptible. It becomes One Temple from the deepest layers of the Earth to the highest spheres, One column of light.

In essence, Kom Ombo concerns evolution, and this process includes both beautiful eras and dark periods of fall. In other words, on Earth, humankind has been locked into a fearful state of being we could never break out of. It is essential to realise that this fearful state of consciousness almost became the trademark of the Earth. For this reason, Kom Ombo symbolises that when we go through difficult periods now, we have a choice to rise again and choose whether to let go of the reptilian part of our brain based on survival, fear, defence, and fighting.

Moreover, Horus symbolises as Falcon God of the skies, our Star Consciousness. Indeed, we come from the sky, and we are Star Consciousness, for now in a human embodiment. So Kom Ombo teaches us to manifest our Star Consciousness again. This gives us a choice to break through the pattern of duality, dissolve the dimensions, enter into Oneness, and become masters of our own lives again. Then, we detach ourselves from the collective unconscious to be master creators of our existence.

Last, Amun Ra calls you back, and you find yourself once again at the back of the wall. You no longer notice any line here. Instead, the entire wall is now golden. They take you back into the temple, where the seat of unity is. Surprisingly, this seat has changed into gold. They invite you to sit on it and enter the small, majestic shrine filled with golden light. From your Golden Diamond Heart, a golden ray leaves for the Cosmos and the centre of the Earth. You connect it to the heart of the Earth and the Cosmos. Similarly, for Sobek and Horus, who joined their hearts, they also come together in your heart. Here your heart area transforms into a black gate through which you can travel. The vortex within it pulls you magnetically inwards, and so you fly outwards through the temple across the Nile, speeding towards the heavens.

In only a moment, you arrive at a place with a golden disc. The Angels of Creation transfer it to you. You take it in your hands, and the disc feels smooth, of solid gold with no inscriptions, and about twenty centimetres. You descend with it and you pass through several dimensional Creational wombs, each of which consecrates this golden disc. When you are back in three-dimensional reality, this disc has gone through all the dimensional initiation processes and carries all the dimensions. It carries Oneness within.

Now, the core of the Earth calls you. It has reserved a place for this golden disc. As you descend further, you place it on that exact spot, and it locks itself in place. The disc clicks into the Earthly-Sun Disc, and the reflection of Kom Ombo Temple into the night sky is complete.

We acknowledge Kom Ombo Light Being, Horus, Sobek, Thoth Hermes Trismegistus, Amun Ra and Amunet and the Light Beings of the Venus Light Path.

Retrieval Amun Ra's Golden Earth-Sun Disc

You walk the path alongside the Nile bank. At the main gate of Kom Ombo, a Light Being, seemingly a gatekeeper and protector of the Kom Ombo sacred site, allows passage towards the Nile bank, but not the temple itself. So you walk on with Kom Ombo behind you. While you gaze at the Nile, the temple and its green reptilian energy permeate you through your back. At this instant, you stand quietly at a distance, and the primordial green reptilian energies mingle, yearning to imbue every corner of your body with their energy. Sobek's energy embodies you as he accompanies you through this rite of passage. Briefly, you turn around and gaze at the temple. An astonishing sight of all the Light Beings, Gods, and Goddesses bewilders you. Until now, they were observing you from a distance. You recognise Amun Ra's Light and Horus hovering in the surrounding air. Khonsu, Isis, so many are there.

Meanwhile, as the green energies embody you, their vibration increases and your body shivers. You can no longer control it. At first, your upper body trembles and shivers, and now the energy disperses forcefully in all directions to your hips and pelvic floor. A violent purging occurs, old emotions dissolve, and the freedom to embody your space, your inner temple overwhelms you. Truly, a desire to manifest yourself vibrates through your body. A *strong desire to be present* in life flows from your pores.

For this reason, the energy of Sobek wants to be present. You glance at the Nile waters and desire to be free and enjoy life, not to be used by humanity or to be worshipped as Sobek, or to be held back as yourself, a human being. The energy slowly descends into the bone marrow of your legs. As you stand here, you purge your sense of power, your sense of manifestation, your sense of claiming your life. Your life is yours and belongs to no one else.

You know who you are and who you are not.

You know what you can handle and what you cannot.

You represent life in its most complete form. And in this capacity, you represent love in its fullest form.

Allow the magic that all elements hold: the water, the earth, the fire, and the wind. The purity of the Earth is about worshipping life. And in life, beings are the real Creations, their powers, passions, and potentials.

Life is about living, being Life, and enjoying its freedom, enjoying the sunlight running through your veins, strengthening and nourishing you.

You sense the choice to be free and move in these waters, to remember the purity of life. When you glance at Kom Ombo, you understand time has stood still in these temples. Life does not take place in temple structures. Life resides in connecting with the Earth, her elements, and all the spirited beings associated with it.

You bid farewell to the idea of a structure needed to worship divinity. It does not belong to the Age of Aquarius. Life is not honouring or looking for something outside of us. It is about honouring our own divinity, our Divine Self.

All in all, the temple we worship lies within our hearts and deep within the heart of the Earth. And you experience such joy now that you have freed Sobek in these waters, now that you have also freed yourself. Life excites you, and the bliss of breathing again, moving your body, sensing Earth currents animate you. The wind caresses you. All the energy movements within Earth's body also run through you, and you intimately connect to her again. This awareness is within our hearts. It does not require a temple. We experience it in our hearts.

You now face up into the sky and see the Sun. Amun Ra sheds his warm light on you. Horus is near him, and he cannot come closer to you as he perceives you are still letting go of the disconnection from life, being alienated from life's true meaning. As a sacred witness, Horus invites and urges you to worship your own pure body, that of the Earth, and the Sun. He teaches you to devote yourself to life. Every day connecting and devoting yourself to life encompasses dedicating yourself to those near you and your heart. You must undergo this transformation. Horus has already mastered this wisdom, and he awaits you. Your Temple of Light resides in your heart. He stays very close to the Sun. From this perspective, he is your teacher, for we all have teachers in our lives who accompany us at certain times.

Horus now slowly approaches. Around you, he creates a vortex of light with a clockwise torsion resembling a healing chamber to restore yourself. Together you descend into this vortex. He has now landed and is standing before you, leaning his forehead against yours. You touch one another, and your combined foreheads create a ray of light shooting upwards toward Amun Ra. He says, "You have mastered being devotional to life and life alone, and its purest expression." He breathes with you at the same pace, and you become One. His gentleness, calm, and patience soothe you. You relax, and he moves through your body. You are One with him. Amun Ra consecrates this sacred union by weaving his golden light downwards around both of you.

You continue to attune your heart to Horus. As you are One, your bodies have fused. Horus raises his head. And so do you. He says, "Invite the fire element of Amun Ra and reawaken your Desire for Life. Say yes to life." Your heart area, your entire chest, your heart chakra from within expands tremendously. A great golden disc comes into existence within your heart. Horus continues to stare upwards as if initiating you along with Amun Ra. Your body transforms into golden light. Horus says, "You are sovereign. You descend from the golden light and have acknowledged and accepted your origin. This initiation will allow you to focus and orient yourself to the Earth. From now on, it is only about the Earth, her heart. All the old stories about the Gods and deities, once healed, we will move on. The most important thing is Life."

He leaves your body again, takes your hand, and guides you to the deeper waters. He says, "Dive in, please." To accompany you, Horus morphs into white light. Likewise, as you plunge into the deep waters, you morph into a water being with a fishtail, seemingly a siren. Something is calling you. In your mind's eye, you see a golden disc lying at the bottom of the Nile River, on the other side of the bank. You cross the river, swim, and take the golden disc in your hands. You try to lift it, but it is heavy and overgrown by time. It must have been here for a very long while. You rub your hands over it and see an inscription. It looks like the footprint of a green reptile, and you hear the words, "Once it was acknowledged that: also, we belonged to the Golden Light."

You know you must bring this to the surface. This disc needs to leave these deep waters to emerge once more and find acknowledgement. So you lift the disc out of the water and carry it to the other side. All the Light Beings from Kom Ombo Temple walk in this direction. The Light of Amun Ra shines on the disc and lasers right into its core. A small golden seed emerges, and while the light continues to shine, it opens. Beautiful green luminescent light radiates from the seed. Softness and tenderness, nurturing and loving energy emanate from the seed. The green energy fills the disc, and it becomes emerald green. The disc teaches about love, nurturing for *All That Is* – the devotion to *All That Is*, for every life. Everything matters. The connection with love wants to be restored. Love is everywhere, in you, me, all around us. Love is within and without, above and below. Life is not about making deviations from accessing our inner divinity in worshipping an entity outside ourselves through temples and their stories. As Above, So Below. As Within, So Without. The One Emerald seed encompasses all this.

With this in mind, you hear the Kom Ombo Light Being calling for the disc. The deities also urge you to bring it inside the temple. So, you leave the waters and move quietly toward the temple. Immediately, the gatekeeper invites you to enter. As you approach the temple with the disc, the construction shudders. Indeed, it knows it is coming. Sobek is about love for *All That Is*, as a dear reptile loving the Sun, the Earth, the water, everything about life. Again, as you enter the temple, you go straight to the back and know you need to place the disc on the central line inside the temple. As you place the disc on the floor, it immediately descends into all the layers within the foundation and beyond, creating a string of emerald-green light. The emerald string forms a circle connecting the right side of the Nile, with the left side bringing them into Oneness, for there is no separation. It is only about life, the human heart, the animal heart, the Sacred Heart, the divine spark.

Kom Ombo celebrates life. This celebration needs to be repeated, the loving devotional side of life, the Divine Heart, and love for life. Nothing more, nothing less. We live under Amun Ra's light. We love his light and love everything that warms to and feeds on this light.

You leave the Temple of Kom Ombo, and as you walk out, you see behind you all the deities waving, thanking you for bringing the disc home. It belongs here, and it will seal the memory of Oneness.

Thank you.

Consecration Amun Ra's Golden Earth-Sun Disc

The Golden Earth-Sun Disc that lay on the Nile's foundation rose to the surface of the Nile's bottom and the Light Being of Kom Ombo recovered it. The temple requested the Earth-Sun Disc to be embedded onto the back of the temple. Kom Ombo Light Being asks you to work with the disc one last time. You tune back into this disc, and it displays a sacred engraved pattern looking like a cross, with a central point. From that central point, you look outward in four directions in distinct steps. It represents a two-dimensional pattern of a step pyramid.

Illustration: Kom Ombo. The Seal.

You descend into the central part, and soon you find yourself in the Holy of Holies. There you see a black cross with the pattern of a swastika. You understand it represents spiral arms that translate the movement of galaxies and universes that revolve around the Sun. This ancient symbol represents the Sun, which nourishes with its light the many stars, planets, and moons in a universe through its spiral arms. The Cosmic Womb keeps within the bounds of this universe One body, and nurtures it with white-golden rays. For this reason, the disc has a golden essence. It morphs into emerald because it becomes a cosmic law governing the Cosmos.

A pearl of wisdom reveals itself to you. In the smallest things lie the most beautiful secrets. And in this case, the rotating motion nourishes *All That Is* with white-golden light. The Sun carries nurturing and loving qualities that provide support, so *All That Is* expands and fulfils the desire to embody higher levels of consciousness to achieve wholeness.

When all motion becomes harmonically orchestrated, a centralisation will occur. All galaxies and universes will converge on the Central Axis of the Cosmos. All will collapse, fuse, and dissolve, and the divine spark will move again as One powerful Light Being.

The divine spark will have enjoyed life and its experiences, like a child who comes back from school to narrate what he experienced, learned, felt, sharing all the beautiful and challenging moments and knowing how to cherish all of them in his great heart.

Activation Amun Ra's Golden Sun Disc

Again, you stand in front of Kom Ombo. The gatekeeper now immediately allows you to pass to the inner temple. You ignite the emerald seal in your heart and walk straight to the temple's back. There the seal is located and well embedded in the ground and foundation. Its pulse vibrates through the temple, and the luminous emerald crystal beats like a heart. If you place your hands on the seal, you can feel the rhythm, the beating Heart of the Earth, of the Cosmos, of *harmonic resonance* connecting us, all right in the middle of that line that once divided the temple.

You hear sonic movements reverberating from the disc radiating out into the Cosmos. This disc profoundly connects to Earth's core. You let the sonic motion act upon you. You tune in to and observe what will happen. The ray of light emanating from the disc swallows you up and incorporates you into its rotation. While it absorbs you, you find yourself at the core of this ray, rotating around your axis. Your upper body is still discordant with your lower body. You rotate at high speed until your body as One undergoes the harmonic rotation.

You now find yourself in the centre, within stillness. The vibration of the ray of light around you irradiates your entire form. In this healing chamber, you undergo the vibration and let your body move with the sea waves. You surrender to this entirely because you know this is a sacred initiation meant only for you. The vibration plays you as an instrument, straightening and stretching your back further and further up into the Cosmos. You reposition towards the Aquarius era, aligning yourself and the Earth with the cosmic heartbeat, which sets the tone for *harmonic resonance and* is most important. This initiation assigns you an important and unique role in this new age.

Your hands and heart radiate green, luminescent light. You hear a sonic sound already familiar to you. It reminds you of a beautiful Light Being you once met with the same luminescent green heart. This pulsating green light reflects *harmonic resonance* and the pulsation of the Cosmic heartbeat. You now radiate the Cosmic heartbeat. From your being, heart, and essence, you are now also emitting the Cosmic pulse. You have aligned with the *harmonic resonance*. You identified with it, and now you exude it. Indeed, you are fulfilled and understand this initiation is coming to an end.

You walk out of the Kom Ombo Temple. As you view backwards, it seems the entire old structure reflecting duality and pain is crumbling. What takes its place is a magnificent, beautiful white temple of light radiating Divine Greatness. All the Light Beings present seem pleased. You acknowledge you have fulfilled your role as Kom Ombo upgraded into the light. The physical structure, which still exists, will allow human beings who visit this temple to undergo a similar process based on their consciousness level.

We thank Horus, Sobek, Isis, Sothis, Amun Ra, the Light Beings of the Venus Light Path, and all other Light Beings present.

II.5 Temple of the Cosmic Ascension Staircase, Edfu

Illustration: Edfu, Temple of Horus.

Pillar of Light

Edfu Temple, in all its grandeur, stands before you. At the same time, it seems you vibrate within a higher octave of this temple. You perceive a higher dimensional presence, and the structure itself appears to float through the air.

As soon as you enter the temple grounds, you perceive a flower is being drawn, petal after petal, in a looping fashion. A clockwise spiral motion sets itself in action, created from the outline, inward, where usually the pistils are located. This pattern is drawn to surround your body. Soon, you will represent its centre. To your astonishment, a birthing chamber emerges.

If you step into this birthing chamber, you will become its heart. So, you decide to enter it and step on some petals to reach the centre. The spirals are thirteen steps going downwards. You now arrive in the central chamber. Here you nestle into the soft petals and hear the sound of a vault closing. The petals enfold you, moving upwards, sealing this flower, sheltering you. Darkness now surrounds you.

Without delay, the flower spins more and more rapidly in a clockwise motion. Horus, is strongly present. Immediately, his energy approaches the birthing chamber. You know he is here. He comes to witness. He sits before you at the entrance to the temple. In your heart, you know he creates sacred space for you to absorb this initiation fully.

Moreover, he strengthens the energy field for you. Thus, he assists you. Now, you can stay in close contact with your heart and consolidate your energy body. You enjoy just being within your heart.

Meanwhile, much moves in your sternum and your spine. Your heart deepens, your ventricles expand to take up more dimensional space. They have also enlarged your spine. It seems as if your spine has deepened itself within your body. You now have a rugged spine in comparison with the rest of the body. It further enlarges and is growing higher and higher, piercing the flower, and going beyond and following the structure of Edfu in all higher dimensions. Horus smiles. He enjoys you. Even more, you grow infinitely higher and higher until you have arrived at Amun Ra. In fact, your spine reaches Amun Ra's bright light, and you immerse yourself within it, allowing your spine to touch his light gently.

You taste freedom and expansiveness in doing so, and as you dive into this cosmic light, you completely lose yourself. From the totality of who you are, you surrender to become One with Amun Ra's light. His light spins and rotates clockwise until you sense this spinning, rotating motion in your spine, which brings his light down into your skeletal structure. Amun Ra's light also reaches your head, brain, cheekbones, forehead, and jaws. Your collarbone, throat, shoulder blades, and shoulders all transmute into dazzling light. The light travels to your hipbones, and the clockwise movement continues until it reaches your legs and the bones of your legs, the whole of your skeletal structure, until deep into the bone marrow. Then, the light descends to your knees, your lower legs, and it slowly approaches your feet, and once it reaches your heels, it pierces and anchors into the three-dimensional Temple of Edfu. And onward to the core of the Earth.

You can effortlessly move up and down along this axis and within your bone marrow. Your spine is so substantial that it has become a foundational aspect of Edfu Temple. You represent the rock upon which to build, nourishing the entire structure with Amun Ra's light.

Horus stands up and approaches you. He lays his right hand on your shoulder and says, "Well done, my dear. However, it is not yet complete. The two feathers of Amun Ra also belong to you, for we are all One. You also have that birth right. For this initiation, you will first need to bring your attention to your heart."

So, you tune into your heart, and it comes across as hardened, as if a layer of concrete is covering it. Horus says, "I know. It is also on the level of your throat, your larynx." With his left hand, he approaches you and says, "Lay it here on my hand. I will take it from you. Give these crystallisations to me." His left-hand approaches, emitting bright light. He touches your heart area. Almost immediately, your heart ejects the crystallisation onto his hand. In return, golden essence energies imbue your heart area, with a thousand lights aflutter, looking like thousands of golden butterflies. Again, you witness yourself morphing from a butterfly into a large golden caterpillar, and then into a tiny caterpillar. At this instant, as you dissolve, you travel backwards in time. In fact, you are developing, evolving, and the only thing remaining is a bright white *Pillar of Light*.

Horus, with his falcon eyes, gazes into this *Pillar of Light*. His falcon eye discerns *One Golden divine spark*. He extends his hand, and your *One Golden divine spark* places itself upon his hand. Horus blows with an out-breath onto it, and out of it emerges a beautiful Cosmic Light Being whose heart aligns with the Sun, Amun Ra.

As can be seen, your Cosmic Light Being is angelic at the same time. It spreads its wings wide, raising you infinitely in the higher octaves of

Edfu Temple. You are entering the vast Cosmos, and here many Light Beings welcome and bless you now that you have come into your Oneness with your Divine Essence.

Behold, this *Pillar of Light* is an ascension staircase and a sacred initiation. Horus says, "They dismembered my father Osiris to be remembered again. You have undergone the same process in the Light of Amun Ra. We must leave the old behind and embrace a novel way of life that holds Light, Hope, and Oneness."

Once you have lifted yourself out of duality – the three-dimensional cage of fear, anxiety, and uncertainty – the Earth is your playground. You have set yourself free, sky-high, towering yourself with Amun Ra's light, leaving behind all that burdens your heart. What remains is to discover who you are and what your soul mission is in this life. As you play in the Light of Amun Ra, you manifest your True Self. Having raised your vibration this high enables you to overview the energies ruling the Earth.

Horus anoints your forehead and welcomes you as a *Cosmic Light Being emanating Amun Ra's light.*

You inquire to understand more about the two feathers. Horus laughs and says, "How do you think you fly so high? The depiction of the feathers as a headdress speaks only of those who possess the highest frequencies on Earth. The frequencies of hope and abundance flooding the Earth, your playground. We raised the vibration so high that we transmute the Earth into a paradise, the resonance of the Garden of Eden." The message that Yeshua brought us is similar. When we illuminate our hearts, we discharge heavy emotions and enlighten ourselves. We gift this to the Earth and set her free. Horus sets the Earth free. You set the Earth free in your essence of a Sacred Being of Light.

Temple of Cosmic Reflection

A place in the innermost part of the Earth reflects the Edfu Temple. To find this place, having the portal of the Edfu Temple at your back, you walk at least two hundred metres in front of you. There abides an etheric hatch on Earth's surface. When you align your heart with the hatch and transmit the requested star codes, star glyphs resonant with the hatch, open it.

You now freefall at least a thousand metres. Beware, it is dark in these deeper earth layers, but this landscape bathes in an enchanting glow of silvery moonlight. The pale light illuminates your path. In the distance, you discern a silver-coloured construction composed of liquid light. The platina substance appears heavy, high frequency. Carrying many light codes, it is shaped like two cones, one next to the other. A curved path leads to the portal of this temple complex, with several gates along the way. When you reach the first gate, you suddenly find yourself in front of a mirror of plasmic light rippling and distorting itself. When you reach out to touch it, your entire hand slides into it and you experience the back of something like a wall you cannot pass through. As your hand explores this wall, you come across several studs, all placed in a recumbent number 3, in the shape of the Source Field. You understand you could dive in with your entire body. This is also a direct entrance to the Star Council of Eight, and every stud offers a communications channel.

Illustration: Edfu. The Temple of Cosmic Reflection.

This is not, though, the reason you are here. The plasmic light merges with your physical system, aligning it with the double-cone temple complex. You now resonate more faithfully with both cones. From within yourself, you undergo a magnetic attraction to the structure. As your inner vision becomes clearer, it allows you to perceive the cones in much more detail. So, you follow the path to the second gate, a pink cone shape, and place yourself within it as it rotates. As a result, you glide to its centre, which looks like a spinning disc containing a central point around which the pink matter slides up and down in rings, like clay on a potter's wheel. You are now being shaped and rebuilt through this second gate creating a pink, angelic essence. The pink essence runs up and down and right through your heart space, creating a surrounding beehive. Surprisingly, golden nectar springs from your heart, trickling out, further crystallising the Golden Diamond Heart into your three-dimensional etheric structure. This renders the Golden Diamond Heart uniquely real, tangible, concrete. You abide within this energy for a while, allowing it to penetrate you fully. The golden nectar represents the infinite abundance of golden light you bring forth at all times. The essence is pure and high frequency because the hive structure provides the optimum sacred geometric storage in the three-dimensional world.

The golden nectar and beehive both represent you as an abundant Creator of your own golden essence. The hive integrates well into your heart and balances you on deeper levels. No matter what happens in your life, you will maintain your balance. Your heart has become your centre of gravity. The door slides open, and you work your way to the third gate. Before you appear, a blue-essence, liquid pool of light greets you at knee height. When you step into it, it ignites within a meridian system of the Blue Sun, which transports Blue Sun energy. The Blue Sun in the Cosmos is the convergence point, a hotspot where all high frequencies converge. It is here where Creation takes place at ultrahigh-frequency levels. This structure proceeds to develop into your body and pierces through your Golden Diamond Heart of infinite golden light, penetrating your crown. You become much more vast than your present self, expanding omnidirectionally, all around yourself, forming an oval structure of intricate Blue Sun strands. This oval is itself a satellite antenna system hotspot transmitting its high-frequency energies to the Earth. You will transmit high-frequency codes when you are in sacred places, with people, or plan to work within Inner Earth realms. By this, you will dissolve imbalances for the Earth.

Without delay, you make your way to the fourth gate, having already passed the main bend in the path that leads to the double-cone complex. It is a huge magenta-coloured circle. You position yourself as the Vitruvian Man within the circle. You take the circumference into your hands, and as a gymnast applying powder to your hands, you hold on to it firmly. The ring does not move. You observe in the distance the double-cone temple complex radiating red light onto you from the summits, etching your divine masculine and divine feminine sides, literally drawing a vertical red line into your right and left sides. The divided energies of your divine masculine and divine feminine sides transform into a triumvirate within this magenta circle. The separation of the divine masculine and divine feminine sides dissolves. All that remains is your heart. Everything related to the divine feminine or the masculine is magnetically pulled away through these two lines. You become androgenic. The double-cone complex pulls the separated energies of your divine masculine and feminine energies out of your heart, out of every bodily cell, like a magnet. You also feel the remaining energies being pulled out of the grey matter of your brain.

The magenta essence slowly and surely takes up all the space in your central pillar within the triumvirate. This is your essential heart energy, your heart presence. Simultaneously, preparation takes place where all the Bodhisattva peonies have previously grown. Magenta and golden threads meticulously spiral inwards towards the energy points where the peonies have blossomed. You observe this on your crown, forehead, temples, throat, heart, navel, and tailbone, as well as the base chakra, the knees, the insteps of the feet, and the lower back. All these systems initiate a spinning motion, and through this, they ignite the Boddhisatva essence within you. The ring you are in dissolves, and this gate opens and takes you to the fifth gate.

Here you calibrate yourself, turning alternately right to left, downwards and upwards. Turning in this way spherically, you feel an expansion from within taking place, opening your heart gate even more as the place to allow the full essence of what you are about to receive.

You now move to the sixth gate. Here, you sit in a thickly textured, pitch-black pool of ethereal water. Liquid when you run your hand through it, the water leaves no black marks on your skin. You immerse yourself, your body absorbing it all. The puddle now empty, black essence morphs around you as if you were wearing a tight-fitting black suit. You disappear into it, now finding yourself within it. The only thing animating the suit is your light essence. You no longer sense your etheric body. You have shifted into another much higher frequency texture, enabling you to match the frequency in this double-cone complex. This preparation phase takes quite a long time. Yet, it is supremely diverse and exciting. With so much preparation, it makes you more curious about what you will find inside.

Proceeding now to the last, seventh gate, you find here the only thing asked of you is whether you choose to enter. You tune in to the double-cone complex to understand why you would want to say yes. It tells you it will ignite within you a black, spiral staircase. The black essence allows you to become transparent, to glide effortlessly through dimensions without noticing they are dimensional. You may glide through on another level, passing through them while abiding as another level of consciousness. Your essence can be much more refined and finely tuned than the frequency on any dimensional level. This seems quite grand, and you clearly say yes.

The gate opens, and many Light Beings welcome you. They wear black robes symbolising the black essence of Orion's thirteenth black-pointed star, which transmutes All That Is. The cone shape radiates the energies of complete transmutation. You walk on until you stand in front of the gate. The door has the same geometric pattern as a turtle's shell, but the lines are golden. You touch it, and the door slides open.

Before you, you behold Horus. He carries the same golden disc as Amun Ra. He has become Horus Ra. Strangely, he mirrors himself. You now behold a double Horus Ra. Here the double cones symbolise cosmic mirroring and the Thoth Hermes Trismegistus Hermetic Principle: As Above, So Below. As Within, So Without. Excited, you enter this Temple of Reflection and perceive that it also mirrors you. Behind you, exist two copies of yourself. You remain, though, within the One essence they had prepared for you when within the circle, in the Vitruvian Man position.

Illustration: Horus.

Meanwhile, a golden line of magenta light awaits you. You follow this light. It guides you up the stairs. You ascend the staircase, where it narrows, and as you approach the end of the staircase, to your greatest surprise you see above you a bath of magenta light surrounded by richly golden decorated walls lit by candlelight. The water in this pool ripples gently. Horus Ra stands behind you. He says,"Step in, please. You will be cared for in an exquisite and deferential manner." You remove your black robe. In your transparent, liquid body, you step into this magenta bath. You immerse yourself because it refreshes you and exudes a sweet fragrance. While you are immersed, you receive images of the Garden of Eden and all its lush and juicy fruits. This is the bathing pool bringing you into bounteous contact with abundance. The two Horus Ras take a seat in the magenta chairs next to the tub. With their heart essences, they project two horizontal golden rings beneath you. When these golden rings fuse, creating a vesica piscis, it hoicks you through. Like a growing mango blossom, you hang from one of the many trees in that lush grove. As you unfold, you sense an infinite source of abundance within yourself, flowing forth as if you were an endless river of light and fragrant energy. You feel golden threads of light wanting to emerge from your blooming flower, just like pistils.

You ask yourself why all this is happening. The Creator Beings of this Garden answer you, whispering the greatest secrets lying within the smallest things. "Just go with it, and trust us," they murmur mellifluously. A bit impatient, you decide to surrender, to trust, to allow the Sun's rays to glide along your pistils to your blossom's Central Axis, to allow them to nourish you, their warm golden light, tenderly intimate, sunlight gliding in, tingling. delightful, caring, nurturing, sunlight unfolding the seed, giving love, recognition, respect, reflecting the birth right to exist, the honour to live, the happiness of existing. Sunlight treats you with as much respect and equality as any other fruit blossom. Indeed, you are as important as any other fruit blossom in this orchard, this Garden of Eden. Henceforth, you feel true and genuinely special and unique. Every day, you wait to be touched by, to luxuriate within this golden sunlight. You know you will feel deeply moved. After all, that is the certainty of the abundance awaiting you, which you know you will receive: golden rays attuning you to this natural flow of evolution, this life, this state of being.

The night has now fallen. You remain here within this tree, now bathed in silvery rays of moonlight, silvery blankets of pale light cooling, illumining you with forest echoes. How gently diffused moonlight penetrates the essence of your essence, igniting, unfolding! She stimulates you to open, silently, softly encouraging you to absorb more and more of her sweet, muted nocturnal glow. Day after day, night after night passes. You become fully infused with all the glow you can carry within. Completing yourself, you find wholeness: your inner soul mirroring that of the Cosmos.

Horus Ra pulls you out of the Garden of Eden, back into the magenta bath. You look at him, and he looks at you, saying, "This abundance, being flooded as a natural state of being, waits you. You will reflect Source and its abundance. There will be nothing between you, truly nothing. There will be no more dimensions. You will be transparent. This thirteenth spiral staircase transmutes you in an instant, and you find yourself above, in Source. Although you are here, you are also up there. Likewise, you radiate absolutely the same thing: Source and its abundance. Even if you take that into your consciousness on Earth within three-dimensional reality, you will emanate this consciousness."

This consciousness will slowly, surely expand, and you will create a grid of this consciousness around you. Indeed, you will transmute yourself and everything standing between you and Source. Yes, you have understood. Now you can leave the bath. No longer do you need the black robe. By undergoing this completed initiation, you are transmuted. As you walk down, Horus Ra walks behind you. Meanwhile, he merges into One because you have understood, and the process is complete. To teach you, he has shown you his reflection. You leave through the gate. In a loving way, he kisses you goodbye. You can stay here for a while to enjoy the moonlight.

Axis Mundi Branches, Secret Gateways

Before you appear the lavishly vegetated avenue leading to the platina double cone structure of Edfu. You walk this avenue. It leads you past this structure. The area's energy is platina in nature. You receive the impression you are walking against a current. Even so, the scenery is charming. Though it is quite an undertaking to move forward, you eventually arrive at a beautiful lake, lotuses abundant around the edge of the waters. Moonlight glistens, shimmering across the water's surface, enchanting the landscape. Your attention has led you to a body of water seeming to comprise various layers, each of a unique texture, yet forming one ethereally fluid body. Within this fluid body the various currents of the various layers swirl, with the border areas between layers drawing your attention, being entrances to other worlds, gateways to otherworldly existences . . . far . . . far . . . away . . .

They speed you up into the entire Cosmos as you move through the boundaries of these water structures.

These layers are stacked one atop the other, unevenly. An atmosphere of disharmony prevails within this harmonious body of water. As can be seen, you are here to understand more about this stacking of dimensions, about this structuring of structures of the Axis Mundi in the Cosmic Womb. Namely, this body of water will explain to you more about how the dimensions connect, about how gateways between different dimensions leading to other worlds, open, about how they are not wormholes per se, for wormholes are tunnels of a different speed of light between dimensions. They run through layers within particular areas in the Cosmos.

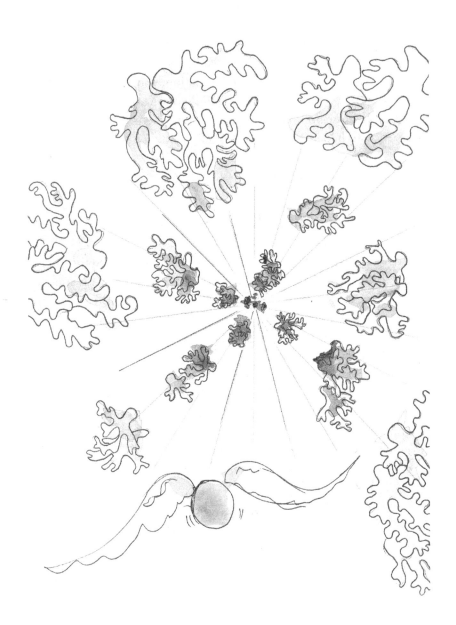

Illustration by N. Van Der Auwera. A sacred Journey into Creation. The Secret Gateways.

Instead, here the boundaries create portals more like windows transcending time and space. Walking through such a window, you find yourself somewhere else, within an immense new structure opening to a vast cosmic view.

Imagine yourself in these layers, moving between them. You take in an overview of All That Is. You oversee Creation just as from a mountaintop, one overlooks an entire valley. The Moon is present, acknowledging these spoken words. In this cosmic overview, you also see tracks you can follow. They spiral inward, bringing you into a completely different quarter of the multiverse. With small steps, you cross vast distances. These boundaries offer a broader scope than wormholes. They oversee a larger space not necessarily connected by a coral branch. They allow you to hop across various coral branches.

Thoth asks you to resonate with and attune your heart to the Moon. Khonsu, Isis, and Nephthys[34] are also present. Even the more ancient Gods from pre-Egypt are visible. Instantly, the water reflects the Moon, and it invites you to bathe multiply its still, singular, perfect lunar reflection. The essence of the entire body of water impregnates itself within you, allowing you to integrate the complexity of the Axis Mundi, its trunk, and branches, into your structure. In doing so, you integrate the means to travel them. Now on your back, floating within the waters – silence reigns – lapping waters allowing you to swirl softly around and around, swirling, eddying all energies within these waters to meld, mingle, fuse, unite within your form. Silvery-white strings of light recreate and replicate within your body the white boundaries you just beheld within watery layers. These layers represent the spaces between the coral branches. They reproduce within your body. Thoth adds that the more you embody the complexity of the whole process, integrating the complexity of the below, the more you obtain Cosmic Ascension. Indeed, by fully mirroring your environment, you dissolve who you are and become only *a mirror, a void, a teacher, a Self-Realised Light Being.*

---

34 Nephtys was a daughter of Nut and Geb, and sister of Isis and God Osiris. She was the sister-wife of Set. She was associated with childbirth, death, mourning, celebration, the night, and the Unseen. She was a Temple Priestess.

In conclusion, you now have a choice. Thoth asks you if you want to be prepared for Cosmic Ascension. You can choose your answer. I have already formulated mine.

You come to understand these waters as reflecting only something you need to see. You have embodied this truth. You now perceive water nymphs and all other water creatures such as the white creature with the huge, soft eyes who led your boat into Philae. You know you can come back whenever you wish. You have eternal access to this sanctuary. They kiss you goodbye, embracing you warmly.

Two Feathers of Amun Ra

Illustration:
The Two Feathers of Amun Ra.

In the foreground of the Temple of Edfu, the ethereal blueprint of the two feathers of Amun Ra is visible, tangible. There will be an initiation for you here. Or you may perform the initiation. It is yet unclear. At this moment, you wear the etheric right feather atop your head. The left feather is not yet active in the temple's blueprint. Therefore, not with you. In front of you opens a braided path of bright white light. It leads you to the entrance. You walk this luminous path, and when almost at the entrance, the path slopes to the left, makes a turn, follows the contours of the original blueprint of Edfu. You continue following this white-braided path of light. For a reason unknown to you, it mysteriously brings you back to the entrance.

The physical Temple of Edfu reverberates with the blueprint of Amun Ra's two feathers. The two feathers in your blueprint also resonate with Edfu's two-feather blueprint. In an intuitive and almost automatic manner, your two feathers raise themselves. On the right-hand side, a feather is present, but the left-hand side shows a void. By circumambulating the temple, you have prepared the sacred initiation, for the two feathers have risen along with the entire Temple of Edfu.

Now you enter the temple, and as soon as you walk through the gate, a deafening silence takes your breath away. You hear each footstep echo in infinite vacuity – and gloomily, darkly, against the walls. You want to remain close to your heart, to direct your consciousness inwards. Gingerly, you step towards the Holy of Holies, the shrine of Horus, suddenly encircled with numerous Light Beings – seeming priests and priestesses who long, long, ago served in this sacred space. With this in mind, they await you, knowing from within the essence of knowledge you are here to consecrate the two feathers. You walk to the head of Horus and lay your forehead on his. Take his head in your hands, you kiss him. Priests and priestesses descend to the shrine, taking it in their hands, lifting it, walking out. You follow falling in behind them in this ceremonial procession. Together, you proceed slowly up to the roof.

The shrine's head aligns with the Moon on the left. The Sun burns fiercely in the sky on the right side. Due to the alignment, moon and sun essences infuse themselves into its body. As can be seen, it is almost like a tabernacle. The two essences meld together in the centre of this object and fuse. White and blue light swirl around one another in magical patterns. You witness. The power of this fusion stuns you, reminding you of the nebulae formation. You stretch out your hands. You reach into the tabernacle. You scoop the swirling essence into your hands.

Here you are. The sphere of light makes your entire body shudder. With your heart, you turn to the Sun, the Moon. As soon as this essence dissolves through osmosis in your heart space – something magical . . . Surprisingly, you experience yourself tree of many branches, sprouting from your heart, your arms, your neck, your head, growing higher and higher. You have known Horus is behind you, witnessing. Your right side is rising to infinite sky. As tree, your branches tower so high they soak themselves in sunlight. Yet your left side holds emptiness. Horus comes. You sense him from behind. He lays his hand on your left shoulder. He asks you to turn around. His appearance changing from falcon's head to human head. You see before a man with golden brown skin, muscular, slim. Beholding you, his eyes are olive green and radiate warmth and strength. He asks you to lay your hand on his heart. You comply. He places his hand over yours. Gazes at the Sun so far away, almost unattainable. He says, he feels trapped within this three-dimensional reality.

The left side represents the balance of how he walks in life. Horus acknowledges the need to manifest himself as strong and masculine. This need arises because in his lifetime he could not yield fully into his vulnerability and engage with his heart. To his regret, he has not been able to unite his divine masculine and divine feminine essences. They represent the void, as if vulnerability would mean being weak, being a prey. The time in which he lived, he had to stand in his power and manifest strength. Horus would prefer to come home to his heart instead of losing so much energy in manifestation, power, and so-called strength. He wishes to balance as one who listens with open heart, connecting, receiving, welcoming, enjoying, celebrating, being together. As he mutters these words, his heart blossoms, expressing love. Horus wants his inner child to become more present in this life. Lovingly, he embraces his inner child with all his uncertainties, worries, questions, doubts, and bewilderment. Inviting his magical child allows him to connect with the mystical side of life, with nature, with Earth, with Unseen parts of the Earth, to be complete, in Oneness. Horus shares that it is time to let go of the struggle, the power. He wants to fall back, to repose within who he truly is, to connect with Earth and Cosmos, in full consciousness. He lets go of the goals he has set for his life's mission, for his ways of living have not yielded the total experience of life. Acting in a lesser capacity, Horus knows he would never experience the whole coronation into the two feathers of Amun Ra.

When these words resound in the endless sky, to his left and to yours, the outline of the left feather materialises in yellow liquid light, birthing itself into existence. Surely, it is not just a headdress. In fact, Horus becomes and morphs into the outline of the two feathers. Embodying these two feathers increases his vulnerability and sensibility to life as he senses the wind passing through them, taking his breath away. As an illustration of this, the strut of the two feathers fills with sunlight. The feathers themselves combine moon and sun essences. They complete the process of Creation. As you stand before him, he asks you to come closer, place your back against his chest while he holds you. Horus says, "Let me initiate you now." Hence, he takes your hands in his. He raises them. He turns to Sun and to Moon. He prays to them, "Transmit your codes into essence. Now, as liquid light, all light codes slide inside you. Your body reacts with chills, inner tingling, calling your two feathers into being. They emerge at your feet, move to your pelvic floor, and rise along your spine. Within the circumference, the feathers expand. It seems as if a breeze blows through you. You behold your ethereal tissue, undulant. The most sensitive energy fluctuations become apparent. You realise you must accommodate to them, accept them.

You both leave behind the blueprint of what you have ignited in the Tabernacle. It shows itself as a miniature of the two feathers. The priests and priestesses lift the sanctuary and bring it back into Edfu's temple. When you tune in to this temple from outside, you become aware of an improved balance, energetic presence on the left side. Namely, the void has disappeared. A balance between divine feminine and divine masculine restores itself. They are merging, becoming One, as the blueprint's energy becomes One. Indeed, by combining strength and vulnerability, you connect to life from the heart. Edfu now radiates connection to live from your white heart sphere: the white-blue light from the heart, the alchemy of sun and moon essences. You decide to stay here for a while with Horus to incorporate everything given to you.

Incarnation of the Divine and the Human Overlay

Horus invites you to sit with him. He has become older. He shares with you the memories he holds of his mother, Isis. As a woman, she had beautiful brown skin, black tresses. She was not too tall. Her body was slim. The well-being of the community empowered her. She gave her heart to all the priests, priestesses, and children. When Horus talks of her, you sense she was more present in life from the same divine masculine energy, than in the void, the divine feminine side. Even though her heart was great, all-encompassing, this masculine side was powered by always being present and alert. Otherwise, she would experience powerlessness. For there was a need to be present, to be powered by external circumstances, people, rather than from within, from heart, from connections with herself and the Earth. The same imbalance translates itself into Isis, mother of Horus. In like manner, it caused within her solitude, and a lack of connection even with the Earth. He explains that even when one of the greatest Goddesses incarnates in tense eras, the overlay of the human aspect can at times be more present than the soul energy. The human overlay can dim the soul's essence.

Equally important, even when a Goddess or a God incarnates, we do the most magical things in bringing about change, caring, nurturing, and balance. So that is what she tried to do. She focused on external balance instead of inner balance because time did not lend itself to inner pursuits. Horus tells you he had a deeply loving relationship with his mother. They were very much together during their lives. Solitude, though, overtook him. Even when he was in the womb, it comforted him that she knew he was there. She cared for him. She wanted to carry him. The outside, however, summoned her. Or rather, she underwent that pull, taking on that responsibility as a visionary, a Merchant Priestess, to be present. Because of that lack of connection and intimacy, she did not allow herself to be true to herself and feel. Horus withdrew after a while, rolling up in the foetal position. He internalised and waited.

At a certain moment, she realised that his essence had withdrawn. She returned with her consciousness to Horus. By doing so, she confronted powerlessness and that she did not know how to find the inner-outer balance. When she connected, almost immediately in her system, insecurity stirred regarding the environment, the instability. By and large, it was difficult for Horus, for her, for everyone. Because he had withdrawn at least until the seventh month of pregnancy, he did not straighten his backbone against her body. He had not been entirely present and embodying his new-born body, which caused him to be inward for a while. He had developed that mechanism for himself. However, slowly, he grew out of that and addressed himself to the Sun, the Moon, to the cosmic elements. He pierced the human overlay to pierce the dimensional layer of human group consciousness. He then infused within himself his cosmic essence, his soul essence. He remembered who he truly was. Today he is grateful he also found that balance between his divine feminine and his masculine energies and brought them into Oneness. Having done so will enable him, as a teacher, to teach people not to be dimmed by the human overlay. As the cosmic day announces itself, it becomes more than ever crucial in Earth's history to merge into One our Human and Divine Essences.

Thank you.

II.6 Temple of the Unseen, Karnak

Illustration: Karnak.

Blue Sun Portal

You would like to absorb the energies of the whole site of Karnak. Equally, Karnak itself would benefit from integrating the energies of all the stones making up all the temples, statues, and obelisks.

At this very moment, Karnak Temple complex seems fragmented. All the energies need to be centralised into one main energy stream so that the temple complex gains strength. As soon as you speak these words, a ray of light collects the energies of all the relics from all the different areas within the Karnak Temple complex. This ray enters your body through the higher heart, within the space of your sternum. As soon as the energies flow through you, you notice Sekhmet's[35] presence. She has seen you, revealing herself to you within your inner eye. She calls

---

35 Sekhmet is the Lioness Goddess. She is a fierce warrior and was seen as the protector of the pharaohs and led them in battle. Even after their decease, Sekhmet continued to protect them and carry them to the hereafter. Sekhmet is a sun deity, also called the daughter of Ra. She wears the Sun Disc.

you to her. You remain with your attention withdrawn for a while. You want to pay attention to how the Karnak energies enter your system. The Blue Sun oval activates again from within, preparing you for your encounter with Sekhmet.

In this Blue Sun oval, you walk along the ram-headed Avenue of Sphinxes towards the temple of Sekhmet. During your walk, you absorb all energies entering your field. You continue centralising them at ever deeper levels whilst you absorb them within. You create one energy flow, one force field.

This place was once most powerful. Truly, it reflected a cosmic alignment. Today, because of many changes, the alignment no longer applies. So, as you walk, you restore the cosmic alignment of Karnak and tune in to the Karnak within yourself. Because As Within, So Without, you are also Karnak. Your heart tells you what to do – to trust yourself. Thus, you walk on. You approach the sycamore tree in front of Sekhmet's temple. Here, in front of the door, you balance yourself. You tune in to your Blue Sun presence instead of your three-dimensional self. For this transmission, you resonate with this energy. Meanwhile, the blue sun essence overlays the totality of who you are. You enter and walk through to her holy sanctum.

Sekhmet's sanctum fills with electric-blue rays. You witness. You cannot see her yet, although you behold her statue. Yet her sacred presence, though, is as vivid as if she were stalking you, staring at you, investigating you. Meanwhile, thoughts race through you that time has taught you: you are worthy of being Seen. And so, in this intense moment, you find your strength. You stabilise yourself again. Strong and lovable, you embody the *I Am that I Am*. Also, you are Sekhmet. She is your very self. By all means, you can remain calm. You continue to find the trust in your heart. Suddenly, a scorching breath heats your neck. Your body stiffens. As Sekhmet becomes less ethereal, more present, her energy radiates enormous power. Time is needed to adjust and attune to it. You turn and gaze into her eyes. Before your eyes, a being of utter beauty becomes embodied. Her eyes open wide, signifying how she welcomes you into her sanctuary. You smile. She takes your hands in hers and revolves around you as you lovingly greet one another.

"Let us centralise and consolidate the entire essence of Karnak here," she requests. "My sanctum represents the centre of Karnak's new created toroid." You acknowledge Sekhmet. She now magnetises your heart, pulling it towards her, creating a vacuum between both your hearts. Thereupon, a light blue conical Creational chamber appears. Within this Creational chamber, a pale-yellow DNA spiral staircase emerges and rotates in rhythm to harmonic resonance, following the Musica Universalis. She tells you that you are both creating with ease and grace. It requires no effort. By drowning in one another's gaze, you allow this process to occur. You allow life to unfold. For Creation can be effortless. Indeed, she smiles.

Meanwhile, in the corner of your mind's eye, you witness the energies of all parts of Karnak being magnetically drawn around the shrine, and a toroid form. Sekhmet continues to smile. You relax. Your hands are still in hers and you ground yourself in her presence as she radiates divine ease and grace upon you. You land and anchor in your own body, and this oval Blue Sun structure is taking you even deeper into your abyss. It morphs and burns away your physical structure and all the etheric structures that comprise your physical structure. It cleanses and purifies your entire body even more than the previous activation did. The oval shape is no longer a wired structure but an oval portal of liquid light. You can sense it undulating, shifting, and morphing around you. The bliss and delight this experience brings are enormous. Sekhmet enjoys your smile.

Meanwhile, the toroid around her shrine becomes denser, more complete, further merged. Sekhmet says the reason she is constructing this is because her statue is in its original ancient place. Therefore, it is a most powerful gateway. As time has progressed, centralising the energy of Karnak will be beneficial. All energies will therefore transmute more easily. As a result, the Creation of the toroid grid nearly comes to an end. The heart gate Creational chamber between the two of you also dissolves gradually. Sekhmet now allows more distance between the two of you, indicating this transmission ends.

From your heart, you express your gratitude, for she has helped you to deepen your blue sun energy and morph into a Blue Sun portal that holds great transmutational power. From her heart, Sekhmet also thanks you for assisting her. She has enjoyed teaching you how to create with ease and grace. By kissing you on your forehead, she bids you farewell and blows her energy back into the statue. Straightaway, you find yourself outside the temple on the bench under the sycamore tree, contemplating and enjoying the Sun and the fresh water.

Secret of Enduring Time. The Vibratory Match.

This time, you enter Sekhmet's shrine from behind the outer wall and pierce it with your etheric substance. Again, you find yourself in the presence of her statue. Now, with your hand, you glide over the material her statue comprises. You kneel and lay your hands on your feet. Suddenly, she pulls you in. Somehow, you find yourself in outer space. Here, you perceive a system of black wormholes piercing through the etheric fabric of the Cosmos. In one spot, numerous wormholes converge. You approach, but when you stand before it, the system of wormholes is tightly woven. You cannot get through. So, you explore the other side. It is the same. You begin to realise that this ensemble of wormholes holds the shape of a whale or mermaid's tail.

Although it seems closed off, you go in as if you were walking into the mouth of a whale, like Jonah. Here you are, wandering into a whale's body. It is dark. You kindle your inner light. It seems like walking in a humid cave. You smell a moist scent. Before you, a body of water. You take the first steps in, and the staircase dives even deeper. You follow the submerging staircase, immersing yourself in an imposing and mighty water world of mermaids. Swimming towards you, they summon you to swim forward, closer, then disappear into darkness. You follow, stroking rapidly, swimming towards a small tunnel, your wet form barely passing through.

Rising on the other side find yourself within a most powerful, deep-blue underwater world. The mermaids in these cosmic waters are enormous. You would fit into their bodies at least twelve times. The environment does not seem so warm and welcoming here. These beings are most purposeful: approaching you, showing what is important at that very moment. And because you are their guest, you follow and allow them to guide you. One mermaid descends rapidly into the deep cosmic ocean. As soon as you also follow and descend, your body must morph because otherwise, it cannot hold the frequencies. The more you descend, the higher the frequencies you encounter. For this reason, you shift to another capacity, in the form of your golden inner light. The mermaid, accustomed to these higher frequencies, retains her familiar form.

You still cannot sense where you are going. It is all dark and deep. But then, in the distance, lights atwinkle wink. You move towards her form. You swim alongside her, swaying within the caressing currents she creates, drawing you comfortably within her inner energy field. She smiles as you adapt so lithely, adroitly, flexibly. You find yourself nearing a huge, expansive golden light. Glowing, forms the shape of a Venus shell. You kneel at the altar, remembering how you knelt before Sekhmet statue, touching at her feet. You place your hands on the altar. It vibrates and trembles like an earthquake. "Please sit," the mermaid whispers. The altar is also a golden chair. "The shivering means, my dear, that it has prepared itself for you." You slide into this chair, huge and deep, all enveloping. Once you have settled within its plush, luminous topologies, the golden light envelops you as flickering flecks of candlelight. A multitude of golden Venus Light Beings appear around you as sacred witnesses. They connect with one another, forming supremely alluring group consciousness fields around you. They hum a deep cosmic hum, moving the candle flame rotate around its axis. You fall deeper into the blue light zone of the flame. The temperature is too high, so you close your eyes. You do not know if you will be able to cope. There is nothing you can do. Now you are here and must surrender. Surely, you can rely on yourself. Moreover, you know you are a complex being. Maybe this resonance is not the right one for this initiation. You trust, though, to shift into the capacity and resonance that enables you to deal with this. So, you morph, shape-shift, and find the right resonance and alignment to fit the energy being sent out. In other words, you move through the different essences within yourself. Finally, you have found it: a silvery restructuring occurs within and around you.

A layer flows out of your system. Different layers release themselves, layer upon layer, like nesting dolls. Your eyes open wide. Your breathing comes even, deep, rapid waves. You can do this. Cosmic sound floods. From within the candle flame, you rise in your yellow essence light robe. The Venus Light has initiated you into its Light Essence. The Light Beings of the Venus Light have given you the opportunity to explore, to understand if you want to work with the essence. This has happened because these are the frequencies ruling Inner Earth as well as all cosmic realms. These are the frequencies of water beings, and their presence is crucial in the coming era. These are the frequencies you also need to hold within yourself to go through certain phases, as you have seen. You have learned through this initiation in a graceful way to pass through various inner essences and tune in to what is required to match a required vibrational frequency. It is a gift bestowed upon you.

Sekhmet now stands beside you. She confides that it takes great strength, wisdom, love, and flexibility to stay steadfast through changes, difficult periods, and devastation. Most important, it is undoubtedly not about struggle. On the contrary, it is about finding the right vibrational match to surpass yourself and Creation, over and over again. Above all, the right vibrational match allows you to ignite an alchemical process, rebirth yourself, transmute all imbalances.

You thank Sekhmet for being here and witnessing. She thanks you for being her student. Truly, you answer her that the honour is all yours. You now both thank all beings of the Venus Light and all water beings. Together, you all rise to the surface. Once again, you kneel before her statue at her feet.

By Amun Ra: Initiation into the Unseen

Sunlight shimmers in the emerald waters of Karnak. The urge to enter the depths of the lake, to soak in its energy, its freshness, overwhelms you. Its emerald essence percolates through your body and your soul. First, you bathe your feet. Soon you cannot resist the temptation to move further and further into the waters. You descend more, down the bottom, to knee height. You bathe your upper body. Relaxed, you float. At the same time, your gaze drawn to the endless blue of the sky, you become expansive, free. White lightning strikes you and these waters. You understand this lake is sacred. It attracts white-light energies. Now, these energies manifest themselves as lightning, moving up and down your body, scanning you, striking you time after time. The incessant strikes activate a clockwise rotation in the waters, submerging you towards the emerald lake's foundation.

When you reach the lake's foundation, you have become so vast you can touch all four corners of the lake with your hands and feet. You embody the shape of a cross, your body at its centre. Your solar plexus moves upwards to the surface of the water, where your entire body bridges the lake. You rise from the water, witnessing an orange essence sphere of light, imbibing its essence. With a spin, you descend again into the waters. You rotate around your own axis, with each spin, enveloping the water around you. However, you also create a motion within the water, producing ever-enlarging waves. Slowly a sphere of liquid light encases you. You have never lived such an aquatic experience before. You even glimpsed a marine Light Being having a tail, but also most furry.

The sphere of liquid light surrounds you, spinning most rapidly.

Lightning continues to strike. From the sphere's crown, it strikes into the sphere, radiating its energies into the inner membrane, drenching the sphere. Simultaneously, the nearby lightning strikes strike the reflecting waters. The white light has now lubricated the inner walls. It continues to weave a second layer of white light across the sphere's inner surface, weaving it in every direction. You find yourself within deeper layers of this sphere as these actions mount. When you project your consciousness into the outer layers, attempting understand what is going on, so much happens. The activity you witness seems wild, dramatic.

As soon as you attune yourself back into the inner sanctum of the sphere, a pulsing calmness brings you into a meditative state. Meanwhile, you notice occasional fluctuations in light from which you can conclude there is much activity outside. The fluctuations are subtle, though, because this white, liquid light sphere envelopes you beautifully. The prevailing silence transforms the sphere into a sacred sanctuary. You are safe and thrive.

By this time, the outside activity has ceased. Calmness has returned. Altogether, you have become different. This emerald lake has changed you, for you are not the person you were before. Moreover, you would like to raise yourself because you keep expanding, and this sphere has become too small for you. Accordingly, you stand up and break free, piercing the membrane, like breaking out of a hatched egg.

As you get to your feet, the water of this sacred lake comes up to your ankles. This perplexes you, for you have become immense, overseeing all the Nile temples, from Abu Simbel until the Nile Delta and up to the Mediterranean Sea. You wonder what happened. During your submersion, it seemed nothing happened at all until the motion and lightning stopped. By the time you left the sphere, you had become an enormous being. Your head reaches the Light of Amun Ra, and you anoint yourself in his Divine Essence. He, in return, envelops you with a grey membrane. Amun Ra is about *the Seen and the Unseen*. The membrane anoints you into *the Unseen*. The shadow allows you to see all that is concealed and cannot be seen.

From this day on, you view the wholeness and fullness of all life's aspects. Hence, it is essential to acknowledge the *Unseen*. When you look at someone from Oneness and in wholeness, it lifts you both out of duality. Then, you no longer focus on one aspect but on the whole. By no longer focusing on one aspect, you are no longer focusing on that which resonates with you in particular. Therefore, all three-dimensional aspects no longer resonate with you. By doing so, you reposition yourself within Amun Ra's Light, namely the *Oneness of light and shadow*. In essence, you have mastered duality.

Amun Ra gifted you with this sacred initiation. Previously, he had already anointed you into the *Seen*. And now, also into the *Unseen*, allowing you to embody his energies and resonate at his level. Equally important, this is the necessary level to balance the Scales of Maat,[36] to keep your heart in balance. Henceforth, you will walk the path of Maat effortlessly. As much as life challenges you, always you will find the right balance between *the Seen and the Unseen*. After all, this balance is in your heart. Your heart will keep you balanced at all times, providing you with a straight path in the direction you desire. Altogether, your life becomes a balanced journey: a life led by a heart that finds its balance in every given situation. Allowing you to walk this tightrope again, a path as you did on Unas' Causeway and at the Sphinx.

At the present time, you look behind you, and Amun Ra gazes at you. He says, "You are ready. I bestow upon you my essence to co-create with the Earth Star. As a master, you have learned and mastered to stay in your heart, no matter what comes your way. In effect, you have mastered duality and follow your heart's string. And, you live your life guided and thriving by love and righteousness. By aligning with your highest potential and the highest mission on Earth, you have aligned to the Light of Amun Ra."

---

36 Maat's scales. When passing into the afterlife, Maat places your heart on her scales. These bear, on the other side, her Ostrich feather. If your heart weighs less than this feather, then you may ascend. If your heart is heavier, you reincarnate on Earth.

II.7 Temple of the Earth Master Stargate: The Golden Disc, Hatshepsut

Illustration: Hatshepsut Temple.

Hatshepsut Stargate

When you stand in front of Hatshepsut Temple, the mighty landscape overwhelms you. The mathematical balance of the temple site radiates equilibrium and harmony. It is a challenge to keep your attention on this magnificent sight, for you experience an entire world beneath the foundations of the temple complex, where restless and unbalanced energies stir.

The temple blueprint shows itself as a Crescent Moon, with rays expanding throughout the entire Nile Valley. These rays carry the high dimensional light of Amun Ra. The blueprint has multiple dimensional layers. When you descend into it, it narrows down, almost like an inverted cone. From the moment you fall into the most profound part of this blueprint, you enter a remarkably distinct world having a vast network of tunnels.

You see in your mind's eye the image of space shuttles travelling through these tunnels at the speed of light. That is how active it once was. You see the network reaching as far as China, Turkey, India, the Far East, Mexico, South America, England, Ireland, France, and so on. This underground tunnel complex allows Light Beings to transmit light codes, information, from sacred place to sacred place.

The underground tunnel system connects all the sacred sites on Earth. They exchange their light codes so they can all evolve at the same pace to expand and raise their light frequencies. Through the different dimensional layers and their respective tones in Inner Earth, star beings enter our planet and travel through this network in dimensional layers we cannot perceive with our eyes. Once, we asked ourselves how it was possible that the same constructions were built on different continents. This may be answered by the fact that, through this network, information flowed freely, operating under the one principle of evolving all together at the same pace, side by side.

Illustration: Hatshepsut Stargate with the Black Cosmic Dragon Line and the Green Earth Dragon Line.

The blueprint of Hatshepsut shows why two streams merge as one, spreading the golden light of Amun Ra into the Nile Valley and throughout the entire Inner Earth network called Anubia. There are three additional points in this Inner Earth network through which Amun Ra spreads his golden codes. Altogether, this makes four points, of which Hatshepsut Temple is one representing the Light of Amun Ra in Anubia.

The blueprint is a cosmological clock with distinct rings and cogs inside. When you turn a cogwheel, you become aligned with certain cosmic constellations. Then, from within the Inner Earth, golden light powers several areas, including several temples in the Nile Temple Valley.

Presently it is not possible to initiate a rotation in this Stargate. It seems to be blocked. This temple and the gate are locked, and the temple complex seems to have sunk into hibernation. Hatshepsut Light

Being now shows itself to you and says that the Stargate needs to be activated. You explore the distinct rings the Stargate comprises, including its centre, and everything is closed.

You move to the outer circle. There, you sense a plasma wall built around these rays. When you touch it, the energy unloads. Codes, patterns, and star glyphs light up. Intuitively, your hand slides down this plasmic wall in an S-shape, several times. You follow your intuition. The more times you move downwards, the more the texture of this wall morphs and undulates and the light texture thins. The star codes regroup like scattered letters repositioning themselves to form a sentence for the code that will activate the gate. Proceeding further, you behold a beautiful diamond geometric pattern emerging from this plasma wall. The diamond brings forth other diamonds. You continue moving. You touch the geometric pattern of the diamond and discover many intricate codes and patterns inside. The plasma wall seems to sink entirely into this geometric shape as if absorbed into it.

The diamond code lights up, and you hear it vibrate, emanating and zooming. Whilst you stretch out your hand, the essence of this miniature diamond integrates into your palm. First you see the rays of the Crescent Moon blueprint pierce the Nile Valley and shoot to the horizon and beyond. As you walk to the centre of the blueprint, you descend into the deepest part. Looking up now, you see all the blueprint layers show various casts of diamonds in all dimensions, revealing that this form is preformed and embedded in this Stargate.

You extend your hand and allow the diamond essence to move because it has its own intelligence and knows what to do. Straightaway, it installs itself within all the respective layers of the Stargate. The layers begin to spin. You hear the sound of an old, rusty ship trying to manoeuvre. The Stargate now moves, and you are jolted as the Stargate descends into the Earth, activating the deepest point, Anubia.

With your mind's eye, you see all the various sacred places around the world. They also activate their light in communication with Anubia. The interconnection is reestablished. The process of growth and expansion into light can once again begin. An abundance of golden light floods these waters and all grounds. It has been dry for a long time. Deep inner cleansing and rejuvenation occur thanks to the life force of Amun Ra's Light. You emerge from the Stargate and stand with Hatshepsut Temple at your back. Your gaze loses itself into the horizon, and you feel fulfilled.

Initiation into Your Inner Sun

Illustration: Hatshepsut. Amun Ra.

You are standing in front of the stairs of the Hatshepsut Temple that lead to the Holy of Holies. The Light Beings of the Great White Brotherhood who have gathered here surround you. At present, an initiation is to take place. As you climb the steps, somehow, you are drawn to the temple's right-side complex. There, you see several columns and feel raging fires. You excuse yourself and say you will be back soon. You now walk to the right side of the temple complex, where the heat of the fire meets you. To your astonishment, you see split dragon tongues coming out of the pillars. Silently, you behold this and walk on. Having already experienced so much that impresses you, you continue to walk until you enter a colonnade and stand right in front of it.

This colonnade emits green luminescent light, which makes this temple section sink down slightly. Gravity is heavy here. You turn around for a moment and see the Light Beings of the Great White Brotherhood are still there. Without delay, you decide to enter the colonnade. As you enter, your essence morphs. Your hands turn into ethereal, green, veil-like mighty wings. They touch each column and pull themselves forward as the raging fire approaches, swallowing and consuming you. Its force inhibits your ability to move forward, as if you were walking into a storm. You decide to shift to your inner layers, to your central point deep within yourself, where you find silence. In this way, you remain turned inwards in a state of vibration where ease and grace reign while your body moves through the fire storm. Still, you cannot breathe, for the fire consumes all oxygen. So, you turn even deeper inwards. You breathe out of your own body, your bone marrow, and your prana system. You are breathing your own essence. As soon as you have it in your fingers, you smile. You have just learned how to be sovereign. Lightness and freedom now engulf you here within the eye of the storm. You are now creating your own essence and feel you do not need those green dragon-like wings of light. However, your physical body still needs them. So you keep moving while each wing takes a column and drags itself along. Meanwhile, the fire continues to consume you, and you burn to ashes like a Phoenix. Somewhere halfway you rise from your ashes and re-create yourself into a beautiful white Light Being, signifying that you have deeply purified yourself.

The fire slowly extinguishes as you reach the end of the colonnade. You become enveloped in a fatherly essence of orange sunset light, blessing you for undertaking this daunting task. When you leave and walk away from the colonnade, you look behind and see Green Dragons preparing the colonnade for someone else. When they look at you, you feel the same fatherly energy you recognised in the orange sunset glow. This experience has taught you how to stay within the eye of the storm, to breathe from your inner core and your own essence, allowing you to be sovereign and move beyond time and space. It also allows you to be separate from everything that exists on Earth and beyond. Your heart hears them say, "Farewell, Cosmic Star Walker."

As you move now towards the temple entrance, you feel compelled to move to the left side. There, a cool blue essence light calls you to go. You cannot resist it. You go to the left side, which is the Temple of Hathor. As you approach, you immediately slide into some water and rotate around your axis, generating circles. Each circle represents an arm, and all the circles together form twelve individual arms. When they overlap, a golden, twelve-pointed star arises. As this pattern descends into the remarkably deep waters, you follow the twelve-pointed star. The mass of water you find yourself in contains various etheric layers. Every layer you pass through is a field that shifts your vibration, forming you and thereby tuning the vibrational strings within your body. Similarly to the Temple of Edfu, here too, you pass through different layers, which prepare you for Hatshepsut's Holy of Holies.

The pattern you created has evolved into a Golden Lotus. This is important. You are attuned to become her seed essence from which everything sprouts. When you click into this Lotus pattern, you fold back into a bud, in the depths of these waters, ready to emerge into the sunlight, into Amun Ra. While this Golden Lotus remains at the bottom of these deep waters, your Light Being ascends and joins the group of the Great White Brotherhood. They have just finished. The timing is perfect.

You walk with them up the stairs, towards the Holy of Holies. There at the top of the temple you see the Sun shining brightly upon you, warming you. The Sun's transmutational power in Hatshepsut is exceptionally strong. You walk on, and this sunlight fills and nourishes you. It vaporises you, and you become a Sun portal of yellow liquid light. You feel merged, consolidated, and centred. In that capacity, you arrive at the door of the Holy of Holies. Here, you enter and see a blue-painted starry ceiling in this sanctuary of Amun Ra. He is present and gazes at you. He sees the seed of your divine potential within your Golden Lotus, which you carry in your heart. He takes it in his hands and blesses it. He transforms the crystal structure into a diamond structure. The Golden Lotus is emanating with diamond lights. He now places it back in your heart, looks at you, and says you have transformed your heart into a beautiful Creation. He ascertains who you have become as a soul and as a new world to explore. Proud as any father, and to honour your achievement, he adorns your heart with countless stars and transmutes you into a starlit sky. He adds that this is his gift to you, the endless sky. You will receive the Earth component in the Temple of Love in the later phase of your sacred journey into Creation. You are the Heart in which only the music of the spheres reigns. Your gift to Amun Ra is the sacred union of your divine masculine and divine feminine energies.

He welcomes you as a Light Being who lives Divinity on Earth, and who may rise to the surface, to the Light, like a Golden Lotus.

"This is so excellent," says Amun Ra, "to behold you because you have attained important levels of purity, strength, and love. You have established your divinity. With all the endless possibilities in every single moment, you chose from the heart, even if those choices were the most difficult ones. You chose strength, courage, and love and transmuted yourself back into a Divine Being, a starry sky aligned by harmonic resonance, always sovereign, even in the most tumultuous moments. You bear your light like a master, and therefore you will reincarnate in your new world. Here, you have the capacity to carry the Earth harmoniously. And, because you gained that mastery, I anoint and deepen your Diamond Heart."

It is complete. You honour Amun Ra as your mentor and as a dear heart friend. You say goodbye. The Sun's rays engrave the energy signature of your deepening Diamond Heart on the cosmic scrolls. The Cosmos has acknowledged, you are a Cosmic Star-Walker.

Cosmic Mirror, Anubia

Hatshepsut Temple seeks a deeper connection with Inner Earth and Earth's primordial forces. In the centre of the foundation, a circular disc in a Y shape shows olive-green essence energies and black essence energies merging into the solar energies of Amun Ra. The two energy streams come from behind the temple area. These are not simply streams of consciousness flowing through the Earth, these lines are dragon lines, a Black Dragon and Green Dragon line merging into Amun Ra's light. It radiates throughout the Earth and, more precisely, Anubia.

The dragon energies concern transmutation. The Black Dragon pushes forward, and the Green Dragon comes up through the pillars of fire.

They represent the energies of Osiris, the dismembered and the re-membered component, merging into the Light of Amun Ra. The re-membering process means merging together with your higher selves and ultimately your One divine spark. You extend your hands, allowing them to touch yours.

The dragons narrate, "This book is about the Earth. It is not primarily about Egyptian temples. Yes, that is right. The Egyptian temples are just a means to birth the New Earth into existence. So, we agree this energy coming through is one you are seeking, is it not? Yes, that is right. We also agree that you seek primordial energy. The raw power is the one that made the Earth into what she is: the raw power of volcanoes, eruptions, earthquakes, waterfalls, oceans, seas, rivers. Look at these primordial energies of Creation from our eyes. You then see green energy running in the foundation of Hatshepsut, throughout the centre, and black energy running below in Hatshepsut's left-wing."

You understand a new balance needs to integrate between the right and left sides of Hatshepsut, to be achieved through the green and black energies. From a purely primordial Creational perspective, this temple is not operational due to this imbalance, the incomplete energetic alignment. Perhaps the temple builders did not take this element into account. However, it is necessary to ground the temple. There has been insufficient co-Creation with stellar energies.

We ask for the presence of the Star Council of Eight, and as soon as these words resound, their energy becomes tangible. The Star Council of Eight mentions that the front of the temple is the Crescent Moon embedded in the bedrock. Equally important, the area behind the bedrock is an additional part. It completes the spherical blueprint of the temple. Consequently, the temple begins to rotate, activated by the Stargate, positioned on the foundation, which introduces this motion.

Immediately the foundational waters on the right side move backwards, infusing it with the element of water. Now, the backside appears to be a void. The energy streams in to nourish this temple. For the most part, the Amun Ra energy is present, nourishing the Nile Valley, but there is no balance between the cosmic and the earthly energies. Seemingly, the void causes this imbalance. As soon as the imbalance is named and addressed, the earthly energies combined with the cosmic energies restore the connection with Earth's primordial energies. Then, this temple's connection aligns itself between Earth and the sky.

The Black Cosmic Dragon represents cosmic energy. The Green Earth Dragon represents earth energy. Neither align. So, Amun Ra's light has only one vehicle driving it. When the black cosmic energy and the green earth energy fuse, a massive deepening of the Hatshepsut Temple occurs. At the genesis of Earth's existence, these energies were designated to help transmute the Earth. They continue to assist the Earth in transmuting, and they safeguard the Inner Earth network. When the Earth leaves her body, the cosmic energies will pull out of the Earth structure this Inner Earth network (Anubia). The Inner Earth network reflects cosmic wormholes: As Within So Without, and so this Inner Earth network represents the Cosmos.

Not only do you travel along Inner Earth lines. You also travel through the Cosmos and between stars and planets. This Inner Earth network also reflects certain cosmic transits. Anubia extends from thirty degrees north longitude to thirty degrees south longitude across Earth's entire width.

Far behind the Temple of Hatshepsut is an energetic area where the two dragon energies have their origin. They have accompanied the Earth since her genesis in this solar system. These dragons always knew Earth's timeline and the blueprint she would follow. They will now take on the responsibility of supporting Earth's transmutation process, consolidating Anubia into a golden disc, and detaching it from the earthly body.

Hermetic Principle of Anubia

The combined cosmic and earthly energies elucidate the Hermetic Principle of Anubia. When you traverse this network and go from Egypt to Turkey, similarly you travel from star to star. The advantage is that you can, in one go, collect energetic codes on both earthly and cosmic planes. As you gather the earthly and cosmic energies and redistribute the codes, all temples balance their cosmic and earthy poles. Within the grid work of Anubia, the sacred sites built on Earth also translate to cosmic counterparts. Anubia is a miniature version of the Cosmos and contains the same energetic pattern, the same sense of reality. From an energetic point of view, the shape of the lines and points that make up this grid work transmit the same frequency as the Cosmos.

Essentially, Anubia is the network between the various constellations of the Star Council of Eight and between their stars and other celestial bodies. The idea of star beings descending from the skies in spaceships is not always the case. Instead, in the Cosmos, they can decide in a nanosecond to take a cosmic route, but in and via the Inner Earth. In a word, they switch spatiotemporal lines. In fact, you will not see them, for, they travel beyond space and time.

As the Earth will transmute, the inner dimensions will also dismantle. For this to happen, all temples will need to align with and mirror their etheric counterparts. Anubia will also be dismantled, intact, because it is a supremely delicate network needing to be integrated elsewhere. Another possibility is that it incorporates into the larger cosmic grid. Most probably, it will not, because there are new planets in need of this structure. The Star Council of Eight prefers to maintain this network because its collapse or dissolution can also exercise a detrimental energetic impact on a cosmic level. Moreover, the cosmic energies transmit the network to other planets or celestial bodies, where inner networks will have to be implemented.

For the dismantlement, the connection between the Hatshepsut Temple and the two dragon lines needs restoring. The disconnected part almost symbolically detaches Earth from its celestial connections. Mankind, the Pharaohs who lived on Earth, mainly mastered dominion and power. We should not generalise, but they often forgot how to connect with the Earth, which has an indispensable cosmic component. Accordingly, there is a gap between the Source of the dragon and Earth's line, and the temple so inhibits humankind from bearing Star Consciousness.

As this is realised and as soon as these words echo, forthwith, two yellow-golden rays of light coming from behind Hatshepsut travel to the bedrock and reconnect with this high-energy spot. A smaller, hollow, conical pyramid is present in this area. Its frequency is high vibrational, consisting of rings. Within, it seems as vast as the Cosmos. The upper part represents cosmic consciousness, and the lower part carries all the energy of the Earth creatures, such as dragons. When the two cones merge at the level of their flat base, they intermingle and project outwards a string of interconnected spheres. These spheres each have a cosmic and earthly counterpart that enters Hatshepsut Temple from behind. They move to the level of the Stargate before dropping and positioning themselves on the Stargate.

The disc at the foundation's centre has a lower green and upper black essence that imbues the Stargate and pierces it straight through its core. The two mighty dragons lead it on from there, and in doing so, they establish Hatshepsut's connection via the Stargate to Earth's core. The essence travels through Earth's crust, the crystal layers, molten lava, and hollow Earth to arrive at the iron crystal. Here, the black-green essence winds itself around the core. The support for Earth's transmutation must occur from her core and then project to the rest of her body to subsequently implode.

The cosmic and earth energies move from the outside inwards and from the inside outwards. Behold, Hatshepsut Temple shivers on its foundation! The black and green energies seep through and permeate all walls. Remarkably, the green essence fully imbues the temple structure, and a pristine earthly temple comes into existence.

Now directly from Inner Earth, a green, pure, and flourishing earthly structure emerges. Its high frequency infiltrates the current temple, and in doing so, allows the surface, the foundation, to crack. The existing structure disintegrates and dissolves. It is replaced by an even more powerful structure. This structure reaches out from the deep Earth, far into the Cosmos, reinforcing the cosmic component of the Temple of Light already constructed. Truly, a sacred union occurs between the cosmic and earthly dragons as they rise spear-like, from Earth's core upwards into the temple's foundation, crushing it to dissolve into golden light.

Illustration: Hatshepsut Blueprint.

As a result, the sacred site is restored. Hatshepsut has found her new balance between cosmic and earthly energies. The balance is necessary to ground the Aquarian initiations the temple offers. Otherwise, if the temple were to initiate you into cosmic energies without a profound earthly counterbalance, your proper foundation may falter.

The Hatshepsut's spirit now walks towards you. She seems more powerful than the warrior she has ever been. She embodies the perfect balance between the feminine and masculine, earthly and cosmic. She genuinely connects the Cosmos and the Earth, embodying greater love and an open heart. Not to mention the beautiful female Queen she already was, she now emanates more balanced governance from the heart, for she has also found a balance between her divine feminine and masculine energies.

Looking back at the Stargate, its two outlines rotate clockwise and counterclockwise, allowing the Y to dissolve and morph into an S shape. A slithering kundalini rises, which in turn allows Amun Ra to release his light. Balancing the earthly and cosmic energies immediately forms a key of power to transmute more energy into the foundation.

The relevance of balancing the earthly and cosmic energies of Hatshepsut Temple lies in transforming the whole planet, not just part of it.

For this same reason, these are profound and essential foundational aspects to work and make transmutation possible. Ascension is unlikely if, as humans, we do not strengthen our foundational level. We therefore need to interconnect with the Earth, our loved ones, our allies, and with our hearts to transmute ourselves.

Thoth Hermes Trismegistus and his Hermetic Principle explain that Anubia resides in our body and in the body of the Earth. Thus, when we clear our subconscious and reflect with the Cosmos, we mirror the above and become the below. Thereupon we embody the Hermetic Principle and become Creation itself. Moreover, we co-create with

Creation, not only because we can assist in Creation, but in effect, we become creators.

As with all Light Temples of the Nile, this temple allows us to birth ourselves into Oneness. Oneness with ourselves, and Oneness with the Cosmos. We can become the Cosmos and mirror it. In the same fashion, we are the I Am that I Am, the avatar of the ultimate Hermetic Principles.

The Mirror of the Cosmos, represented by Anubia, is the Hermetic Principle's embodiment: *As Within, So Without. As Above, So Below.* The Earth carries in her body the entire Cosmos. Likewise, all stars live within her. She represents the I Am that I Am.

I Am the Earth, and I Am the Cosmos, I Am All That Is. This Hermetic Principle thrives on Cosmic Love, for the Cosmos is a reflection of the Earth and Earth, Cosmos. They cannot *not* love one another. Indeed, they support one another, care for one another, and nurture one another.

Earth's Master Stargate, Anubia

Anubia extends from thirty degrees north longitude to thirty degrees south longitude across Earth's entire width. This central band spanning Earth's centre is absolutely one Earth Master Stargate integrated into her body. This Master Stargate attunes itself to the heavens, celestial bodies, and astrological movements. It initiates downloads of specific codes necessary for the Earth to incorporate into her body. It integrates the stellar codes, allowing her to evolve within the whole embracing her.

The Stargate Anubia is like a cosmic clock with cogwheels at various dimensional levels. There are at least twenty-seven levels of cogs incorporated into this cosmic clock. Each turns independently of the others. These individual movements initiate a unique opening of the Master Stargate aligning it with a particular star constellation or grouping of constellations. Specific tuning to open the Stargate is essential for the cosmic clock to align with a particular star. Thus aligned, the star releases its star codes. When released, the Earth can receive them freely.

There will come a time when all the wheels will assume the same position. The aperture of the Stargate will entirely open. During that sacred moment, the entire Stargate will uplift from the earthly surface. For Earth will no longer need her body. She will then have reached her ascension and the Stargate will pass into another celestial body to help guide the growth of other planets, stars, and moons.

Specifically, when we examine more closely the structure of Anubia, how she integrates star codes, we behold a set of points connected by lines or tracks. These specific points represent sacred temple sites on Earth and cosmic stellar representations. They receive star codes, the star codes incorporating themselves into these points. The star codes then flow powerfully, vigorously into the tracks connecting the stellar temple areas.

The downloads of these star codes bring greater connections between the temple areas on Earth until all areas become One band of sacred space. Once fully integrated, the energies between temple areas run through one another. As One temple area covering Earth's width, they now radiate the most powerful Golden Source Codes. The pulsing of the Golden Source Codes as an in-breath and an out-breath of the earthly body brings about more dimensional space from within. The heart of the Earth quietly feels the call more and more clearly, and responds. Her heart leaves its inner temple, its body, to build another life in another place. For her, she is enduring this process with ecstatic bliss.

When she departs from her physical form, all those near her will receive her blessings: the light codes of her Temple of Love. When we integrate these into our hearts, we will always remember her and all our co-Creations. This loving connection will forever remain between her and every Light Being, no matter which cosmic projects we may later engage in.

Anubia, as can be seen, is not merely a network of movement at the speed of light. It is so much more. Most of all, it represents the cosmic clock, the Master Stargate of the Earth, responsible for uniting all temple areas on Earth to function as One and radiate the Source

Codes for herself and the Cosmos. Equally important, Anubia offers a transcosmic passage for all Light Beings to assist the Earth, coupled with the Cosmic Ascension project. With this, the Earth indicates she is ready to embark on her next incarnation.

In this journey, we learnt that Hatshepsut Temple was attuned only with the cosmic component and not with the earthly one. By and large, the temple could not take on its role in the framework of Anubia. It had lost its connection to the network. So it shows us this: if we neglect the earthly component in an ascension process, the transmutation process cannot occur. This reasoning also applies to our earthly human body and the horizontal axis of our life, which we share with those we love: animals, plants, and nature.

Within the grand story of history, we are also describing here the state of consciousness of Queen Hatshepsut, whose temple is a reflection of her being. By this, we mean she was keenly attuned to the stars, devoted to deities, and her role in that play. She might, however, have had too little heart for the Earth, Earth-and-Cosmos equality, and the integration of cosmic energies within Earth's body. We can all learn from this.

II.8 Temple of Sacred Geometry, Dendera

Sacred Geometry Creation

Illustration: Dendera.

Oddhe Rheia Earth's Group Consciousness

You are standing before the Dendera Temple. A dome of plasma covers it so you cannot enter. You walk around the circumference of the transparent dome, sliding your hand through it like a veil. By doing so, the essence of this plasma dome creates a certain lightness in you. You feel enabled to descend into the Earth beneath Dendera Temple. Hence, the essence composing the dome is the access code to the sacred place you are led to.

Meanwhile, you descend powerfully and drill down into the Earth. You pass through all Earth's strata, the Hollow Earth and beyond. Then, close to Earth's core, you see a plasma sphere. Intriguingly, it seems to be made of a different material than the Earth. You recognise in it the same essence as in the half-dome shape. Be that as it may, you know you must be here.

So, you approach it. It is surprisingly small. You fit right in. While you are in this transparent sphere, the landscape changes. As in an elevator, you shift to another dimensional reality, and a completely unfamiliar landscape appears. Hence, this plasma sphere is a portal to a multidimensional realm within the Earth that is not within Earth's physical body but in a cosmic space on an inner multidimensional level, within Earth's light structure. Although you find yourself within a vast space that seems to be unbounded, a quantum cell encloses you within a fractal branch of Earth's inner dimensions. We know that fractals are infinite replications of the main blueprint from which they emerge.

Sounds also echo in the far distance. The atmosphere is airy. It strikes you that this vastness feels empty. You cannot recognise any earthly forms here. Everything seems abstract. You can perceive colours, lines, shapes. Then . . . in front of you, appear two large round eyes. A being lowers itself to your level and looks you in the eyes to make you understand it is not empty at all. They are here. You look at her. She tells you she belongs to the group consciousness Oddhe Rheia. Her name is Fnomiea. She has a flattened, round face. Her head appears substantial compared to the slenderness of her body. Her skin appears pinkish, tender. She does not have a firm, consistent, muscular body. She is rather delicate, with a little more skin tissue, which in her neck is more folded. She is tall and slim. Her eyes large, round dark, with clear-blue crystalline light shining from within them. Her heart, too, radiates a light blue, luminous light. She loves how you observe her. She asks if there are certain of her features you would like to see in more detail. Her openness makes you smile. For she shows you she very much wants you to get acquainted.

Behind you, you see many beings just like her, some smaller. There are also children. You can recognise masculine and feminine creatures. Though they are androgenic in their expression, they either translate as feminine or masculine energy. You notice they work with the primordial white strings, the energy essences through which the golden seed of the Earth can unfold its blueprint, manifesting itself in a certain density. We had seen this when a new Cosmos came into being in Source Field. The seed descends into the new Cosmic Womb, and meridians comprising vibrational white strings create a toroid field. They show you they work with the primordial geometric pattern of the Earth. They work with the white vibrational strings, the transmitters of vibration, building blocks of the Cosmos. With their hands, claying, shaping, and playing with these strings, creating with them.

When playing these strings, they adjust the vibration. The strings attune differently, depending on which movements they perform, causing a regrouping of Earth's matter on multidimensional levels. By working with the vibrational strings, they affect earthly matter in every density within which it expresses itself. They affect all dimensional levels making up the body of Earth.

You wonder if this wording is correct, and it is precisely so because they are nodding. Yes. All right, you feel confident you have understood. You are, therefore, ready for the next phase. They show the Earth as a spherical, geometric pattern of various geometrical forms: the octahedron, dodecahedron, icosahedron, and vesica piscis, which is located flat on the equator. They increase the frequency of vibration, which allows these geometric patterns to accelerate. You witness the particles within these geometric patterns accelerating. They shift from one geometry to another: the vesica piscis procreating from its centre, with sprouting circles swirling around one another creating the flower of Venus love. From this, the Flower of Life can grow. You can always recognise the basic pattern, the vesica piscis, which remains underneath.

Fnomiea works the sacred geometry. She shapes, clays it as on a potter's wheel. Moreover, she creates with it, bringing it up to higher frequencies. This is so because she wants to attune the Earth to the cosmological environment so that Earth will evolve at the same pace, side by side with the group consciousness to which the Earth belongs. For the Earth does not belong to the solar system or to our galaxy. Our Earth belongs to a group consciousness, a soul group. Although the Earth is alone in the solar system, even so, it is connected to its specific soul group consciousness. Thus, Creational Light Beings, including Oddhe Rheia, work with the sacred geometry of the Earth so that it remains connected to its group consciousness. This is essential because it inhibits alienation and the decay into low frequencies that would otherwise make it increasingly difficult to resonate with that group consciousness. The Creational Light Beings respond to the influx of light codes originating from their soul group. These souls can embody as stars, planets, or moons, or as any manifestation. It is all possible. There is an interconnectedness that represents a grid mapped onto itself. We have seen many times in the Sacred Journey into Creation that the grids exist on themselves. But this is actually a grid of their group consciousness within the larger cosmic grid.

There is an interplay in this soul group. The Creational Light Beings are playing with the geometry of the Earth, being the vibration of the Earth, bringing it into alignment with the group consciousness and finding the vibrational match with the group consciousness to allow it to evolve and ascend together, as a group. This group consciousness carries the Earth in a certain way, for when there are souls who have evolved, they carry the Earth, and the Earth itself carries other entities. Moreover, within this group consciousness, there is a constant exchange of information, of light codes. And this place where we are offers a constant update for the Earth to be in vibratory match with this group consciousness.

Fnomiea takes your hands because she wants to show you something. While she holds you, you sense her heart luminous and flaming, making a continuous motion of an infinity loop. This movement also creates a humming sound. You have difficulty bringing your attention to where she takes you, for her heart essence makes you curious and distracts you. She shows you a blue crystal in the distance. Also, the blue crystal shimmers like flames. They have an essence that waves within. Likewise, her heart seems to be the same essence. There are blue crystals positioned on various levels on the Earth. They give direct access to this group consciousness present throughout the Cosmos. There are also light-yellow crystals positioned more on the vertical axis of the Earth. They indirectly download the information from the group consciousness on a cosmic level. This information has more to do with the weaving of the horizontal strings in the toroidal field of the Earth. Thus, it involves the etheric tissue composing the Earth. These yellow wavy crystals actualise the blueprint tissue.

The tissue of the blueprint accordingly aligns with that of the other members of this group consciousness throughout the Cosmos. The Creational Light Beings are playing with Earth's sacred geometry, to update, uplevel, and ensure it remains in harmonic resonance with All That Is and, more specifically, the group consciousness to which the Earth belongs. As soon as the blueprint's fabric alters, a repositioning takes place both within the Earth and on Earth's surface, according to the cosmic firmament. Hence, whatever moves in the celestial firmament reflects within the Earth. In addition, the Creational Light Beings show you that in the Cosmos, new paved stellar highways form.

Moreover, these specific Creations provide momentum for star beings such as the Earth or other stars to jump on and enjoy that momentum to manifest quantum growth. Truly, this group consciousness is profoundly focused on these new Creations, providing the necessary momentum to make a quantum leap in growth and expansion. These stellar paths are created instantaneously and disappear shortly thereafter. They are springboards for the group consciousness to ascend to increasingly higher levels via the cosmic Central Axis.

Initiation: Creational Seat

To initiate you, the Creational Light Beings bring you to a final space. A place where there is a golden seat. As you stand before this seat, you see through the golden energy the same wavy blue energy present in her heart and in the blue crystals. She invites you to sit within it. Instantly, the power of this chair startles you. So, you proceed slowly, for the energy the chair radiates is most powerful. The emanated energy field radiates to such an extent that even if you lower yourself, you do not immediately sink into the chair, for it penetrates your body, preparing you. As soon as the rays lower you, only then can you settle on the chair.

Now seated and still, you feel the radiated light pervading you. Truly, this is the most peculiar situation you have ever experienced. The light reorganises your inner system. Meanwhile, you are fiercely shaken. Your vibrational white strings are modified, aligned with your Central Axis and correcting the previous disharmony. Your eyes undergo a slight change. They enlarge like the eyes of the Creational Light Beings around you. Your body shifts and morphs. You stretch and see yourself with a similar long, slender body and enticingly soft skin. They want to let you know what it is like to live from their consciousness, or perhaps they want to tell you that you are one of them. What could it be? You continue to sink in. When you do, the bright blue light in your eyes radiates outwards like crystals to the other beings in the same group consciousness throughout the Cosmos.

When, through these eyes, you gaze up into the heavens and connect your heart with the Cosmos, you hear all the Cosmic Sounds between the stars, planets, and Light Beings. You can hear Light Beings and stillness and order through sacred geometry, through vibration. You experience the Musica Universalis.

Moreover, you now understand that Cosmic Sound is always present. When sounds express themselves and are not immediately received, they remain in our enclosed multiverse. Thereupon, the Cosmos contains Cosmic Sound, so whatever one creates remains generated within this structure. Time is equally irrelevant. Although distress decreases with time, sound does not. Sound is pure energy abundant in the Cosmos.

As if you have a sonar system in your eyes that can track them, you now know where all members of this group consciousness reside. You hear sounds of information sent to you, and from you to them. Forthwith, you receive and transmit the constant stream of sound information flowing into the Earth. You have direct access to the primordial white vibrational strings of the Earth, and even to those of our Cosmos. You can feel them. Clearly, you feel connected to the White-Stringed Omega Ω. You tune in at a cosmic level from this capacity to a vast, expansive area and network.

With this in mind, you look at all the Creational Light Beings who surround you. They are supreme Divine Light Beings on the level of Creation. You can see that some of them have yellow eyes and others blue eyes. You now embody the blue-eyed beings who resonate with blue crystals. They match the vertical primordial white vibrational strings of Earth's toroidal field. Whereas the yellow light crystals resonate more with the horizontal bands between these vertical grid lines, being those bands weaving the etheric fabric of the toroidal field. You stand before them. They are immensely proud of what they have shown you. This is what we create. We are present in a quantum sphere within the Earth, a direct access point to this vast cosmic world. In like manner, in the smallest of things reside the greatest secrets. What would happen if you were to embody the yellow-eyed beings? They suggest you try.

Thus, you repeat the same procedure: you drop into the chair and allow yourself to be pierced by its lights. When you open your eyes and your body restructures, your eyes radiate yellow light. As a result, you indeed resonate with the core of the Earth, but with different levels of matter, and with the earthlier components: rocks, waterfalls, bodies of water, plants, animals. It is the matter making up the Earth and filling the Earth, beyond its geometric outline. You can hear squirrels. They also have a vibration. The yellow energies determine the vibrations of water, rain, animals, falling leaves in the wind, a human voice. They prepare the frequencies that will determine how matter manifests itself in form and sound.

In the capacity of these Creational Light Beings, you feel you can be water. You feel the vibration: you are seeping through water, its tingling feeling. The tingling feeling life gives can be sweet but also ecstatic. The more you go through this sacred journey of Creation, the more it comes to Bliss. This tingling is generated by cosmic sex, the ectasis of the splendour of existence you experience when allowing life force to flow through you. You allow life to flow through you. You allow ecstatic bliss to nourish your soul, you allow yourself to live from cosmic sex and experience that day to day. It must be remembered to experience the smallest things in life: to enjoy a breeze, listening to a drop of water falling into a mass of water. You allow yourself to experience life through your eternal I Am Presence. It permeates all etheric fabric at the vibrational level and frequency.

She now shows you through these eyes how the vibrational frequencies fully permeate the Earth. They convey a tingling emotion, tingling sensations, ecstatic bliss. This abundance of ecstatic bliss is also accessible within ourselves. You feel these pearls of wisdom given to you allow you to sink deeper into your body. You deeply anchor yourself in this life and in this Earth. You genuinely desire to shape your life, fashion the Earth and create something beautiful with it and something beautiful in your life. You wish to obtain mastery in your life. You slowly leave the golden seat. As you stand, you know you still have the yellow and blue essence in your eyes. They are Creational capacities activated. A higher Creational divine potential now emanating from your own eternal I Am Presence enables you to create with the prima mater of sacred geometry. You can do so at the level of outline with the blue essence and at the level of in line with the yellow essence. Your Creational divine potential also elevates your consciousness into the Creational worlds, giving you a much wider range of consciousness. This divine potential strengthens you in your Divine Creational work.

Sacred Lotus

As if to show you her heart, the Temple of Dendera unveils herself layer upon layer, unfolding and delving into deeper and deeper dimensions. You approach the deeper layers within this temple. As you walk, you hear sand grinding beneath your feet as the warm sunlight gently caresses your body. This experience is palpable. You feel Dendera Light Being reaching out to you. The palms of your hands are moist. Curious as you are, you do not understand what she wants you to see.

Illustration: Dendera: Hathor.

Meanwhile, the temple structure in our third dimension has unveiled and unfolded itself fully. The construction is no longer visible nor tangible. Instead, you witness a vast landscape of lush green meadows bathing in sunlight. This paradisiacal place is a haven connecting intensely with the animals grazing on the grasslands and sipping the refreshing waters.

In the centre, you see a circular platform with a crystalline structure of white essence. It has been built according to the Fibonacci sequence. The first part of this structure extends rather low. As you follow its construction, the etheric walls become higher and higher. Moreover, you notice the shape like a shell, a spiral spiralling out towards the outline as the structure heightens. You observe this form emerging as you approach. Once the structure arrives at its last phase, you can see the top forms into a sharp point. At this moment, Dendera Light Being invites you to enter this white crystalline structure. You approach. You first touch its essence by rubbing your hand against the wall. A high-frequency sound echoes throughout the structure and the surrounding environment.

You have witnessed a resonance chamber coming into existence! Without delay, you enter the spiral-shaped temple from its outline and walk inwards, penetrating deeper and deeper into this sanctuary. As you move towards the Holy of Holies, Dendera Light Being spins you around your axis in a sensual dance, enveloping the white crystalline essence around you. Her white essence surrounds your hips, belly, and legs, truly urging you to descend into your own deeper essence. Still, the white crystalline essence swirls around you, forming strings that make an up-and-down motion around your hip area and legs. Each downward movement brings you deeper into your own multidimensional structure. At the same time, the Cosmic Sound echoing from the crystalline essence purifies you with a power you can hardly resist. As a result, you see yourself becoming clear as crystal quartz.

The high-frequency sound cleanses and purifies you, transforming you into a high-resonance temple. Your legs and hips are almost transparent. Gradually, this transparency moves up from your belly towards your stomach, heart area, neck, and head. Finally, you feel you must align your crown with the top needle of this temple. As you do so, Dendera Light Being responds with a sound resonating with the apex. Each emanation of sound creates an additional layer resembling a snow carpet on the top of the temple. You continue to tune in to the white essence snow carpet designed uniquely for you until it falls on you, imbuing you. In response, your crown opens, out of which smaller white crystalline clusters emerge. Your entire body shivers as it tries to align with the energetic structure activated in your crown.

Granted that the whole of your skeletal structure repositions and aligns with this high-frequency crystalline structure, it requires considerable shifts in your spinal column. During the repositioning, you hear the high-frequency sound initiate movement from within your body. With each shift of your skeletal structure, more dimensional space is created within your body, allowing you to embody more white light. Altogether, this structure will help you clearly hear the stellar voices so many light-years away. Indeed, this unique structure provides you with clairsentience, clairvoyance, and clairaudience. Also, it aligns you with all the stellar constellations, for they now are part of you. The Cosmos is in you. They are not outside of you, dispersed in the Cosmos as entities you can connect with. Instead, they are within you, sending their energies through you, nourishing and nurturing you.

Meanwhile, your skeletal structure becomes heavier. It wants to descend deeply into the Earth. You feel the gravity on your entire body. The stellar essence you have embodied permeates to the level of your bone marrow. Due to this integration, your skeleton feels exceedingly open, light, restructured, and resonant, knowing it is receiving the presence, support, and guidance of stellar consciousness.

This ancient temple most likely predates even Lemuria, when star beings created with the prima mater. Here in Dendera, they used sound and crystalline energy. These ancient energies were still detectable to the ancient Egyptians. As an ode to the powerful Dendera Light Being, the Dendera Temple came into being to give a new structure to its Light Being on Earth. Dendera Light Being is primaeval and older than the three-dimensional Temple of Dendera itself. In ancient times, there were no deities present, no Gods worshipped. Instead, there was total equality. Everyone wished to enjoy earthly life as a cosmic being who created paradise on Earth. More so, the pure essence of Creation worked with all earthly beings, enabling them to be resonant and in *harmonic resonance* with *All That Is*. Purity is centred on living your Divine Essence and Potential on Earth while feeling wholly nourished and guided.

As soon as you embody these energies, your consciousness shifts. Although you perceive you are here on Earth, walking about and living your life, you are aware of what prevails above you. You feel you belong to a larger cosmic structure. You can choose to live it, hearing the voices and receiving the information. Or you can decide to actively co-create by asking yourself these questions: What does the Earth need? What can star beings teach you or show you that resonates with your unique soul mission?

You immediately understand they are connecting with the Earth through you while you live here: guiding, inspiring, motivating, and helping you. As you sit in this temple, they work with various sound strings. Each reaches a specific octave in your body. These sound strings move up and down, left and right. Foremost, they want to descend into your structure to clear old, outdated energies so that you gain more grounding and more multidimensional access to Earth's core.

This temple provides you with access to Earth's core. Hence, you enter this inner sanctum and spin around the axis, being a pillar through which you can descend. Gradually you approach the Inner Earth and arrive in the 144th dimension. Here, you perceive infrared light in this part of the temple, identical to a womb. The space is narrow, bottle-shaped like an Omega Ω. You want to draw shapes. As you sketch on this inner wall, you feel a tingling in your body as if you were drawing within yourself. You understand you have descended into your deeper self. Each movement you make in this cavern is discernible in your body – As Without, So Within – and so materialises itself before you.

You request the presence of the Hathor, and they immediately appear in your inner sanctum. They say, "Yes, this is about self-love. The softness of this membrane teaches you to be gentle with yourself. It teaches you to think before acting, to avoid abruptness, allowing you to be very mindful of what you do outside, as the slightest act reflects on the inside, on your inner self. You are Cosmos, and Cosmos you. Harmonic resonance teaches you that if you care for what is outside you, you also love yourself. You have understood."

As you sit there with your hands cupped, a beautiful pale yellow luminous Lotus flower lays itself in your hands. This fairy Lotus feels almost surreal. The Hathor continue, saying, "This is your gift because you are the proper foundation upon which everything can grow and thrive. Indeed, you are the fertile soil giving birth to life. Life entwines itself with you, enabling you to feel this Lotus's fragility. My dear, you resonate with the fragility of life and All That Is. This resonance allows you to take care of and nurture the Earth. We desire this energy as the cosmic perfection for Merchant priestesses and priests, as this is Divine Love. Divine Love creates wholeness and Oneness in your outer and inner environments. You govern life from the heart and connect with the heart of All That Is. Please integrate this beautiful Sacred Lotus into your heart and let it descend as your sacred altar into the pelvic region to stretch out fully. The Sacred Lotus ignites the foundation within you, which you seek."

For now, you have completed this initiation. You thank Dendera's Light Being and all beautiful Light Beings, such as the Hathor and the Light Beings of the Venus Light Path.

Last, you bid farewell to this beautiful, sacred place.

Sacred Geometry Creation

The first quarter of the Moon resonates with the temple seed of Dendera. In fact, the seed of Dendera lies hidden deep within the core of the Earth at the 144th dimension. Here it exists as the geometrical pattern of the seed itself. From that point upwards, it radiates its codes and essences to Dendera Light Being and the area around the Temple of Dendera.

At this moment, you descend with your consciousness to this point. In this dimension in Inner Earth, you travel to the temple seed of Dendera to align your temple seed with hers and to co-create. The Dendera Light Being expresses her delight to have you here with her and leads you into her inner abyss. As you move closer and closer and dive into the depths of Inner Earth, you feel as if you are diving into a deep blue ocean where before you all is blue. Surely, you must trust your guidance. In the far distance, you perceive a shimmering-bright, yellow-white light. Hence, you know you have arrived. From where you are now, the light seems quite large. The closer you approach, the more you see that the light reflects its geometric pattern with flaming energy.

This place in the 144th dimension is exquisite. The temple seed in front of you radiates blue light from its core. You hold it in your hands as if you have found a treasure on the bottom of the ocean that you long to cherish. Your temple seed also resonates with it and recognises the same geometric pattern within itself. Thus, it ignites your blue light at its core. In the blue core of your temple seed, you see the sphere of the twelve-pointed Star again, with a thirteenth circumferential point. Outside the sphere, you see many spheres. They surround the thirteenth point of your twelve-pointed Star. There is a whole spherical system of dimensions within this seed's blue light core.

The core of this geometric pattern catches your inner eye, your divine spark, a tiny golden light. Both yours and the divine spark of Dendera Light Being connect. They exchange their codes and information. Subsequently, Dendera Light Being tells you about her life here on Earth, through Earth's history, and about life in all the dimensions in Inner Earth. She holds all that knowledge within her, for she has been here since the Earth was a new-born celestial body. She is passing on all this information about Earth's history to you because you also need to know her history to attune yourself to her fully. When you understand the Earth Star, you can co-create with her. Dendera Light Being knows about all the changes that have occurred on our Earth and that those changes affected Earth's surface. Dendera Light Being tells you she also has a window to the outer worlds beyond Neptune, out to the Cosmos. In her existence, she has always interacted with the outer worlds.

She tried to work with Earth's geometric blueprint to keep herself balanced, sovereign, and healthy as best as she could.

Dendera Light Being is still a significant presence on Earth. From the blue core of her temple seed, strings of light flow to you and envelop your blue core as well. This is her way of inviting you to co-create with her on these profound levels of geometric Creation. As a matter of fact, these are the blueprint levels, and she invites you to co-create with her in aligning the Earth with the cosmic grid, so that *harmonic resonance* permeates all. Equally important, she creates with sound, which she emanates from her heart and her entire essence. As Creation occurred through the first spoken word, so she also expresses the first sound. By doing so, she balances and restores the Earth within the cosmic grid.

She shows you that the Earth is already outside the solar system in relation to the cosmic grid. In physicality, we are still within our solar structure, but she has already brought the Earth towards her future position as an Earth Star. Similarly, the Earth Star moves through her sound, on this cosmic grid, toward her future position as an Ultraviolet Star. With each step the Earth takes, Dendera Light Being balances and opens the way, clears her path, and provides dimensional space so that the Earth continues her evolution with ease and grace. Again, Dendera Light Being not only supports the Earth Star in her position within the solar system but clears the path for the Earth to evolve. Dendera Light Being is truly loyal to Earth and, like a Boddhisatva, guides her to her destination. She invites you to do so the same. If you love the Earth as she does, you can choose whether you accompany her on her path. By doing so, your inner knowledge of sacred geometry and sound rekindles. In this lifetime, you can contribute if you feel willing to do so.

Moreover, Dendera Light Being reveals that you incarnated on Earth because Divine Love connects you to Earth, a Love bond that transcends time and space. As she returns with her attention to you and away from the window out to the universe, she examines how your temple seed is evolving. Her observation pleases her. A golden spiral string surrounds your temple seed and offers it the golden essence of the Source Codes of Creation, clustered structures through which the divine seeds of life move. You understand that this string is like the clusters within the coral structure transporting divine sparks to destined places. Your temple seed is ready to move into your own 144th dimension, and she initiates you to create at the level of sacred geometry, the level of blueprint and sound. In sum, Dendera Light Being teaches you the way she creates. If you so choose to co-create with her, she will prepare you. Already by deepening your temple seed to the 144th dimension, she gives you the gift of sacred geometric Creation. Proudly she looks at you as an equal. "We are ready, my beloved," she says and allows you to ascend to Earth's surface. You find yourself back in your physical body.

II.9 Temple of Transmutational Power, Abydos

Being a hologram for the Cosmic Axis, you embody the cosmic mainframe, attuning you perfectly to the harmonic resonance of the Cosmos. Henceforth, you represent its evolution.

Axis Mundi Stargate

By Thoth Hermes Trismegistus and the Light Beings of the Venus Light Path.

On the foundation of the Abydos Temple rests a huge circular field. It is the blueprint of a Stargate, communicated by Thoth Hermes Trismegistus and the Creational Divine Light Beings of the Venus Light Path. The texture of the upper layer of this circular field is light blue, with wavy liquid light rippling in various directions. When one descends more deeply into this field, an enigmatic calmness and stillness reigns. It is reminiscent of the White-Stringed Omega Ω and the birth of the Divine. A quintessentially magical atmosphere prevails here. Within this outer circular perimeter, eight smaller conical shapes, each carrying diamantine energy, reflect flaming white and rainbow lights – a mesmerising sight.

Golden stardust descends into these smaller diamond cones, entering first into their circumferences. When these outlines are filled, the golden stardust spirals upwards from the lowest point in the cone to the top layer. Here the coordinates of the various star constellations vibrate like a star map. The stardust changes its coordinates. The smaller diamond cone then aligns itself with another cosmic field within the spectrum of the Star Council of Eight, similar to how a satellite tunes in to various frequencies. These eight smaller diamond cones are the eight representatives of the Star Council of Eight.

Cones are optimal conductors of vibrations. The upper part of the flat base is layered. The layers make it look like a diamond. Here, the con-

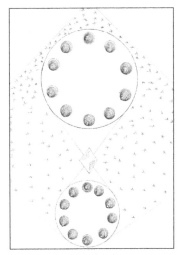

Illustration: Abydos Temple.
The Stargate Blueprint by
Thoth Hermes Trismegistus.

stellations convey their light codes, and they alchemise. The frequency of the diamond ray is omnipresent and runs through the cone. It has a keenly sharp, high-frequency vibration and continuously restructures the cones' content, updating and aligning it according to their stellar constellations.

Because of its high frequency, the diamantine essence can ultrasonically download the frequencies of stellar constellations with tremendous speed, into the cones. The quality of these frequencies is high, pure, and enlightening. Thus, the incoming information remains pristine, pure, and unaltered.

These eight smaller diamond cones position themselves within this larger circular field, which also bears a cone shape with diamond essence and whose apex in the Earth is under the Abydos Temple. All in all, the diamantine essence permeates the entire Stargate. In short, the larger cone shape is the Stargate. It contains all eight smaller diamond cones. The Stargate reaches the bandwidth of all star constellations represented by the Star Council of Eight. And, the incoming cosmic energy is enormous, high frequency, and pristine.

On the foundation plate of Abydos, from this flat base and upwards, a gigantic plasmic field, encompassing all star representations of the Star Council of Eight, radiates outwards into the Cosmos. From the top of our Cosmic Womb, its cervix, and downwards, an additional similar encompassing plasmic field overarches the same star representations. From top to bottom and from bottom to top, like a hermetic shield, two plasmic fields surround the star constellations of the Star Council of Eight.

At present, Thoth asks you to stand here on the foundation plate in Abydos Temple, in the middle of the eight smaller diamond cones. While you stand here, you look up into the wide Cosmos. Emerging out of the diamond Stargate, you see the ethereal outline of a cone shape with its apex rising into the Cosmos. It is the Earth Cone, the geometric blueprint of the Stargate. This apex meets the apex of a Cosmic cone. From that point, its flat base shoots even more deeply into the Cosmos. The Cosmic cone is the same hologram, but on a cosmic level mirroring the Earth Cone on the Abydos site. Both cones positioned one atop the other constitute the Stargate. It must be noted that at the converging point where the two apexes meet, an octahedron shows, also being a cosmic window. When you run your finger along its circumference, it makes a shrill sonic sound. The energetic field around this window rotates and appears silvery, like a galaxy bearing many nebulae. If you observe more closely, you will see yellow spiral arms which, similar to branches, fractalise. Two-dimensionally, it seems to be a spiral-galaxy structure. But multidimensionally, you discern a cosmic herringbone structure. It becomes clear that, like a mirror for the Earth, this window reflects the evolution of the Cosmos. Therefore, the plasmic shield containing all star constellations of the Star Council of Eight also anchors in the highest point of our Cosmic Womb.

Thoth encourages you to look more closely at the octahedron. In fact, it is a mirror, a most powerful gateway. He asks you to stand within it. When you do so, you receive all the information present in the Cosmic Womb's Central Axis. As already depicted in the Cosmogony, the Central Axis contains all the data that further replicate and fractalise in the Cosmos. Indeed, you can compare it to a cosmic mainframe, which you now attune to.

To put it another way, this window of plasmic light initiates your body to hold the Cosmic Axis mainframe. With this in mind, your heart expands and deepens spirally. Even steps in your heart area appear at different levels. In fact, your heart takes on the same shape as the stepped Stargate of Hatshepsut, or conversely of the Step Pyramid at Saqqara. Meanwhile, within your heart gate, smaller octahedra appear. These are replicas of the window you are now in. These octahedra give your heart gate the same appearance as the gate with the semiprecious gems you have already experienced on Elephantine Island. It slowly becomes clear to you that all the initiations in previous temples have prepared you for this moment. Now you can carry the Cosmic Axis and all its wisdom within your own structure.

"Why is this happening?" you ask Thoth. He tells you to keep listening while the Light Being of our Cosmos tells you everything. Then you hear: these octahedra are the representations of all sixteen segments of this Cosmos. For this reason, each representation of the Star Council of Eight has two representatives. In due time, when each of the sixteen segments coincides with its respective cosmic mirror, the Cosmic Axis will dissolve and the herringbones will descend, bringing our Cosmos into full bloom, budding and ready to ascend into the Source Field and beyond.

As Cosmos Light Being has spoken, you feel all sixteen octahedron segments flowing into your body. They converge in your heart. As a result, you are transforming into a downwards cone, your head is on the flat base, and your pelvic floor represents the apex of your cone. All the incoming energy of cosmic golden stardust blends into your apex and fills you. Then the golden stardust spirals up your body. When it arrives at your head, your flat base aligns you with the mainframe of the Cosmic Axis. This alignment makes you shiver. You feel how the crystalline structures present in the Cosmic Axis (which reflect the sunlight from the bottom of a seabed) are restructuring you. The coral's trunk is now the outline of your body. In your body, you feel cosmic information. Being a hologram for this Cosmic Axis, you embody the cosmic mainframe attuning you perfectly to the harmonic resonance of our Cosmos. Henceforth, you represent its evolution.

Thoth says the process is incomplete. Seshat, his consort, is also present. She documents and stands at your side in her leopard dress. Seshat comforts you by saying you can do this. In addition, she lays her hand on the back of your neck to support you. More than anyone, she knows how difficult it is to tune in to these high-frequency energies. You allow both their hands to reinforce you while they are at your side. Now it becomes easier to ground these energies within your body.

At the same time, the cosmic mainframe energy sinks through your pelvic floor and down into your legs. These white crystalline energies are descending all the way down. Thoth shows that you must carry and embody this knowledge because it is necessary for the Earth to receive this energy. What the star people, the Earth, and all those involved in the Cosmic Ascension have been doing during all these millions of years is all about attuning the Earth to the evolution of the Cosmos. With this knowledge, you stand on your own. You are sovereign. You need not function under the umbrella of the Star Council of Eight. You will share this with others. In fact, in ancient times, people tuned in to this knowledge. In Egyptian times, the Maat energy allowed us to balance and live according to cosmic laws. At least, that was told. She attuned us to harmonic resonance but did not directly support the quantum ascension of the Cosmic Axis. Hence, it transcends all Egyptian rites of passage. Now we access the expanded Maat. You are outside the framework of time and space, of the hierarchy of suns and moons. There are only eight divine beings who carry this knowledge. The missing two represent the two golden orbs in Abu Simbel that were not finished.

As the initiation continues, you feel in your body the liquid light of the same texture as in this octahedron window. You have become the quantum point between the two cones. As soon as you breathe in that liquid light and exhale it, you perceive this field, being your body, as undulant. Your body has become this essence. You ask Thoth if this has anything to do with the Emerald Tablet. Thoth answers that yes, the Emerald Tablets are the foundation, yet this goes beyond. These are the shared Creation Codes for the Aquarian Age. The Star Council of Eight has again released them for humans to understand, tune in to, and co-create.

As you stand here, the contour lines of the Cosmic cone extend up-wards from this window. In the Cosmic cone itself, eight smaller di-amond Cosmic cones show and exchange information from the star constellations. When this cosmic information enters the Cosmic cone, it descends into its multilayered structure, comprising seven layers and the eight smaller diamond Cosmic cones. Furthermore, the information spreads from smaller Cosmic cone to smaller Cosmic cone. The golden stardust falls one layer deeper each time, to merge as golden stardust in the lowest point of the larger Cosmic cone. It then slides into the outline of the octahedron window towards Earth's cone. The cosmic sound resulting from this process is shrill and high.

From the circumference of Earth's cone, it descends further into the circumference of Earth's Stargate on the foundation plate. The golden stardust enters its flat base with its eight smaller diamond earth cones. Here it moves from smaller earth cone to smaller earth cone. All cones randomly exchange gold stardust with one another, assimilating the evolution of the Cosmic Axis. This precious information will enable the Earth to make a quantum leap. This is the difference between the Emerald Tablets, or the Maat, which represented a cosmic balance. Here is the information of stellar pathways that are the springboard to climb and ascend the Cosmic Axis. This window above the Abydos Temple provides this information for the Earth. It is not just about balance, which is a prerequisite. Now we go a step further and gain access to the Cosmic Ascension plan.

Who creates the cosmic springboards? Thoth answers that these are various stars or constellations coming together in different Star Councils, and each time a different constellation provides cosmic insights, teachings. If you tap in to those, you make a quantum leap. So the mechanism is to tap in to one's victories, knowledge, and wisdom, and use this momentum as a springboard to evolve at the same pace, side by side. These are the realities of the Light Beings of the Venus Light Path.

Once we all spiral upwards, like the golden dust whirling upwards, we reach the highest point of the Cosmos. It is knotted to contain the prevailing energies. In due time, when it unknots, the herringbones loosen and our Cosmos comes into bloom, opening its petals to reveal the accomplished Central Axis. The Star Council of Eight specialises in gathering information from all energies present in our Cosmos, including you, in imparting wisdom and knowledge so that all may benefit. By sharing cosmic information, we all work our way up, untie the cosmic knot, and depart. With all the information entering this

Earth Stargate, it brings the Earth into a transmutation process. The information stirs and shakes the Earth and you see the black energy transmuting everything, making the Earth even more crystalline. With each flow of information, black energy transmutation rings surround the Earth. These black transmutational rings magnetise and extract from the Earth what she no longer needs. They take from Earth what is no longer needed. It is a de-warping from matter to spirit.

The Creation of the Stargate predates the construction of the Abydos Temple. Even more, the Stargate does not even resonate with the temple. Due to this powerful energetic place, the temple site found her nestling. The Stargate energy is even discordant with the Abydos Temple. They are two different energies.

Hologram of the Flower of Life

The Flower of Life hologram, hangs from the top of the downwards cone of the Stargate of the Cosmic Axis, under the Abydos Temple. When you tune in to this Flower of Life, you can see the twenty-five intersections permeated by the diamond energies. Of the whole hologram, these intersections are the most important aspect of the Flower of Life Grid. They have the power to penetrate matter and break it down.

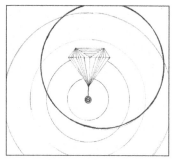

Illustration: Abydos Temple. Flower of Life Mother Hologram surrounding Earth's core.

The Flower of Life as a hologram is situated around Earth's seed of life. It thrives on the black essence of transmutation and shows you its multidimensional and fractal nature. From the mother hologram, infinite flowers of life sprout, creating infinite diamond-like intersections. They rise through Earth's body and travel through all Earth's dimensions towards the surface. The diamond essence cuts through the Earth body and gradually breaks material density down. The black essence transmutes from within Earth's Light Body into whatever density level it is in. This structure will leave the Earth with only a crystalline body, which will then unfold and dissolve.

Dismantling and dissolving dense matter into crystalline energy will allow the Earth to awaken her divine seed of life. Observe and allow these flowers of life to pass through all Earth's layers. You are witnessing a high intensity of purification. The flowers of life are emerging from the mother hologram surrounding Earth's core. The matter at this depth transmutes first, and dimensional space is created from within. Around Earth's core, her seed of life, an ever-expanding and enlarging aura of powerful white light grows. This white light veil also moves upwards from within Earth's surface. Its energy is high frequency, creating even more momentum in the transmutation process, accelerating time incrementally.

In essence, the flowers of life transmute matter. This transmuted high energy resulting from this process creates dimensional space in the form of high-frequency white light, which is constantly increasing. Moreover, the coefficient of the white light is considerably higher and helps with the further transmutation of the earthly body adjacent to this veil. So, the flowers of life do the preparatory work by breaking down matter and making it less dense. And the high-frequency light surrounding the earthly seed of life transmutes it into golden light and returns it to the Cosmic Womb. She gives her body back to the Cosmos, her Creational Mother.

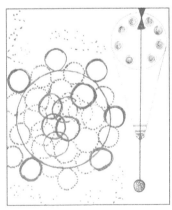

Illustration: Abydos Temple.
Flower of Life Hologram transmuting Earth's matter.

The Flower of Life is neither a pattern nor a grid: it can transmute matter. When this white light ascends from dimension to dimension, it dissolves the dimensions and unleashes the horizontal vibrational strings. These intertwine with the vertical vibrational strings, the first blueprint contours of the evolving seed of life. When these horizontal strings release, all dimensions collapse because there is no longer a grid to hold them within. Only vertical vibrational strings remain, which form the underlying structure of the interlocking herringbones of the Cosmos. Once all the horizontal woven strings dissolve and all the dimensions collapse, the herringbone will also loosen its latches. Just as we spoke of the Cosmos unravelling and unfolding its petals, so too the Earth's Central Axis will rise and blossom. An ultraviolet-coloured seed rises through its central passage, ready to be guided to its future incarnation.

Seven Solar Kingships

Illustration: Abydos Temple. Vaulted Chapels.

Abydos Temple emanates powerful bright light, projecting it outwards to the front where you stand. It also tries to project itself upwards, toward the Cosmos. Curious about this bluish essence light, you decide to enter to find out from where this light originates. The Abydos Light Being calls you, pulling you in. You speed up your pace. As you enter the sacred grounds, Abydos Light Being guides you towards the seven vaulted chapels from where the blueish essence light seems to radiate. She telepathically shows you that this light desires to revert upwards toward the Cosmos.

When you stand before the temple, the light radiates upon you to call you forth. It requires your co-Creation as Sacred Architect. So, you now turn to the first vaulted chapel. Strangely enough, while you are there, this blue essence light does not originate from these vaulted chapels either. This space is empty. However, there seems to be blue essence light piercing through these walls. So, it must come from behind them. You project yourself behind the walls of the vaulted chapels, and from there, Abydos Light Being leads you deep into the Earth towards the temple's foundation. The blue essence light bundles itself into a ray of light enveloping you and descends into its profound foundation. In your descent, you drop your consciousness into the Earth. However, with part of your consciousness, you also remain at the surface to understand what happens. Here you see the blue essence light has disappeared, withdrawn into the Earth. You are now all set to co-create. You hear sounds of heavy doors and locks opening and closing. These must be the energies of the vaulted chapels, providing access to something in Earth's core. Now it becomes clear to you that the actual three-dimensional vaulted chapels merely represent the multiple Inner Earth Chambers through which you travel and upon which the Temple of Abydos rests.

With each level you descend, you hear heavy locks opening and closing again: opening to provide access into the lower one, closing as the upper one closes to prevent unwanted visitors. You descend vault after vault after vault until you arrive at a circular pit. Once you have entirely dropped, you become aware you have been spinning during your descent. The spinning motion gradually subsides, allowing you to find your stillness. All around you is dark and damp. You do not know where you are. You ask Abydos Light Being to guide you. Immediately, your attention is drawn to the Star Council of Eight, with whom Abydos Light Being co-creates and always has co-created. To connect with you, all the sixteen representatives surround you in this Inner Earth space. They telepathically explain and initiate you in preparation for what is coming. Three out of eight representations of the Star Council of Eight position themselves behind you, and five place themselves in front of you. You are lined up as the fourth representation, and they ask you to attune to themselves.

As you undergo this line-up initiation, you feel your etheric hip area detaches itself from your etheric upper body. Your etheric lower body moves to the front of the line. The first representation situated there infuses energy into your etheric lower body. Then the second representation infuses energy into your hip area. Followed by the third, fourth, and fifth representations, and so on. Your structure seems to imbue itself with the energy of all sixteen representatives. Now this part of your body finds itself again before you. It asks you to do the same thing. So, you transmit your essence to your etheric lower body. And then, to complete the cycle, it conveys essence to the three last representatives behind you.

As your body parts merge again, you embody the energy of the Star Council of Eight. Here you stand, greater than ever imaginable, you rise, piercing Earth's surface, transcending the Cosmic Abydos Stargate, and aligning your crown with its centre to penetrate it as well. As you do, the energies of all constellations interconnected with the Star Council of Eight pervade your body and bestow their codes of light upon you. You reach the Light of *All That Is*, and it endows you with a crown of its essence. You wear a Solar Crown for the first time. All the Light Beings related to the seven vaulted chapels appear before you in your mind's eye. You see King Seti, Ptah, Re-Horakhty, Amun-Re, Osiris, Isis, and Horus. They all embody the same solar essence and wear the Solar Crown. They were all initiated into the highest level of Solar Kingship. They all govern the Earth through the pure essence of their hearts and in co-Creation with Amun Ra's light. You realise you represent the channel transmitting light codes of all constellations of Abydos Stargate to permeate the Earth. The above becomes the below as all starlight codes percolate through you and imbue the Earth Abydos Stargate and its eight diamonds.

Each diamond in the Earth Cone of Abydos Stargate resonates with specific constellations. As they receive the starlight codes of respective constellations, they ignite and power themselves with them. Each diamond within the Earth Cone of Abydos Stargate has several multidimensional layers. The starlight codes permeate all layers and fully activate each diamond. Each diamond is responsible for radiating its starlight codes throughout the Nile Valley, and beyond. The Solar Kingship represented in the vaulted chapels embodies solar governance. They were and continue to be conduits for the Star Beings of the Star Council of Eight to make their starlight codes tangible and applicable on Earth.

The upper structure of the Earth Cone of Abydos Stargate, comprising several layers, begins to move. The various layers rotate upon one another, initiating a deepening towards the diamond's lower part. This part of the diamond is the alchemical cauldron where all starlight codes of respective constellations merge, recode, and imprint to serve the Earth. The rotating layers stimulate the essence fused below to rise to the surface of the Earth Abydos Stargate. As the upper part of each diamond begins to rotate, the more deeply fused essence rises and becomes accessible. As it rises through the surface of the foundation of the Abydos Temple, it permeates all the pillars in the halls, which become conduits for these starlight codes. They ignite again into pillars of light.

The alchemised starlight codes rise through the Light Pillars and the temple itself, evaporating, undulating, and soaking all the walls harmoniously. The starlight codes take the form of an orange essence light. All the Light Pillars imbue themselves with this orange essence, and so do you. Now you also discern that each pillar comprises cones clustered in a string shape. These cones rotate clockwise and counter clockwise, igniting and further opening themselves because they were dormant for so long. All these pillars rekindle and breathe again. The entire Abydos Temple breathes and pulses gently. A subtle vibration is apparent as the energetic blueprint of Abydos undergoes a cellular restructuring of its crystalline energies and its light essence. A reformation occurs also of the Abydos foundation plate. The latter energetically is composed of three rectangular layers. These decrease in size as you descend. The deepest layer represents a downwards-facing four-sided pyramid.

Truly, the power of this pyramid is not comparable to its size, for it bundles within the entire Abydos light structure in merely one ray. Then the pyramid radiates the bundled Abydos Light essence up through the centre of the Cosmic Abydos Stargate. There it seeps into the circular disc. Abydos Light essence pervades the whole circular disc and fuses with the Star Council of Eight's essences. New upgrades ignite the Now-dispersed Abydos Light essence. This Cosmic Abydos Stargate is a cosmic alchemical cauldron in which Creation occurs. Once the Star Council of Eight has given their starlight codes to the dispersed ray of light, a swirling clockwise motion restructures and reorganises the Abydos blueprint throughout this entire Cosmic Abydos Stargate. Following motion creates a new blueprint, forming all the encoded clusters. Now, the light essence of Abydos Temple is ready to descend again. Finally, the Star Council of Eight sends the Abydos Light essence back through the Cosmic Abydos Stargate to where the apexes of the two cones meet. There the essence of the diamond shape adds itself, merging with and claying the Abydos blueprint into a seed. This *One Cosmic Seed* descends further into the three-dimensional realm piercing Abydos foundation. It nestles into the small downwards pyramid. Here the *One Cosmic Seed* integrates.

Soon, a beautiful white-yellow flowered pattern unfolds into existence. It contains numerous spheres within. Abydos nestles in a colossal Flower of Life sphere containing the Path of the Venus Light's white-yellow essence.

The spherical Flower of Life stimulates the replication of the essence within the Abydos Temple. This initiation's blueprint carves into the walls of the Osirian Temple. Physical representations are often a reminder of the true essence a temple embodies. You witness how this beautiful spherical Flower of Life develops from the centre where the Star Council of Eight planted the *One Cosmic Seed*. Golden essence light emerges and fills the outlines of each of the nineteen spheres within this larger sphere. The golden essence imbues every outline of all nineteen spheres within this Flower of Life. Simultaneously, as this expansion occurs, the spherical Flower of Life envelops the entire Earth.

The Temple of Abydos physically represents the Earth body integrating its spheres into Inner Earth and enveloping the Earth as a grid.

This sacred geometric reorganisation is perfect. It complies with the primaeval blueprint of the Earth. It represents the pure Earth's blueprint when she birthed herself into existence. The Earth regained her original blueprint, not just as a grid on the upper structure, but also as an internal geometric structure.

As the entire Earth body reorganises, it also repositions itself to gain a stable, autonomous balance within the solar system. The Earth also experiences a shift in sovereign awareness. Although she is physically orbiting the Sun, she seems to reorient her consciousness towards herself as Earth Star. In her perception, she no longer resonates with a revolution around the Sun. She instead embodies the energy of a star. By doing so, she creates a pattern around herself of the One Divine Spark. She creates spiral arms. These fan out from her core into all the other multidimensional spheres she embodies. She imprints herself as a star having an entire system of stars, planets, and moons orbiting her. By imprinting her new *blueprint as an Earth Star*, she shifted the timeline from a planet to a star, bridging her existence and embodying Star Consciousness. All future celestial beings in each of her spiral arms – suns, planets, and moons – she already invited. She also created their blueprints. She called for all the Light Beings who desire to embody in her Light Body structure on the spiral arms forming her new structure.

You now witness her white-yellow light essence stretching, becoming elliptic. This elliptical motion invites her to construct her Cosmic Axis. This Cosmic Axis is a replication of the Axis Mundi. When she replicates this structure within herself, she enables herself to resonate with the Cosmic Axis at every given moment. By doing so, she will always resonate with the evolutionary path of the Cosmic Womb. She envisions fusing with the Cosmic Axis and fuses her structure at the same pace prevailing in the Cosmic Womb. By applying the *harmonic resonance* of Cosmic Ascension, she completes her blueprint when the Cosmic Womb fuses into One Golden Light Being, as seen in the Cosmogony.

This *harmonic resonance* and cosmic perfection is the holiest initiation you have ever witnessed. The sacredness of Earth's love for *All That Is* overwhelms you. The cosmic intelligence operating through the cosmic blueprint is beyond words. All this, imprinted by the Star Council of Eight, is within this *One Cosmic Seed,* which contained the Abydos reorganisation, the cosmic reorganisation of Earth as a Star in *harmonic resonance* and sacred union with the ascending Cosmos.

All starlight codes are active, installed. The golden essence in the Flower of Life's spheres restructures Inner Earth, percolating through her, powering her. She is a complete and uttermost beautiful potent being of light, omniscient and all-encompassing. As for you, you have completed your role of Solar Kingship because each period required an update. Those who knew represent these vaulted chapels as the Star Council of Eight. You represent the earthly eight giving access to a central Ennead sphere, a passageway for humans to move at the same pace with the Earth Star.

All is perfect. Close your eyes and surrender. You fully understand in all the cells of your body that the Earth nurtures and takes care of you, that she makes sure that you evolve as you need to with the Star Council of Eight's co-creative help. You are part of her divine blueprint as co-creator, as her friend, because your heart resonates with hers. Divine Love thrives within you, connecting you, bringing you into sacred union.

Now that the Abydos Earth Stargate has reignited, a thorough process can occur, enabling the Earth to ascend completely. We can depart from our bodies and move on. The way we ascend makes a difference and enables us to achieve Cosmic Ascension. It is the quality and the perfection in which we evolve that is of importance. If we move in *harmonic resonance,* we are complete, whole. However, we are not always in *harmonic resonance.* Even so, it is what we should envision.

At last, you return to your three-dimensional form and stand again before these seven vaulted chapels. While you walk through these spaces, you touch them. Each vaulted chapel whispers the pearls of wisdom of the Light Being embodying Solar Kingship. You honour each of them. You are now part of them, interconnected. You form an earthly Star Council of Eight, representing the cosmic Star Council of Eight.

It is an honour and a gift to be a member of this earthly Star Council of Eight.

You behold these seven vaulted chapels. You thank them as they welcome you into their lives, and you include them into your life.

The Abydos Light Being is with you. She holds her etheric hand on your shoulder. She blesses you. You feel emotionally moved. She senses your emotions and stands by you to comfort you as a mother comforts a child. When you have allowed and accepted this great honour into your heart, she will guide you out.

Your life will continue, but it will never be the same. Abydos Light Being endowed you with Solar Kingship. You are a co-creator of the Earth. As you walk out, Abydos Light Being says goodbye. She says, "I will be in your heart at all times. I am here in my temple and within you." As you walk, observe the palms of your hands. White-yellow essence light emanates from them in the forms of butterflies fluttering up and circling you. They are creating a DNA-strand pattern slowly descending and integrating into your energy body. You feel a need to stop. When you look back, you see Abydos Light Being standing before the temple.

In your bones, down to the very marrow, you are integrating her essence. As a result, you embody the essence of the Abydos Temple. By doing so, you understand you will co-create with her eternally, wherever you are, in this incarnation and all embodiments to come. This rite of passage symbolises Oneness, interconnectedness, *harmonic resonance*, the Hermetic Principle of the within and without. You have come into sacred union with Abydos Light Being. She asks you to be mindful, for you are an extension of her. You both know in your hearts you will be. Otherwise, this divine gift would have never occurred. As you acknowledge her, you send from your heart a white-yellow ray of light, confirming to her you will be as mindful as all seven other Solar Kingships who have preceded you.

"Thank you," she says.

Solar Kingship Initiation

Here you stand in front of Abydos Temple. You are somehow hesitant to enter these sacred grounds. An inner voice invites you to turn inwards for a moment. As soon as your gaze turns inwards, a gush of calmness and inner peace wells up. You understand this specific initiation requires you to be sensitively attuned to the energies to come. You focus on your Central Axis, feeling blocking energies on your free will, your free choice. These must dissolve to attain access to higher levels of consciousness. You deeply inhale, exhale. You envision your Central Axis as an upwards-unfolding Jacob's Ladder. The three-dimensional part of your cosmic Jacob's Ladder you are dwelling in needs to be liberated from the lack of freedom, the lack of choice, so you can connect to your higher soul levels.

Immediately you feel Abydos Light Being responding to these words. From a distance, her essence emerges as a bright light tuning in to you, radiating into you, helping you dissolve these blockings. The initiation to come requires you to sense freedom and clear access your cosmic Jacob's Ladder, your soul structure. Then you will welcome into your three-dimensional reality all the essences of your higher dimensional selves. For now, you bathe in the light which Abydos Light Being radiates upon you. You enjoy receiving it, feeling how it is to be cared for. Soon an orb of white light envelops you as if she has projected her essence upon you to dissolve all that inhibits you from accessing all codes this initiation will offer you. Increasingly attuned, your vibration immediately entrains with hers, perfectly in phase, perfectly equalised. At that moment, a portal . . . opens . . . allowing you to access the Abydos Temple.

You begin walking. Upon entering the portal, you take in the majestic colonnades, pervasive, mysterious energies in this sanctuary . . . time stands still. All these divine beings are ever-present, imbued within these walls, vibrantly alive. The voices of temple creatures guide you through the shrine to where Thoth and Seshat's energies await you.

Their hieroglyphs are present on almost every wall, Thoth scribing and Seshat at his side. He tells you all your actions will be accurately scribed. Walking between these pillars almost seems as if walking a pilgrimage trail allowing you to become initiated and cleansed. You continue towards the central hallway. Somewhere halfway an etheric breeze, divinely instructed, nudges you to the left side, where the seven vaulted chapels reside. You are guided to start with the chapel of King Seti. While you approach, the presence of the Light Beings of all the other seven chapels surrounds you.

Illustration: Thoth Hermes Trismegistus and Seshat.

You enter the first chapel, strangely void, sounds seeming of underwater vibrations, essences of waters omnipresent. An etheric drop of water envelops, repositions, continuously searching out the most central place, aligning with the energy of the ensemble of all chapels present.

A direct line points forward, connecting all seven chapels with you. All is set. Your initiation begins.

You know you are to raise these seven vaulted chapels within your structure, more specifically within your spine, as if remembering your very self. The energy of Osiris is present. Golden liquid light fills your spinal column. With your mind's eye, you observe all vertebrae tilting inwards, towards the spinal column. Your attention is drawn to them, and through this, you understand this positioning must change.

As you stand here in the vaulted chapel of King Seti, you feel the first vertebra resonating, opening horizontally, sonic petals of a blooming flower. As it orients outwards, golden liquid light flows via the vaulted chapel, permeating the vertebra, percolating into your tailbone. The point of your tailbone receives lubrication. Instantly from your tail-bone, the golden liquid light projects upwards into your thirty-third dimension. Abydos Light Being has now set the blueprint of this initiation ignited within you.

King Seti is here, beside you, in the first vaulted chapel. With his hands, he magnetises the first vertebra, providing warmth and security. Your vertebra feels relaxed and opens fully, as does your entire Cosmic Axis. Energy surges upwards, encompassing your entire Cosmic Axis, then surges downwards, integrating the Cosmic Axis essence within your first vertebra, then essence descends further into your tailbone. You witness many golden rings installing themselves around your spinal column, holding within the essence of your Cosmic Axis. The golden rings move in upwards and downwards movements, magnetising the lower part of your spinal column. When the calibration completes, the rings position themselves again at their rightful positions along the spinal column. A spinal column of golden rings comes into existence, and your spine aligns with this golden column of light. Each vertebra stretches to match the golden ring it resonates within, simultaneously stretching and enlarging your spinal column.

King Seti, with his attention on your spine, shows you a cross-polli-nation between all your vertebrae. When golden liquid light exchang-es itself between vertebrae, they increase in width, increasing each vertebra's dimensional space. In each vertebra, a multidimensional structure unfolds. Each vertebra carries within itself the essence of all thirty-three. The multidimensionality in your spine activates. Each vertebra has all your dimensions within. As a single vertebra, simultaneously, it represents the whole. You embody the *I Am that I Am.* This multidimensional energy enables you to live your dimensionality with ease and grace. A multidimensional life becomes second nature. You thank King Seti for deepening this initiation into the cellular structure of your body.

The second vaulted chapel presents itself to you. Ptah[37] stands at your side. With both of his hands, he magnetises the second vertebra of your spine. It also opens fully, allowing the golden liquid light to permeate the vertebra itself. A replication of the golden rings in the outer structure surrounding your spine is now also visible within. From within yourself, Ptah ignites fractal procreation. By resonating with your external environment and replicating its codes within you where appropriate, you will always evolve at the same pace as the Cosmos. Your body becomes a reflection of what happens outside of you. You are *the embodiment of As Within, So Without.* Ptah adds, saying, "The construction of your light-body structure as an incarnated human being will automatically update and upgrade according to cosmic evolution. You find yourself continuously on my potter's wheel."

You thank Ptah for igniting the cosmic evolution within.

The Light Being of the Third Vaulted Chapel calls you. Re-Horakhty is present with his two hands, magnetising the third vertebra. As he lays his hands around your vertebra, etheric veils unfold. The vertebra becomes a fairy lotus with soft etheric petals fluttering and floating. The softness, gentleness, and lightness are alluring, the slow, harmonious motion resembling jellyfish tentacles afloat in softly undulant waters, your vertebra responding instantly to the slightest energetic currents, like the feather of Maat responding to the slightest whispers of change in the surroundings. This light essence aligns your crown with your

---

37 Ptah, the Master Builder. In the triad of Memphis, he is the husband of Sekhmet and the father of Nefertem. Ptah is an Egyptian creator God who is said to have existed before all other things. He designed the world and brought it into being by the creative power of the word, according to his heart's design.

forehead, pineal gland, throat, heart, solar plexus, belly, and pelvic floor. It then retreats inwards and integrates into your body. Now you can just *be*. You can surrender and move with all vibrations, responding in sublime surrenderings. The Re-Horakhty initiation allows you to evolve at the same pace with evolution. He emphasises you become *One with All That Is*, because the essence you float within is the cosmic grid. It allows you to dissolve fully and to become One with your environment. This essence permeates each vertebra in your spinal column.

You thank Re-Horakty for igniting the Oneness with All That is within you.

The fourth vaulted chapel is that of Amun Ra. As his light envelops your fourth vertebra, the Hathor are also present with their sacred vibrational sounds. Using sound strings, they assist in opening the vertebra. As the vertebra resonates with the vibrational tones, two multidimensional layers are already emerging from within. The vertebra continues opening and unveiling other layers, limitlessly, a Thousand-Petalled Lotus ever-blooming. Amun Ra exclaims you have embodied Amun Ra's light, thus, this multidimensional divine structure. Your spinal column shows an extensive expansion already present. He and the Hathor now replicate that expansion into the other vertebrae. The same profound structure becomes visible there as well. Because of this, you deepen into your cellular structure, your *Pillar of Light*.

You thank Amun Ra for deepening your Pillar of Light within you.

The fifth vaulted chapel beckons. Osiris awaits. As soon as you enter, he lays his hands around you and attunes himself to your fifth vertebra. He calls forth the essence of the Tree of Life and its cosmic counterpart, the Jacobs 'Ladder, with its deep roots in the Cosmic Womb. He calls upon its essence to ignite within yourself eternal life throughout all embodiments. The essence offers you a safe passage from one embodiment to another, allowing your whole soul essence to travel with you. You will always be One, throughout incarnations, without ever leaving behind your energy signature codes. Osiris shows you that in your Tree of Life, you find yourself in the trunk. From here, you reach out to all the realms contained within, as they are your soul extensions.

Then, from the One divine spark positioned in the trunk of the Jacobs' Ladder, you draw to yourself the aspects of your soul extensions that are important. This enables you to integrate your soul extensions back into your own structure. You bring them home. You are a sovereign master of your own multidimensionality. The essence of Osiris replicates itself in all other vertebrae.

You thank Osiris for igniting and deepening your Tree of Life and your Jacob's Ladder within you.

Isis, in the sixth vaulted chapel, magnetises the sixth vertebra. She wishes to model with the prima mater of your essence. She creates from your energetic clay, the inner Divine Child. She is the Divine Mother. She explains you can embody this attribute of divine motherhood only if you feel your Divine Child within. Only then do you experience the vulnerability, the love of your inner Divine Child. You resonate in the outer world with all beings on Earth. For a Divine Mother, the Earth is inclusive. You see the love, strength, and vulnerability of all surrounding you and live accordingly, with thoughtfulness. The essence replicates itself in all vertebrae.

You thank Isis for igniting the Divine Child within you.

Last, Horus welcomes you in the seventh vaulted chapel. His hands surround your seventh vertebra. With his beak, he carves into this vertebra the all-seeing falcon eye – the *Eye of Horus-Ra*. The shape looks like that of a daffodil. Your carved *Eye of Horus-Ra* points upwards to the Cosmos. It oversees All That Is, all stellar connections, stellar vibrations, and stellar pathways and their intersections. These intersections are high-frequency cosmic hotspots where energy merges. Here, often we see blue sun energies coming into existence. The *Eye of Horus-Ra* also allows you to see the multi-layered structure of the Cosmos, built almost atom-wise. You now witness the herringbone structure of the Cosmos. You then travel brilliantly, using these pathways, hovering on cosmic currents. As you pass through, you imbue their light codes in your Light Body, as you did in Anubia. This gift replicates her essence in all these other vertebrae.

You thank Horus for igniting the Eye of Horus-Ra within you.

The additional twenty-six vertebrae build upon themselves and cross-pollinate. They interconnect and build your etheric structure, remembering all your core qualities to embody your Solar Kingship. They are about sacred geometry, aligning with the cosmic, being a mirror of the cosmic. All these vertebrae enable you to incorporate the divine potentials characterising you as a soul and integrating them into your earthly existence.

As Within So Without. As Above, So Below is the overarching Hermetic Principle. The upper twenty-six vertebrae now fold back down onto you in a double layer, onto the vertebrae or golden rings one to seven. All these essences to embody the Solar Kingship can now cultivate and deepen within you.

You thank all Light Beings embodying Solar Kingship for having initiated you. You thank all other Light Beings present for their support as sacred witnesses.

Initiation: Moon Disc

The Moon Disc shows cycles as multidimensional. A cycle evolves from New Moon to Full Moon and through the third quarter back to the New Moon. In a moon cycle, you ascend from matter to spirit or descend from spirit to matter. Both are important and trigger a new process and allow us to fine tune our soul essence. One can feel more pleasant than the other but both have the same effect: to come into Oneness. When we embody a new phase in New Moon, we move through the moon cycle, and we embody the seed the New Moon holds. The Moon Disc, carried by many ancient deities, represents the moon cycle. Through the Moon Disc, we carry this cycle within our heart sphere, consecrated as a Birth Gate: Our Diamond Heart. The latter allows us to create ascension and descension processes.

The Moon Disc describes the beginning and the end. You are the link between them. You are the initiator of the beginning and the end – the point where the tail and head of the feathered serpent[38] meet. Here at the quantum point, you abide, holding quantum energies of Creation that race through the cycle of Creation. The cycle of birth. The moon cycle.

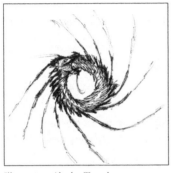

Illustration: Abydos Temple.
The Ouroboros.

In essence, the Moon Disc is concerned with creating. As you create, you embody the gift of opening the seed. You are the opener of the seed, the opener of the path allowing the seed's development into its full potential. The seeds are sown and given life force. This impulse of Creation is very much connected to the Omega Ω, which provides sacred geometry, structure, essence, and sound allowing Creation to blossom and open fully.

With each further opening of the seed, this awakening Creation absorbs the Light of Amun Ra even more deeply. In this process, the Alpha α and the Omega Ω fuse their essences. Only then can you experience bliss. One cannot sense it before. There will always be lack, sadness, and meaninglessness until you reach a point where you expand to your full potential. Only then will you dance in the Light of Amun Ra.

Amun the Omega Ω and Ra the Alpha α coming together allow you to experience the Eternal Bliss of Life.

---

38 The name Ouroboros comes means *tail-eater*. As an alchemical symbol and one of the oldest mythical symbols in the world, it It is found in Aztec myth, Chinese myth, and numerous others. It depicts a snake or dragon biting its own tail to create an eternal circle. It symbolises the cyclical nature of nature, its eternal return, and the unity of everything.

Part III

Full Moon

III.1 Temple of The Infinite Creator, The Great Pyramid, Giza

Illustration: The Great Pyramid.

The Great Pyramid of Khufu at Giza is closed off in its vertical axis from the Earth and Cosmos, thus holding energy endlessly as it pulsates with a gust of sadness from within. It has been in this state of being for thousands of years, neither surrendering nor letting go. However, this purification is necessary to complete an old phase and usher in a new beginning. This energy trail translates into the waters under the Giza plateau. They are stagnant and do not flow into the Nile valley to transmit the light codes.

Silent, and for thousands of years awaiting those who have eyes to see, the Thousand Petal Lotus longs to burst forth, to invite the cosmic sky and its energies to flow through her body again. She longs for the Divine Light to envelope her. She longs to interact again with Cosmos and Earth. She feels as much as we do: it is time to give birth to a divine Earth, a Garden of Eden.

The Infinite Creator. Moon and Sun Fusion.

The Light Beings of the Pyramids of Khufu, Khafre, and Menkaure are present. Their underground structures, their three respective earth pyramids, perfectly reflect their overlying solar structures.

Thoth asks you to attune to the underground pyramid ensemble uniting for this transmission. Open your heart gate to connect and be the sacred witness to this sacred initiation. You now hold the underground triad structure in your energy field. You see how the solar and earth pyramids separate from one another. As these two octahedra separate and dissolve, you see each carries in its inner structure a cylindrical column of light. We will refer to these as Pillars of Light. These three Pillars of Light connect, carrying important values within themselves. In the upper part of the Pillar of Light abides the solar energy of Ra, in the lower, the lunar energy of Amun. The solar and lunar energies merge, uniting light and dark, divine masculine and feminine energies. When they come into Oneness, the Light of Amun Ra ignites. The divine feminine and masculine reinforce one another and significantly raise one another's vibrations.

You extend your hand to the three bright Pillars of Light as they invite you to receive their energies. From them, a yellow string of light enters

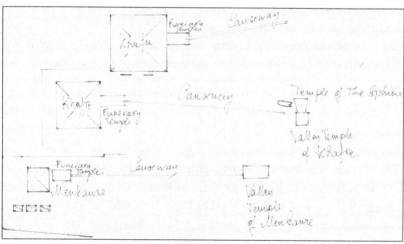

Illustration: Map of Giza Plateau.

your left hand, moving toward your heart, enveloping it like a vein. A vein system of yellow light surrounds your heart and fuses divine feminine and masculine energies, solar and lunar energies. The yellow-light vein weaves from the left to the right side of the heart, encompassing the whole. The arteries continue to proliferate, the network moving to your arms and hands. The fusion of energies entering you stirs up your entire body and activates your pelvic floor. Old energies testifying you would not be powerful enough to live up to your divine potential on Earth are now dissolving. Your bones and bone marrow also require cleansing.

From this alchemical process arises your Pillar of Light, the fourth Pillar in this present structure. Your Pillar of Light contains the perfect balance of lunar and solar energies, enabling you to embody your Divine Creation. The lunar energy brings about a never-ending Creation, showing us the same pattern of a Thousand-Petal Lotus always blooming. Both energies come together harmoniously, perfectly balanced. They teach you to balance your divine feminine and masculine energies. The feminine energies ignite a blooming process, the masculine energies a nurturing one. To create infinitely, you must maintain this balance.

The three Pyramidal Light Beings observe you, satisfied with this work. Whatever energies you manifest in this world, the underlying rule is to embody solar and lunar energies to manifest your full potential. You now have these energies in balance and can create with ease and grace, in never-ending alignment with Amun Ra. "This wisdom is also scribed in the Scrolls of Truth of our beloved Maat," says Thoth.

Throughout Egypt, you have temples dedicated to Amun Ra, mainly above ground, and in some temples, we descend underground for the lunar aspect. Here at Giza, both consolidate and find balance. You can initiate or activate a Moon or Sun Disc, but if they lack balance, you, as a creator, will not create with abundance, and the Creational flow will stop. Because either there will be too many seeds unlocked and not enough solar codes to nourish them, or there will be too many solar codes and not enough seeds unlocked. In the latter case, all those codes are at a loss.

Even if you know you are doing great things, you must maintain balance. That is why they call it the Scrolls of Maat, a Pillar of Truth. It is all about balance: allowing infinite and Divine Creation to take place. These are the codes for the Garden of Eden, the Codes of Abundance, growth, prosperity, and love. We achieve these only through balance.

Thousand Petal Lotus
Receiving your Divine Potential

You witness the Great Pyramid of Khufu. Halfway up the pyramid, light-blue ethereal rings constantly move towards the top and purify the energy. The lower part of the pyramid becomes heavy as silvery old energies accumulate there. All four sides of the pyramid unfold, and the energy flows away. Now, the top and the ground are visible, but the first half of the pyramid is transparent and flows empty. Then, the top part and now even the whole pyramid dissolves. What remains is an ethereal outline of a cone. This cone shape represents a vibrational birthing chamber resting on the Great Pyramid's blueprint, restructuring it into higher frequency and vibrational architecture. Red vibrational strings move up along the cone, to the top. From all sides, the red strings resembling branches, rise to create a large grid that then closes off this cone.

The cone now retreats into the pyramid's outline and around its Central Axis. An ever-opening kaleidoscope comes into being, constantly distorting the four sides, each time providing deeper and deeper access to the downward-facing earth cone to reach its full capacity. Then the pyramid can download the frequencies of the star to which the Great Pyramid was aligned. Shrill sounds resound as it aligns with the respective star.

As a result, the Great Pyramid straightens its backbone. All the upper dimensions of this pyramid collapse and slide down around its Central Axis. This kaleidoscope of the four sides of the pyramid deepening and expanding fractally represents all the petals of the Thousand Petal Lotus. So, by deepening into the earth cone, the higher dimensional structures of the Pyramid of Giza become activated in each dimension.

The corresponding dimensional Lotus present there reads the corresponding light temple, then also descends along the Central Axis. As a layer of petals, it settles into our third dimension. This is the Thousand-Petal Lotus descending. Its layers slide down onto the foundation of the Great Pyramid. All the interdimensional light temples of the Pyramid are unfolding, now within three-dimensional reach. The last upper temple contains a golden seed. Through the Central Axis of the Great Pyramid, the golden seed descends and solemnly installs itself within the core of this Thousand-Petal Lotus, which morphs into a Golden Lotus. The Golden Lotus radiates white light, with all the interdimensional petal layers rotating independently of one another. This rotation stirs the Nile Temple Body as all energies in the area undergo this rotational movement. The Thousand-Petal Lotus breaks open the etheric fabric in our three-dimensional reality in Egypt, making matter more ethereal, increasing the light coefficient, and creating dimensional space for each Creational Nile Temple. In response, each Creational Nile Temple activates the descent of its own interdimensional light temples, and the upper golden seed also descends. This Golden Lotus on the Great Pyramid of Giza represents the crown within the Tree of Life. The Nile represents the central pillar, and the banks of the Nile the left and right pillars.

All golden seeds, divine sparks from all the Creational Nile Temples descend into the respective temples and merge with the three-dimensional temple seeds present in the Holy of Holies. The cosmic mirror of the upper seed and the three-dimensional temple seed fuse, giving the temple back its divine potential. All these Golden Lotuses rotate, setting the Nile aswirl. Abu Simbel pushes the energies upwards, and the Great Pyramid of Giza pushes the energies downwards to deepen this process even more towards Earth's core. The Nile, as the Cosmic Axis of the Cosmos, coincides and merges with the Central Axis of the Earth. This process allows the Earth to merge and align with the Cosmic Axis. The Great Pyramid of Giza and Abu Simbel provide a deepening. It brings the energy of the Nile closer to the Central Axis of the Earth. The Central Axis of the Earth coincides with the Central Axis of the Tree of Life. It is ready to slide into the larger part of Jacob's Ladder: the Axis Mundi, the Central Axis of the Cosmos.

Illustration: The Pyramid of Khufu. The Thousand Petal Lotus.

Creator Beyond Space and Time

The green essence light of Abu Simbel is also present within the Great Pyramid, surrounding its Central Axis and imbuing its foundation plate with light. The Great Pyramid Light Being invites you to step into this green essence light ray to consolidate the Within and the Without. You walk towards the Great Pyramid, and once you enter the sacred pyramid field, it feels vast, as if space does not exist. There is this one pillar of green essence light and the nothingness, the void. This sensation feels holy. You feel you are all that matters. This experience is only and uniquely for you.

You approach the green essence and slide your hand through it. The Great Pyramid Light Being giggles. It makes you laugh as well. You ask permission to enter. She consents. You take the first step into this emerald field. Soon you know the outline comprises at least seven layers. You find yourself in this first layer, within the central pillars' outlines. In front of you is the membrane of the second layer. You touch it. It is plasma morphing and moving its essence according to the movement you induce.

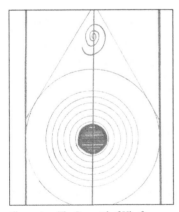

Illustration: The Pyramid of Khufu.
The Cosmic Ancient Rite of Passage.

The molecular structure of your body has changed. It has straightened you out, repositioned you. Now, this plasma membrane opens like a gate, and you move through, entering the second layer, where you enter an unknown world. The rose essence is omnipresent, and gravity no longer exists. You float and spin around your axis. The Great Pyramid's Light Being is delighted. You surrender to the Now. The spinning motion with rose essence also prepares you as these strings of light weave themselves around your Central Axis, redefining, imprinting, and encoding it. The Great Pyramid Light Being initiates you in the divine potential of the Pyramid, so you embody her ability to work with stellar consciousness.

Your etheric structure is now being prepared for that to happen. You will become One with the Great Pyramid's Light Being and embody her divine potential. Soon, the weaving of rose essence strings completes. They consolidate and create a solid structure around you. Then you bring your consciousness again within the Great Pyramid, in this second layer. You get back on your feet, and the membrane of the third layer opens.

Upon entering the third layer, at your feet you perceive black liquid of a thick substance. This black liquid substance is alive as it sloshes against your feet with its body. Clearly, it wants to tell you something. So, you decide to act on it and walk in the direction it urges you to. It asks you to circle this third layer seven times. You walk in circles seven times through this layer in the Central Axis of the Great Pyramid.

By doing so, you have created the geometrical cone shape comprising this black essence. You have ignited an initiation chamber with the same functionality as the sarcophagus of the King's Chamber in the Great Pyramid. You move to the cone's apex and align with its energy, feeling safe and nurtured. The energy is soft, the Great Pyramid Light Being respects your rhythm and approaches you. Black essence strings spiral downwards from the cone's apex and encircle you. In your mind's eye, Osiris reveals himself. He recounts having undergone the same initiation.

The black essence strings consolidate into your energy body around the rose essence. You embody cosmic essence. When it merges around your spinal column, its essence becomes granular. The grains are golden nuggets and breathe and pulse gently. You come to understand that you embodied the Cosmic Light Being of our Cosmic Womb as its breath resonates within you. You softly pulse, resonating the cosmic breath of Cosmos Light Being.

As you allow this breath, two golden clusters emerge within you. They open, transforming themselves from crystallised to golden liquid light, flooding the black essence that has consolidated around you. The golden liquid light activates as you perceive shimmering lights. While it is working within you, the stellar paths, and their intersections in the Cosmos replicate within you. You also recognise the herringbone structure. To your astonishment, the entire structure of the Cosmos replicates itself within you. All intersections, as converging high-energy spots, find themselves now within you. You embody this cosmic system in ever-changing motion.

Osiris says, "If you want to know how it functions on a cosmic scale, you must first embody it. If you want to work with temples and represent cosmic energies, you must first embody the overall structure. You need to understand them and the vastness in the overarching totality and allow them to operate fully."

We move to an area that goes beyond astrology. This is about cosmic architecture and applying it on Earth to work with light temples. The whole cosmic structure that has unfolded within you is now coalescing and consolidating as golden liquid light, as one central string into your Central Axis. This golden string is the first layer within you, offering you an overarching perspective. You operate from an overarching principle. As we come to an end, all pearls of wisdom implode within your heart.

The membrane towards the fourth layer opens. You enter. You see Yeshua. You see Marie Magdalene's Sacred Heart within your own heart. You feel it has three segments: a triad. This heart feels warm, vast, fragile, but most of all, all-encompassing. Yeshua stands before you and gazes at you with a gentle glance.

He holds your two hands in his and brings them to his heart. His heart area pulsates forcefully as if it could erupt from his chest any moment. You are dazzled. You do not understand. He laughs. His heart makes a clockwise spin, pulling you in, his heart gate opens. You move through this tunnel and emerge from water on the other side. Afloat upon these waters, you become aware of creatures shadowing profound depths. They try but cannot access you. You understand you enjoy high protection, for the action underwater is quite violent. Floating on the surface, you feel one with the Cosmos. A stillness, calmness, governs you. You cannot even begin to resonate with what is happening below. You feel it is the old timeline with which you no longer align.

You have understood. Yeshua brings you back. He lays his hand on your Sacred Heart. He fuses it with the same essence of Oneness and cosmic alignment. Your heart pulsates forcefully. You encompass the light, the darkness. You remain sovereign, in Oneness aligned with the Cosmos. He adds that you include it all because the darkness is also love. Darkness deserves to be loved. As soon as we see the darkness attempting to shift to the light, we allow the creatures to come to the surface of the water, to heal, to come into Oneness, to undergo cosmic alignment. Then they belong and resonate again with the harmonic resonance of the cosmic grid and stellar energies from which they have disconnected. That is also your mission to accomplish. Duality does not exist. There is only Oneness. We are all on the path leading to Oneness. Some move rapidly, others slower. Everyone walks at their own pace. Everyone may walk at their own pace.

Yeshua kisses you on your forehead.

The fifth membrane unlocks. You undergo vivid currents of light-blue essence energy. They govern this membrane, swirling you around your axis, your axis around you. Your whirling body collapses and transforms into a disc-like a spiral galaxy. From the disc's core, where all resides, light-blue essence travels to the outer outline of your spiral galaxy and back again. This interchange of energy alchemises and transforms you into a golden disc. The stellar pathways, all energies, essences you have embodied, integrated from these membranes, consolidate into this disc. The disc is the same as the one seen in Anubia. Only this one is yours. You breathe into every stellar pathway interconnecting stars and galaxies. You breathe into each star. You live it as if you are the Cosmos, as if you are the Cosmic Womb. With your Sacred Heart, you encompass All That Is and embody Oneness as well as the path to Oneness everyone walks at their own pace.

This pulsating structure feels powerful. The Cosmos Light Being is present. She says, "If you desire to co-create with me, align with me, align with my evolution. You need to be me to understand and feel evolution. We must interconnect, so we do not need to talk nor explain. You will know telepathically and move with me at the same pace. I am you, and you are me. We are One. We will be One in time to come. As Within So Without. As Above So Below. Time and space do not exist. We operate from this framework." The essence of this golden disc now withdraws into your heart as a tiny golden spark softly pulsating, all-knowing, all-encompassing. She continues, saying, "We gift you free will and sovereignty. It is your choice every day again to resonate with it or not. And if you do, it will stay with you. I will stay with you during all the embodiments you will take in the future time."

The membrane opens to provide access to the sixth layer. You walk through, and all the Light Beings of the former layers are still here, supporting you, aligning with you, lining up with you. The space between the sixth and seventh membrane is minimal. The Great Pyramid Light Being says it just wants you to choose, as you are a Sovereign Master. We want you to choose consciously as you have embodied the Cosmos Light Being and its sovereignty. You decide now whether to move forward.

You close your eyes because your mind says, "Yes, why wouldn't I? Of course, I choose, and I say yes." However, for a moment, you withdraw within your heart to feel what it truly means. What does sovereignty indeed mean? At first, as you do this, you feel that the seventh sacred space is holy, that it deserves all the conscious respect. It deserves a heart that understands what this is about. The seventh layer requires all-knowing, responsibility, engagement, and thoughtfulness. Your body feels it because your skeletal structure enlarges as if you will carry the Cosmic Axis around, which All That Is revolves. This knowing, the responsibility, the love, the honour, requires a conscious ignition in you. There will be consequences. This journey has taught you so much and has brought you home to your Heart Light. This step will bring you even closer to the origin of You.

The membrane opens as these words are spoken. You step through it. Yes, you choose to resonate on the most profound level with the origin of who you will become. A vault opens before you. You fall into it and drop in the earth pyramid apex of the Great Pyramid. Then it shoots you up in the Cosmos through Source. You move beyond Source into Source Field. Once you arrive there, you curve downwards and make numerous spirals embedded in one larger spiral staircase, like a cochlea.

You created a spiral multilayer structure. When you arrive at the apex of that cochlea, you know you have completed the sacred geometric pattern. There are spirals within the spirals imbued in golden essence. A fractal procreational process begins by creating other spirals in the same pattern, beyond space and time. Here you create the Master Blueprint. It is unalterable and not compliant with space and time. The Earth is in alignment with space and time, causing the delay in her ascension. Space and time have caused the Earth to deviate from the Master Blueprint. By creating at this level, you avoid deviations. You create an evolutionary pattern outside time and space. As an overarching principle, this is essential because it provides stability in manifestation. This overarching principle allows free will and sovereignty and simultaneously offers the main direction. There is space to procreate fractally, create timelines, make choices, and be a Creator within that main direction. For our main direction, you will set that outline like the one resonating with the Master Blueprint, the guide, to bring everyone back in the same direction.

You are again within the Central Axis of the Great Pyramid of Giza. The golden cochlea, with its multilayered spiral structure, integrates into your heart. You have understood. The only thing remaining is the link with Khufu. Khufu does not connect to this initiation. The energy of this ancient site and its remnants are energetically still present. The Great Pyramid of Giza holds part of this initiation within itself, but not the entire seven steps as in ancient times. We, the Star Council of Eight, emerge these ancient codes of wisdom because we envision everyone on Earth embodying and becoming this Divine Being of Light. We desire the perfect organisation, harmonisation, positioning within the cosmic grid, and the reflection of harmonic resonance.

Part IV

The journey to the New Moon

Illustration by N. Van Der Auwera. A Sacred Journey into Creation. New Beginnings.

New Beginnings

Around the Great Pyramid, two golden rings shimmer from afar. You can discern their vibrational sounds, almost like those of singing bowls. The vibration they emit initiates and leads you into a solar transition ceremony, an alloy of seven metals, seven celestial bodies,[39] seven cosmic segments. You celebrate the transition from the end of your journey in this solar system, this Cosmos, to a new beginning.

Like the sound of singing bowls, the overtones and undertones now give you the chance to release old energies and touch something deeper within yourself. The rings strike. First, you hear the chaos of sacred sounds, and only then do they become sequential. Your body recognises this system of tension and relaxation, contraction, and dilation. You can move within this rhythm, especially because the transition between chaos and harmonic rhythm is soft and natural.

These rings engrave themselves more and more deeply into the ground around the Great Pyramid, becoming a pillar of golden light connecting Earth's core with the vast cosmic sky.

You can still distinguish the two distinct rings as two walls moving independently of one another, yet still as One. This sacred geometry around the Great Pyramid feels supremely high frequency. From the foundation of the pyramid, countless blue spheres connected through liquid Light move upwards together like waves in water. These remind you of Nun and Nunet and how they introduced themselves to you at the beginning of this journey. Only here, the waves are more alive, more playful, seeking your attention and asking you to come closer. The joy of this blue essence makes your heart sparkle. Your presence excites it. As you come closer and closer, you understand these two rings have been transformed into a double-faceted golden column of light. The pattern reflects the blueprint of the Flower of Life: only it is not static but animate.

---

39 One for each celestial body: gold (Sun), silver (Moon), mercury (Mercury), copper (Venus), iron (Mars), tin (Jupiter) and lead (Saturn).

Illustration: The Flower of Life.

It amazes you that a sacred geometric pattern can become alive. You wonder what can animate it. As soon as you utter these words, you recognise a being with an Egyptian appearance. He has golden-brown skin, black hair down to his shoulders. He wears an Egyptian *schenti* or kilt. His name is Sita,[40] so he carries Sita's essence within him to guide you through this initiation. He asks you to move close to the Pillar of Golden Light. While doing so, you also move your hand through the golden essence. You hear it respond to you by emitting a shrill sound. Sita nudges you to slide your hand along it in a waving motion. As you do so, the blue spheres follow your movement. Sita says, "It is time." He asks you to sit close to him in a lotus position. He places his hands on your knees. You feel his heart beating, his warm body. He asks you to breathe in phase with his breathing because you will do magical things by uniting your breaths. You close your eyes and connect deeply with him, with his breathing, his heartbeat.

You follow his inhalations and exhalations and slowly become One. As your breaths merge, your bodies also fuse. Just as the two rings of the Flower of Life became one, he will work through you. He asks you to communicate with this wave of spheres. It begins to envelop the Central Axis of the Great Pyramid, moving up and down. Now, the energies are mostly diverging downwards, like a child ploughing its way down through the narrow cervix. Meanwhile, the connection of the downwards earth pyramid is slowly separating from the upper cosmic pyramid. The top of the downwards earth pyramid moves horizontally

---

40 In Hinduism, Goddess Sita is an avatar (incarnation) of Lakshmi, a Goddess of wealth, fertility, agriculture, and vegetation. She is the wife of Vishnu; whenever Vishnu incarnates, she is with him. She is also described as the daughter of Bhūmi (the Earth), where she returns to her mother's womb, the Earth, for deliverance from a cruel world as a testimony to her purity.

Vishnu is one of the supreme Gods in the Hindu triumvirate (or Trimurti). Along with Brahma and Shiva. He is the keeper and protector of the universe. Vishnu returns to Earth at pivotal moments to restore the balance between light and dark. He protects the people and restores order in the world. His presence can be found in everything in our Creation, in All That Is. By some Hindus, he is seen and revered as the divine being from whom all things emanate. Vishnu is represented with a blue-coloured human body and with four arms.

and lies flat on the surface, then rises to merge with the top cosmic pyramid of the Great Pyramid.

They spin more and more rapidly in their fusion, propelling the golden Light Pillar more profoundly into the Earth and the Temple of Love. You realise this is happening through your breathing, as a sacred witness in co-Creation with the Great Pyramid's Light Being. A deeper connection continues to form with Earth's centre. Now you feel the same in your body, and your Central Axis deepens towards Earth's centre. The energy of the Golden Lotus, activated within you, descends via the Central Axis to Earth's centre.

Here, it lays itself upon the steps of the Temple of Love as an offering and a request to be blessed. The doors of this Temple of Love open. A beautiful being receives your Golden Lotus and brings it inside for a moment. Inside this Temple of Love is a patio with a pond decorated with lotuses and many other aquatic flowers. This beautiful being places your Golden Lotus in this pond of deep blue liquid Light. You see your lotus grow roots of intricate filaments similar to the tentacles of a jellyfish swaying in the water. While breathing in phase with Sita's breathing, you observe and feel that sometimes he makes a more powerful exhalation, which heralds a new phase in this process. In the centre of this Golden Lotus, a tiny chamber opens, from which green essence emerges. The beautiful being takes it into her hands, for this was what she was waiting for.

It seems to be a green scroll reflecting the lush green vegetation of Earth, the Garden of Eden. She takes it to her altar. There she scribes on it. You are eager to know what she writes. She explains it is an update of your earthly soul contract. You have brought your fully blossoming Golden Lotus to Earth's centre in her Temple of Love. This means you bring her the greatest gift you could have possibly offered, as it will give the Earth strength and help her complete herself. For, if everyone brought the essence of their Golden Lotus, a new beginning would be ushered in right now. The gift, the energy, the light codes represent the completion of your earthly soul contract. All these light codes of Golden Lotuses of Earth's inhabitants will at some point come together in the Temple of Love within Inner Earth. Together they will merge and transform into a new blossoming Lotus knob. As a creator, you create with the Earth, and the wisdom you gained during your time here is of significant benefit to her. It will also speed up her growth process. Strange as it may seem, you both share a soul contract in which you help one another and in which Divine Love connects you. As the Earth evolves, you evolve with her. As you evolve, she can evolve with you. In this divine partnership, you have just helped her prepare for her new beginning by giving this most beautiful gift. This is one of the most beautiful things you have now fulfilled. We thank you and love you for this. Now, dear one, I have scribed the accomplishments you gained in your co-Creation with the Earth. I now return it to you, she says.

She finishes her scribing and rolls up the scroll, inserting it back into your Golden Lotus. It assimilates into your energy and spreads into your petals like a golden glow with sparkling diamonds, making your Golden Lotus even more divine than it already was. Your Golden Lotus has reached the level of mastery once attainable on Earth. She takes your Golden Lotus out of the water and guides it back out onto the steps of the Temple of Love. She bows her head upwards and tells the Light Being of the Great Pyramid to rise it to the surface again.

Almost immediately, the Golden Lotus introduces itself into your pelvic floor and flows into your heart. The new light codes in your body initiate a new era. In your pelvic floor, the same Lotus knob shows itself. This is your new beginning. You are evolving with the Earth at the same pace, side by side. Deep gratitude overflows you, making you feel close to her. Recognition and love heal your heart in the most profound of ways. You feel she is your divine partner, your friend. You can trust her and rely on her. This beautiful relationship with this level of integrity, forged by Divine Love, is eternal.

The blue wave of the Flower of Life's spheres is beholding you, showing her joy for you. To share his happiness with you, Sita slowly withdraws from your body and embraces you firmly and lovingly.

This initiation is ending. Somehow, you remain unsatisfied, for you would like to know who animates the Flower of Life, who has brought you so much bliss and has stirred your heart. You approach it, and you hear these words: "I am Mut,[41] Amun Ra's wife." She comes towards you in her leopard dress and holds you in her arms. She says, "My dear child, you have done so well. You are carrying your new beginning. You have ignited the essence of the New Moon, having completed the Full Moon cycle wonderfully. You have contributed to Earth's evolution, and we thank you for that. We want you to know that we remain connected: you, I, and all of us who thrive on Divine Love for the Earth. Because we are the ones who remember the Garden of Eden in our souls and carry that resonance, clear and discernible in our soul essences and bodies, we will rekindle it by consolidating all Earth's energy back into her Temple of Love, her heart. In the same way, humanity will be brought back into the heart."

We dearly thank Thoth Hermes Trismegistus, Vishnu, Sita, and the Light Beings of the Venus Light Path, and all other Divine Beings for this initiation.

---

41 Amun Ra was known to the Egyptians as the Supreme God, the Sun God. He not only created himself, but he was the creator of the entire universe. Mut is his wife, just as Sita is Vishnu's wife. This transmission brings together the energies of various religions because these are universal and One.

IV.1 Temple of Cosmic Time, The Pyramid of Menkaure

When I stop rotating time, and time stops, everything will be pulled into this black hole and dissolve. I will also dissolve as soon as everything has passed through my body. - the Black Scarab.

Illustration: The pyramid of Menkaure, Giza plateau.

Black Scarab: Timekeeper

The Pyramid of Menkaure, the smallest pyramid on the Giza plateau, is the most out of balance. Tuning in to this, suddenly you become extremely tall, surpassing this pyramid. On your knees, you have your hands around its four sides, and you bring your consciousness to its Light Pillar. You feel a heartbeat inside, sensing a life wanting to be born. You recognise lunar energy wanting to emerge through the solar energy of Menkaure Pyramid. You act as a midwife.

You connect the Golden Seed within your heart to Menkaure's Light Pillar. The Unseen surfaces to be Seen. Menkaure's earth pyramid fully merges with its sun pyramid, becoming One and ready to ascend.

When the lunar energy births through the One Pyramid, the pathway clears the way for the Earth to pass through. You bear witness to the opening of the way. The Earth births herself through the Pyramids, in co-Creation with the Moon, birthing Amun Ra's solar essence.

Menkaure's Pyramid is small. As the crone, it does not need to manifest itself, for it already carries all wisdom within. The Earth has now found her gateway to give birth to herself into solar consciousness. This symbology reveals that the Earth, and all structures, are prepared and ready. The Aquarian Age is significant in this regard. There will be no other era.

Also, she carries the black energies of the thirteen-pointed star, which assisted in the transmutation process in the Great Pyramid where Osiris's backbone sought to rise. This symbolically cleared the way for the Cosmic Axis to open, transmute, and give birth to its Cosmic *Pillar of Light*. Menkaure will now occupy that space as a sacred witness and represent the process as a crone.

Inside her etheric body, the energy of a Black Scarab lives. When you align your Golden Seed to the Black Scarab, you see it making a pivoted motion, moving the wheel of seasons, cycles of death and rebirth, and of new beginnings. The Black Scarab turns this wheel with its legs. In doing so, it wheels us into Oneness. The Black Scarab powers the Giza Pyramids, which function as a portal taking us into another world.

Illustration:
The Pyramid of Menkaure.
The Black – Golden Scarab.
Cosmic Timekeeper.

As the Thousand Petal Lotus unfolds in the Great Pyramid, the Earth can access a portal to join the Cosmic Axis or any other destination. The Lotus also represents the head of the snake. Both the head of the snake and the Lotus provide us with access to new worlds. When the Thousand Petal Lotus opens, a huge *Pillar of Light* emerges. In essence, this represents a Cosmic Ascension gate enveloping the whole Earth. The gate widens so far that it takes the whole Earth into its body. Then it teleports the energetic core of the Earth to her new destination, where she needs to be.

Oddly enough, when this Pillar of Light emerges, its shape resembles the Omega Ω, the white vase taking the Earth to her next incarnation.

Thoth asks you to stay focused on the Black Scarab. You have your hands on his back, and he asks you to touch him. As you caress him, a golden colour emerges. He is a Golden Scarab. He confesses it asks energy to keep the cycles and time running. He manages time as a Timekeeper. These golden legs feel divine, precious. He says a time will come when he will know he can stop. At that moment, an implosion will occur. When this happens, the thirteenth pointed Star will pull the Earth with its swirling black energies through the Pyramid of Menkaure to the Pyramid of Khufu to then ascend.

"When I stop rotating time, and time stops, everything will be pulled into this black hole and dissolve. I will also dissolve as soon as everything has passed through my body," – the Black Scarab.

Earth's energy, shaped as a White disc, passes underground to the Pyramid of Menkaure, to be blessed by it. The Pyramid of Khafre forms a bridge using an underground lake whose waters connect the energies of the pyramid. The White disc proceeds to travel through these waters beneath the Pyramid of Khufu, rising upwards through its backbone of the Central Axis. The White disc appears to be powered by Earth. Once it is above the apex, it rotates.

The created torsion field opens the Central Axis, igniting the entire etheric Earth body yet to be transmuted. This White Disc carries Star Glyphs to open the way to the afterlife for the Earth. In this manner, it acts as an Opener of the Way to the Cosmic Axis for achieving Cosmic Ascension. It also functions as an Opener of the Way to dissolve fully with cosmic consciousness. At that moment, the Earth shakes and trembles on her foundations. Physical life will no longer be possible. The whole Earth stirs as if consumed in the belly of Sekhmet. A centrifugal movement within the torsion field tears the Earth apart and renders matter ethereal. Only ethereal matter, her essence, remains. All the rest transmutes into light. These three pyramids and their moon essence help dissolve Earth's physical body during her Cosmic Ascension.

Honeycomb Divine Light Being

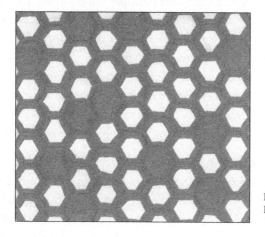

Illustration:
Honeycomb Light Being.

Here you stand before Menkaure, the smallest pyramid on the Giza Plateau. A black door emerges out of nowhere on one of the pyramid's four sides. The Menkaure Light Being invites you to enter. The black essence presenting itself is already familiar to you. You walk towards the doorway and enter the black space filled with the thickly textured plasmic essence. As you proceed through the doorway, this thick layer of black essence of about two meters in circumference attaches itself to you and follows the silhouette of your body. Being enveloped by this essence, you feel the need to position yourself within the pyramid's centre, right at the middle of its Central Axis, aligning it with yours.

You remain in stillness as this thick essence enters your body, clearing you from within. Your Central Axis becoming golden. You now fully harmonise with the axis of the Menkaure Pyramid, which opens and increasingly expands your Central Axis, stretching it in all directions. On your Central Axis, three pranic centres appear at your forehead, heart, and belly button. Moreover, these pranic centres situate themselves on your Central Axis, its front and back. However, they do not align exactly with one another.

Menkaure Light Being asks to align these six points. That being said, your higher dimensional selves thriving on an enlightened grey essence descend like a veil in folds on the back of the Central Axis of your body. Your whole etheric multidimensional structure, containing all your higher angels in your higher dimensions, fall together into your three-dimensional body. Just as the Creational Nile Temples are multidimensional temples with a presence in each dimension with Light Beings still active there, so too you carry the same structure. You are a sacred site. Your Central Axis now reaches so high that you can see the Central Sun, and from there, your multidimensional structure descends. This process continues, and the more these presences descend, the more your pelvic floor is calibrating to be able to accommodate it.

To bear all the energies, your pelvic floor now becomes larger and firmer. You feel your legs becoming sore. You clearly notice your bones and bone marrow are too dense to allow in and bear the light. Your enlightened, silver, multidimensional essences are your higher divine capacities that you have not had access to. You have been unable to unfold these energies in your present life.

These enlightened silver essences want to redeem themselves. And so, your body expands and expands, becoming a beacon of your being that works now in conjunction with the essences of the Moon, which helps unlock the capacities of your multidimensionality. As a result, your higher dimensional selves pour into your body. Slowly, you hear what sounds like a rusty ship moving. This means we are almost done calibrating and installing the multidimensionality within you.

The three front and rear prana centres on your Central Axis align and merge. First, attention goes to the heart prana centre. From the rear, your temple seed enters this prana centre at the front, piercing your heart and bringing in moon essence, making your heart bloom. Multiple layers emerge from your heart, similarly to the Golden Lotus at the Great Pyramid. Here too, multiple layers arise from within and rotate independently. They create more and more dimensional space, causing your heart to expand. You feel your rib cage expanding spherically. The light coefficient increases considerably, powerfully affecting the area of your navel and pelvic floor.

Your pelvic floor feels pressure for the blockage of not unfolding as your divine potential is building up. The pelvic floor is for allowing your Creations, your divine potential, to be birthed in your current existence on Earth. The energies that cannot unfold your divine potential slowly descend via your heart area, to your navel and pelvic floor. Slowly they glide down, and as they approach your legs, they try to move through the bone marrow, but it is too dense and tight. In response, your Heart Light now expands, moving more and more into your pelvic floor, into your legs, and into your feet.

As the underside of your body clears, you feel your Heart's Light pressure rising to your throat and head. Despite the imbalance in your head, you feel your spine and your Central Axis have become straight. You have just raised your spine. You are firm and have an expanded Central Axis. Your right and left poles, which represent your divine feminine and masculine energies, almost no longer exist. Only a few faint chalk lines remain visible, and these are gradually fading away. Your Heart Light is slowly approaching your throat and liberating your larynx and your head. Amun Ra comes to help you with your crown. He magnetises it and literally pulls out the blockage to your unfolding. Your Heart Light now pierces your crown, bursting it open, and your Heart Light splashes out powerfully like solar rays.

Your attention moves swiftly to your pelvic area, and your lower body glows a blinding white light. Throughout your body, an abandoned, outdated, and porous grey honeycomb structure is crumbling, falling apart. This honeycomb structure once actually received and housed your divine potential in your body so that it was always available to you. However, like an old, abandoned matrix, it has weathered over time.

The white light continues to unfold energetically within your body, and your heart is also expanding. As the Divine Light finally enters through your crown, its nectar of golden essences slowly flows in and descends down through your head, neck, chest, stomach, abdomen, pelvic floor, legs, and arms. From within, the nectar settles into a new honeycomb constructing sacred geometry. It is as if your body is being built in accordance with a hive. This new honeycomb grid becomes the updated structure in your body, allowing you to store your divine nectar.

As of now, your higher dimensional selves receive the nourishment needed to function here on Earth when connected to a three-dimensional body. The honeycomb structure is a sacred etheric tissue transmuting all energies hindering you from unfolding your divine potential. It creates more dimensional space, making you energetically and exponentially more significant than your physical body.

You take on the true greatness of your own Universal Cosmic angel, carrying the Light of Amun Ra. You cannot express its size in kilometres, but in the sense of multidimensional space from within, it can be compared to a quantum cell like the place Oddhe Rheia residing at Earth's centre. It is not to be grasped with your mind.

You freely provide the divine nectar to your higher dimensional selves and anchor all these higher dimensional essences into your body. As a result, you now feel your skeletal system, your bone marrow, and the grey essences within your bone marrow crumbling and descending, leaving you with crystalline structures. Within these structures, the golden strings of your divine spark are now visible, running through your body like threads. They also remind your three-dimensional energetic system of who you really are, of your One divine spark. It stays with you always and only with you. The process continues, and your higher dimensional structures continue to descend within you to a more profound level. You can hear this taking place. You can feel it. You are becoming solid and complete.

Thoth tells that Lemurian people radiated this golden essence. They had exactly the same honeycomb structure and were intrinsically connected to their golden light. They could levitate and lived on prana.

The honeycomb structure you embody now is the energetic body of that same state of consciousness. This form holds your multidimensional structure in this reality and allows your multidimensionality to descend. Thoth also points out that your Heart Light has descended to your pelvic floor and now encompasses your entire body. Your entire physical form has become your heart, the essence on which you will thrive. There is no divine masculine or divine feminine. There is only you, your heart, and the golden light enabling you to birth into wholeness and unfold your divine potential. That is all you need, all that has been mentioned above, you have brought into unity within yourself.

Your balance and your Heart Light illuminate your Unseen seeds, bringing you into harmonic resonance. You have arrived at the New Moon. Gradually you come to embody your I Am Presence. You love being here on Earth. You love to feel the wind and hear all the sounds of animals, waters, breezes, Sun, rain, and clouds. So this is the paradise on Earth Yeshua told us about. Heaven is in our heart, and the heart contains All That We Are, all our higher dimensional selves. Our whole Tree of Life. Our whole Jacob's Ladder.

You thank Menkaure Light Being and Thoth Hermes Trismegistus for providing this initiation for both you and for the Pyramid of Khufu. We are all aligned, the Creational Nile temples, the Earth and you. Thoth says, "My dear, rest now."

Sacred Heart

Illustration: The Sacred Heart.

Menkaure and Khafre Pyramid find themselves before you. From their earth pyramid, they weave patterns of black essence strings. These reach your feet. They will help you embody the greater essence of the Great Pyramid of Khufu. They are part of the Sacred Heart. They are the two wings supporting you to radiate the essence residing within your core. When you tune in to the essence of these black strings, they feel hollow, like wormholes, yet strongly woven, elevating you to the highest levels, allowing you to embody your creatorship beyond time and space. You allow them to elevate you. Each takes one side and elevates you, symbolising the path to Oneness. Thus, you walk with ease and grace and come into wholeness and full resonance with the Great Pyramid of Khufu. As the two threads elevate you, they also open your left and right sides. From that inner line separating right from left, an entirely unknown world emerges. A vast space, a void, opens, and endless space of light-blue essence emerges in the Great Pyramid of Khufu.

The cochlea structure from beyond space and time comes forward. All structures of existence swirl within it. They undergo restructuring according to *harmonic resonance* and cosmic laws. Each spiral in the overarching cochlea receives the essence for functioning beyond time and space and adopts an invariability and steadfast structure.

You will now stay aligned with the *Master Blueprint* and with *harmonic resonance* to be embodied at all times. The cosmic law and Hermetic Principles are now accessible to you. The entire time-space structure re-organises in this cochlea structure and thrives beyond time and space. You now reposition the entire Cosmic Womb according to the *Master Blueprint*. It dates back to the genesis of our Cosmos. You witness the alchemical process occurring within your own heart space. Once you feel the *Master Blueprint* of the Cosmos imprinted, you implode the cochlea structure into your heart.

The Light Being of Source Field folds its hands before you to thank and bless you. You govern your life and all existence from your Sacred Heart, which is all that matters. You have found your guiding string always guiding you home. You will always find your home with ease and grace, in the most efficient way. The two Light Beings of Khafre and Menkaure descend with you back down to the Earth. They withdraw their black essence strings and tell you they will be at your side as part of your Sacred Heart, assisting you in bringing Oneness to the Earth.

Tree of Knowledge: Earthly Mirror

Below the Giza Plateau stands the rooted system of the three pyramids and the Sphinx. At each end of the roots within this rooted system, there is an emerald pearl or seed. There are many roots. Within each, the emerald pearl receives the pyramids and the Sphinx's codes, transmitting them through this rooted system. The emerald seeds hold the codes in safekeeping. Each emerald seed represents a Creational Nile Temple. Thus, each Creational Nile Temple always connects holographically to the three pyramids and the Sphinx as a landing strip for Cosmic Ascension.

In this space, you feel a maternal atmosphere, for the sacred nature of conveying codes from these pyramids and the Sphinx into the seeds is so nurturing, comforting, caring, loving, protective, and devoted. The sensitive seeds gestate tenderly in their birthing chamber, reminiscent of the Tree of Knowledge, where the three pyramids on Earth mirror the knowledge of the Tree of Knowledge. They carry the Tree of Knowledge in their roots as emerald pearls, seeds of life. They represent the Tree of Knowledge via the Cosmic Axis through which we ascend.

While we were able to birth ourselves anew in Philae through the initiation of the cosmic Ovus, here at Giza, the energy allows the whole Earth to also ascend, for it symbolises a reflection of an essential runway for Cosmic Ascension through the trunk of Khufu's Pyramid. The seeds represent the various Nile Temple Bodies, and the trunk represents the One Nile Temple Body. The roots are the temples that come together in this triad and transmit their codes into these roots. They reside in the deepest point, akin to your root chakra, the deepest point representing incarnation, embodiment. They embody and nourish the Tree of Knowledge, lending it an emerald glow.

As the Creational Nile Temples collect their codes, they co-create with the Cosmic Axis and womb, replicating the same process. Each temple is a multiverse in this replica, one of the coral branches represented as a multidimensional structure. As each temple representing a certain multiverse comes into Oneness, the energies move up to the triad pyramids at Giza.

This process then replicates itself simultaneously throughout the Cosmos.

As Within So Without. As Above So Below. The Creational Nile Temples reflect the branches of the coral structure. The Nile itself reflects the Cosmic Axis. Cosmic Ascension implies the unfolding of our Cosmic Axis to unveil its *Pillar of Light.* On a planetary level and multidimensionally, the Creational Nile Temples co-create with humans, Egypt, and the deities of Egypt to enable them to ascend. On a cosmological level, they co-create with the whole Cosmic Womb because we are all One. It is all reflection and mirroring. Each fractal contains precisely the same energy as the larger structure, faithfully mirrored. The Earth, as a fractal of the Cosmos, embodies cosmic energy. Each fractal or pearl in a root does what the larger structure does. It is all One mechanic moving together at the same pace because we are all One.

The Nile Valley mirrors Cosmic Ascension. The pyramids of Giza represent the Tree of Knowledge through which we ascend. And within the Nile Temple Body, there is replication on different dimensional levels. In Philae, you have the cosmic Jacob's Ladder, the Tree of Knowledge with the Boddhisatva Light Body, allowing us to move through it. In various temples, we have worked and initiated our own Cosmic Axis and brought all our spirals into our own system as One. Each temple has prepared us to come to this point where we can just be and dissolve. When we sail up the Nile, we move through the Cosmic Axis and birth ourselves into a Divine Being of Light.

The Holy Triad, or the Sacred Heart, also counts three chambers, the feminine and masculine as a vesica piscis and then the birth canal as the third chamber, through which we create the most beautiful Creations. Here, we give birth to the Earth and ourselves. In a larger multidimensional perspective, we are initiated to give birth and create at different density levels, in or beyond the paradigm of time and space.

The Nile Valley initiates us to be Creators in Divine Creation at various levels of density. We are also initiated with and by the temples to birth the Earth into an Ascended Light Being. We birthed our Diamond Heart as a gateway through which we also ascend. The twelve-pointed

Star is a gateway through which we move to Oneness, to the thirteenth point, the Pyramid of Giza.

Illustration by N. Van Der Auwera. A Sacred Journey into Creation. Ascending the Axis Mundi.

Thoth Hermes Trismegistus initiation: Ascending the Axis Mundi

Thoth says he will now stand behind you. He wraps his arms around you. He kisses your head, and you rest against him. You now breathe with him. Everything around you dissolves. As you spin, you become vertiginous. Thoth is here, and you pass through the coral trunk he embodies for you. While you are in his arms, you dissolve and rise upwards into the ether. You span the cosmic sky. It seems as if you *are* the ether connecting all the stars, but truly, you are not. You are a supremely expanded Light Being who has dissolved into Oneness with *All That Is*.

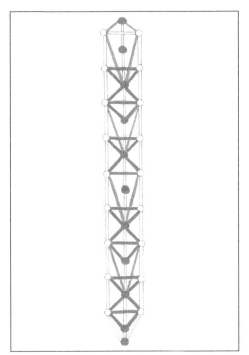

Illustration: The Jacob's Ladder.

You can be the grid connecting all. You can wrap yourself around a star as a protective grid. You can travel and be of help where needed.

IV.2 Temple of Cosmic Aquatic Beings, The Emerald Mother Temple, Bermuda Triangle

Ignition Secret Sacred Places on Earth

As a torpedo whale, a cosmic whale was sent through the Great Pyramid's pit, together with a cosmic mermaid, to ignite all the pyramids worldwide. Through its passage across the Great Pyramid's pit, the Great Pyramid reconnected with the Cosmic Axis. After so many thousands of years, it is time again to pave the way to Divine Unity.

Our Creational Mother, the White-Stringed Omega Ω, sends the cosmic whale, awakens all sacred sites Seen and Unseen, and kindles their lights. They hold their positions on Earth with a mighty grid that holds all energies during the transmutation process, enabling energies to remain high frequency. All Earth residents shall feel supported when undergoing such a difficult transmutation process. For it requires courage, righteousness, compassion, love, self-love, softness, and of course strength. Once all the sacred sites that have sunk to the ocean floor, or are buried deep below Earth's surface, reactivate their seeds, a new grid of sacred sites will then emerge and become anchored within the Flower of Life grid. The kindled light of the sacred sites forms a vibrational grid radiating ever stronger vibrations outwards. These sustain the pace and raise the vibrations on Earth in such a way that it supports Earth's Cosmic Ascension process. The grid of the sacred sites is preprogrammed to increase the energy each time. It is important for all residents of Earth to tune in to this grid, align to it, and enjoy it.

The Earth shall become a high-frequency space in this solar system and galaxy. More and more Light Beings from other stars and planets will join us. They will find it much easier to help us, as the high frequency on Earth allows them to remain present. We will make quantum leaps. There will be no stopping us.

The cosmic whale speaks, saying, "I am a Creational being. I originate from the upper part of the Cosmos. In this area, the energies are divine, and there are many divine verses. Ultrasonic sounds, Creational sounds imbue the liquid etheric waters present there. These are not the primordial waters, but liquids highly conducive to transport sound and geometry throughout the multiverse. We provide the universal codes to create new worlds. I carry everything within me. We are many Light Beings. We are aquatic beings who work with sound similar to the Hathor. Through sound, we create sacred geometry and blueprints. As can be seen, we take part in the Creation and fractal expansion of our Cosmos. A cosmic whale is complete, and our essence travels throughout the multiverse.

As cosmic whales, we move through Earth's inner depths, close to Earth's core, resonating with Earth's Temple of Love. Our presence ignites veiled sacred venues around the world, and we resonate with the Mother Pyramid of the Bermuda Triangle.

We also work closely with the Venus Light Beings. Their essence creates from within, just as the Moon ignites seeds from within. The Venus Light creates a conducive environment and provides everything needed for the blueprint to unfold. The Venus essence brings everything back into interconnectedness, into *harmonic resonance*, into the primordial frequency of our Cosmos. The Venus Light as sacred essence brings everything into the fundamental harmonic frequency from which everything can unfold. As cosmic whales, we are less of a sacred witness and are more active from our divine masculine energy. We are truly the master builders and creators who invent new sacred geometry. From within our bodies, we create new patterns, which is our divine potential. We work with the temples of the Earth. We ask them to radiate the frequencies we provide. They reflect our sounds and geometric patterns. Thus, the geometric patterns radiate out through the sacred sites. We support the Earth in this way. This is partly a resemblance to the Venus Light because we also create from within."

Provenance Cosmic Aquatic Light Beings and Golden Disc

The cosmic whale is here with you. She stretches her body, enjoying this moment with you. You lie beside her, aligning your heart with hers. You see light-blue light emanating from the core of her heart. This light-blue light expands throughout her body, runs towards you, making the come-hither gesture. By enveloping you, she gently nudges you to enter her whale's body. As you step over the threshold. You feel yourself enter a whole new world. The energy feels sacred and ancient. You bring her uttermost respect. You thrive in this blue essence light in this chamber to which she has opened to you. The more closely you approach this chamber, the more it seems a Stargate will transport you to another place. You stop for a moment. You would like to feel her and be with her for a while. She is here on the earth plane. As you embody her, you also feel a vastness of cosmic nature. You realise she is a hologram of Star Consciousness present here, a hologram of light-blue essence, represented as a whale.

You perceive her as a whale. Through her sound as Star Consciousness, she communicates with us. She sheds light on our role in raising the ancient sites worldwide, from the oceans' deep waters. We will ignite, activate, and raise their energies. These energies will thereby co-create with the sacred temples still present on the land. As she speaks, you see lights of temples igniting and activating on a planetary scale at the bottom of the ocean. They open multidimensional layers to release their essence to cocreate with us.

The element of time explains that the past is essential in the Now and future to attain wholeness and completion. When all these ancient temples on Earth co-create, each sacred temple represents a star in the cosmic blueprint of Anubia's disc. We need each of them to activate the Oneness of all ancient sites as One Light Being. When this happens, the earthly representation of the cosmic disc also ignites. Then, the earthly disc can merge into the cosmic disc. They then lean into one another and merge to form a circular passageway, a Cosmic Gate for the Earth to move through on her ascension path on her way to her next incarnation.

All these codes in both the Earth and the Cosmic disc fall into place and resonate with one another. Thoth Hermes Trismegistus's Hermetic Principles are fulfilled. The Earth Star has completed her trajectory in this quadrant of the Milky Way. The cosmic whale and its light-blue essence will achieve the earthly representation of the Cosmic Womb blueprint merging the above and the below. From that point onwards, a transmutation process occurs. She transcends her body and ascends. In essence, the Golden discs of the Maya adopt the same principle. The Earth has a disc, as do all other planets. The thirteenth is the one we merge with. Our solar system dissolves, and Helios Light Being ascends. Each planet's disc needs to merge with the cosmic grid's blueprint to ascend and match the underlying cosmic laws.

You are still in her chamber. She wants to bring you into her world. You travel with her. She looks like bright light travelling throughout the Cosmos. We travel far away, very close to the Central Sun. You are approaching it. She enters the Central Sun's orbit, entering its energetic field, and spirals right through its core. She shows you it is a spiral, and the outline is moving inwards. If you follow that inward movement, it is a gate that leads you to its core. You move along the spiral arms and funnel into the Central Sun's core. Here you already feel the Bliss of the Omega Ω of Eternal Bliss.

You hear her laugh. "Yes," she says, "this essence is pure. My blue essence light is special. Here is the repository for this blue essence." You no longer have a whale before you but a beautiful Venus Light Being. She is so passionate about what she does. From her heart, she truly wants to share, to show you everything. She brings her essence in her cupped hands. She stirs it to show you the structure, which is almost metallic and has a shine. You ask if you can touch it. "Of course," she says, suddenly nudging you all the way in, and she follows. You dive into this lake of beautiful blue essence light from the Omega Ω of Eternal Bliss. You float with her in this liquid light, enjoying being with her. Bliss unites us all into Oneness, and there is nothing between us. We "remember" ourselves as One, enjoying our existence and one another. Humanity has forgotten to enjoy one another, to see one another as a new world to explore and enjoy the journey. You are in this liquid blue light on the foundation of this lake. You breathe a deep sigh, and you look at one another. She says, "This nears the end of the journey of the Enlightenment Codes."

"I know," you respond.

She says, "It has been an adventure. I hope it has given you joy, bliss, awe and enchantment rekindling your Foundational Desire for Life."

You tell her, "It is the most beautiful experience I have ever had." As you respond, you see her heart lighting up. She loves your answer.

"And it is true. It has been the most beautiful experience ever lived. Now come, let me take you back," she says.

Emerald Pyramid and Eight-Pointed Earth Star

The Emerald Pyramid in the Bermuda Triangle joins all other underwater pyramids through a similarly rooted system.

There are eight pyramids on the Earth Star, which together form an eight-pointed Stargate. These pyramids and their formation in an eight-pointed star also reflect the Cosmic Axis allowing Earth's ascension. They form a larger gate, and each one of those eight pyramids needs to be functional for the entire gate to work properly to allow Cosmic Ascension. Each Creational Nile Temple can embody the whole Nile Temple Body, but it will also embody it on a certain multidimensional level.

For instance, the Ovus at Philae ignites the same principle on a more human level, whereas at Giza, it represents the planetary (Nile Temple Body) level more. Like a star in the sky, each sacred place on Earth plays a distinct role in Earth's Cosmic Ascension. As formations of sacred places embody a greater ascending power, they reflect the groupings of stars. They all represent cogs in the cosmological clock, Anubia.

The eight-pointed Star forms a planetary Ascension Stargate. Each star activated within this structure empowers this Stargate. Once all eight stars are powered and activated, the Eight-pointed Star ignites as a portal. It enlarges from inner Earth and outward, ingesting the Earth into her being and ejecting it on the other side of the portal. The temples that carry the eight-pointed star energy are the Pyramid of Khufu in Giza and the Emerald Pyramid in the Bermuda Triangle. There are six more, three above ground, three underwater.

IV.3 Emergence of the Garden of Eden on Earth

Cosmic Reflection on Earth

For this transmission, we ask for the co-Creation and presence of the Cosmos Light Being. We ask she be present with us with her etheric body and project her energy onto the Nile. Golden shimmering diamond lights now spread into the waters of the Nile, aligning it, stretching it, consolidating it into One Pillar of Light.

The right and the left banks of the Nile withdraw into this Pillar of Light to be absorbed, assimilated, and brought into unity. There is no longer a right or left bank of the Nile. There is no divine masculine nor divine feminine energy. Oneness dissolves these polarities. We have achieved completion. There is no more separation. Within us, without us. Now, the Nile River sends the energy of Oneness within us and through the waters of the Earth. Oneness thrives in every drop of water worldwide and is spread by all the aquatic creatures all over the world because they too are all part of a resonance grid that transmits information.

By bringing Nile banks and its temples into wholeness, this energy transmission becomes accessible and is projected on a planetary level. The Nile's Pillar of Light slides into the Cosmic Pillar of Light of the Cosmos Light Being. It has poured its codes into the Central Axis of the Cosmos, just as we have poured the codes of our Golden Lotus into the heart of the Earth. Slowly but surely, the Garden of Eden will arise from the memory of the Earth.

Creational Source Codes One Light Body

The cosmic Light Pillar asks to be deepened through reconnection and alignment with the three Omegas Ω. Therefore, the Nile's Pillar of Light needs to be initiated into the cosmic cauldron of Creation.

Asking the Earth Light Being's help, she settles down next to you. She holds the Pillar of Light within her hands, magnetises it, and fills it with milky-white moon essence. It now carries moon essence and embodies that which we do not see. She draws in this Pillar of Light with her etheric hand. She stirs all Creational Nile temples, and from their core, they ignite their inner Lotuses. The Lotuses rise from the temples' roots to the surface, up to their multidimensional temples. The Lotuses unfold their petals and bloom until the pistils are open and unfolded to receive Amun Ra's light. Earth's Light Being gazes at you and smiles. She says, "Now they're fully ignited. They are ready to merge into One. All these Lotuses converge and line up along the central line, representing the Nile. We have often worked with lineup initiations. Here it happens again: all Lotuses line up on one Central Axis."

Each Lotus positions itself. The topmost one is rotating clockwise and the lowest counterclockwise. These rotations allow them to find the correct alignment to the specific constellation or distinct stars of importance. She then locks herself in that position. When all Lotuses, or Light Temples, have fully positioned themselves and locked themselves in, their cosmological clock or their Stargate aligns with the respective stars with which they resonate. Consequently, the Central Axis experiences a transformation process. The Lotuses ignite with milky-white bright light, intermingling their energies.

Meanwhile, the lineup is alchemising. The Lotuses now position themselves in a circle. They continue to evolve as a spiral, spiraling down the Nile Valley into the Egyptian soil. The Lotuses descend into Earth's core, where the Earth representation of the three Omegas Ω lies. As Within, So Without. The three Omegas Ω situated beyond space and time, this Cosmos, and the Source Field, all hold an energetic reflection within the Earth, a mirror.

The Lotuses align with that reflection and spiral downwards. They twist around the first Omega Ω, wrapping it. Then, the second Omega Ω, enveloping it, and the third Omega Ω, encircling it to anchor themselves fully.

The three Omegas Ω resonate with this light string depicting the Creational Nile temples. Each Omega Ω conveys its true essence to this light string. Each Light Temple receives the light codes. Each Light Temple now carries within the remembering of its proper existence. Together, they all share the Creational Enlightenment Codes. All Creational Nile Temples resonate as One because they remember their origin. They recognise and acknowledge they are One Nile Temple Valley initiated into One Pillar of Light.

IV.4 Temple of the I Am Presence

Blessing of your Inner Thousand Petal Lotus

You desire to make intimate contact with your heart. Amun Ra is present, enlightening you. His cosmic light pierces your whole heart down your back and permeates you. Allowing him, you feel a vacuum in your upper body, filled with white-yellow light. This vacuum represents your inner Sun, increasing in size, frequency, and vibration. Gradually your inner Sun dissolves its essence into the whole of your body. You see its rays of light climb toward your throat area, penetrating your throat and head, permeating your eyes. Rays of white-yellow light shine through them. Your spinal column is twisting and turning restlessly, not knowing how to cope with these intense energies. Your hip area is also not accustomed to undergoing this pure light force.

With intensity, Amun Ra has chosen to be fully present within you. His white-yellow light permeates the whole of your skeletal structure to envelop it, mummifying it into a healing chamber for you to transmute your bones into light. He smiles and enjoys all of this.

From your heart area, you feel a pull to move your chest forward. Amun Ra says, "My Dear, you have worked so hard and igniting each Creational Nile Temple so that its Lotus emerges from the dark waters. Now it is your turn." Your body engulfs in an in-and-outward movement of your heart area, causing your Thousand Petal Lotus to bulge out of your etheric body more powerfully than ever, yearning for the blessing of Amun Ra. Its petals are subtle, satin-like, etheric. Your Lotus unfurls, aligning itself with any energy it beholds, trying to acclimate to what surrounds it. Incidentally, she harmonises the external energies to create a balanced environment for you. Your inner Lotus moves smoothly and majestically, accelerating the seed's growth. The main petals on the outline take shape. Now all inner petals also unfold.

You witness the blessing of your own Thousand Petal Lotus by Amun Ra. This emerging process appears never ending, recreating itself from within until three pistils are present and visible. They turn like a lock clockwise, counter clockwise, aligning you with the Cosmos. The pistils position you towards your highest potential according to your soul mission, according to your proper Jacob's Ladder, so that when you ascend, you will arise through your Jacob's Ladder in the same majestic, streamlined, never-ending way. At each step in your ascension's process, you will rebirth yourself, recreating yourself again and again until you birth All That You Are into existence. You can then merge as a golden disc with the golden disc of Amun Ra, the Central Sun encompassing the whole Cosmos and providing it with light force. Just as the earth disc will merge, so will yours. You are now prepared. Everything is ready. You re-enter with your consciousness in your heart area.

Amun Ra Light Being approaches you and kisses your heart, sealing in your Enlightenment Codes. He looks at you with a gentle gaze, saying, "My child, I will see you soon."

True essence of the *I Am* and Amun Ra

Bright white light shines upon you as if you were moving through it, ascending, crossing the threshold into another existence. You are approaching this bright white light, and within, you see Light Beings present, gesturing you to come closer. Slowly, you advance because you want to imbibe this bright white light. You want it to permeate your energy body fully. You breathe in profoundly, each ray it holds welcomes your Light Body.

Diamond rays radiate from this bright white light core. They move among themselves, and you notice that this action transforms your body, preparing it for every step you are to take. The diamond rays molecularly re-imprint and recode you. They create the dimensional space you need to allow this light in fully. Your body dematerialises as they restructure your energy body, allowing the newly created dimensional space to absorb the white light.

Your earthly body dissolves completely. The woven patterns of all your light bodies are being restructured and dismantled. Your body's essence restructures and morphs. Crystalline energies open their membranes and release their codes. You will no longer need them. They have served you well and accompanied you throughout all your incarnations, providing you with the wisdom and knowledge you required to enter your ensuing embodiment.

You now release all crystalline codes making up your existence and this Cosmos. It is time. You open the inner vaults of your Light Body. The crystalline codes rise from your Light Body, and above you. They gather and cluster into a crystalline scroll. You attempt the trajectory of the Alpha α and the Omega Ω, the beginning and the end. This divine spark that chose existence embodied all codes of wisdom throughout its journey, including all love codes. It has completed the trajectory of bringing itself into completion and has manifested its full potential, therefore completing the circle. All that was present in the beginning has manifested. The seed has fully blossomed and shows Creation its true essence. This trajectory entails enjoying life: enjoying the beauty, enjoying the laughter, enjoying Being you, exploring and discovering All That You Are and manifesting it, bringing it into the light, bringing the Unseen into the light.

Amun Ra embodies the Seen and the Unseen, the Alpha α and the Omega Ω, the beginning and the end. Amun Ra symbolises the enlightenment of the Unseen. As such, he guides the pearls of wisdom within a seed into the light. Amun Ra enjoys seeing that you have brought into the light All That You Are and All That Is Unseen. As such, he knows he has accomplished his mission. He knows he has guided you well. He knows you have understood, because that is who you are. That is the true essence of your I Am Presence. Beautiful being of Light, walk your path and bring All That Is Unseen within you to the light. Flourish. Blossom, and just be present. Like a Thousand Petal Lotus, keep unfolding yourself until every aspect of you has realised, because that is who you are. The I Am Presence.

Your beloved Amun Ra.

IV.5 Tower of Babel, Mesopotamia (Iraq)

Illustration: Pieter Bruegel the Elder - The Tower of Babel (Vienna) - Google Art Project

Earthly Pillar of Divine Love

When the Tower of Babel was built as a physical structure, it contained abundant energies of unconditional love. Through time and during the dark periods the Earth and all its inhabitants experienced, these energies of unconditional love withdrew from the Tower of Babel into an etheric sphere above the tower. A process of dissociation took place. When there is too much pain and suffering on Earth, one can decide to leave one's body with its consciousness. If we do this, we then stop embodying and feeling ourselves. We become dismembered.

At a certain moment, The Tower of Babel also stopped embodying its physical structure. This Light Tablet's primary mission is to resurrect the Garden of Eden, which has withdrawn into the Inner Earth, and the hearts of all people.

We can retreat into the Earth or the inner or higher dimensions. However, that means we are not present in the here and now. Whichever era we inhabit, we are not living within the timelines we are supposed to in order to accomplish our mission. The Tower of Babel concerns our incarnation and truly embodies the love and divine potential we carry within our souls. In this way, we transform ourselves, the Earth, and resurrect the Earth as a Garden of Eden.

In essence, the Enlightenment Codes represent the chalk outlines for reconstructing the Tower of Babel to revive the key for all inhabitants of Earth to speak the same language again, the language of Divine Love, to transforming the Tower of Babel into a tower of Divine Love, a portal of Divine Love, a beacon radiating that message across the Earth and other dimensions while infiltrating the etheric outer sphere of Earth's Light Body. The ethereal pouch stored above the Tower of Babel descends back into its foundation. It provides a solid surface. All ethereal walls of the Tower of Babel fill with the golden energies of Amun Ra and the magenta essences of Divine Love. From there, it infiltrates the whole outer structure surrounding the Earth, infiltrating all inner layers all the way to the Temple of Love. From this Temple of Love, the magenta rays radiate outwards as a star of Divine Love. A white dove circles the Tower of Babel three times, declaring: "So, it is said, so it is done." We give thanks for this transmission to Thoth Hermes Trismegistus, the Sphinx, Mary Magdalene, Mother Mary and the Light Beings of the Venus Light Path for their presence.

IV.6 Temple of Love and Venus Light

You witness the Enlightenment Codes gathering and forming One Ray of Light, then further evolving into a bright white-yellow Angel of the Venus Light. You also discern the energy of the Pegasus as she wants to fly you out into the Cosmos. She says, "It is about time that you receive these codes." You fly out into the Cosmos to suffuse them into the Earth as the moon essence has done at the Apis Temple. The Enlightenment Codes spiral and envelop the Earth. In a whirling motion, they turn inward into the Temple of Love.

An up-and-down pulsing movement from the heart of the Earth delivers birth to her Thousand Petal Lotus, unfolding herself to show the Cosmos. Here I am – I am present. With three pistils propelling her to an anchorage, she swirls through the cervix of the Cosmic Womb, enveloping the three Omegas Ω with her energy. They bless her and are thrilled she has come home. They bestow upon her a unique Source Code to celebrate who she genuinely is and to acknowledge that the Earth has remembered herself. She has resurrected her true Divine Essence. She has remembered her origin.

Your consciousness returns to the Venus Angel of Light carrying all Enlightenment Codes. She says, "All blueprints are ready. We have worked multidimensionally and beyond the framework of space and time. These blueprints containing the Enlightenment Codes are immutable and unchangeable. Each of us has our own free will and sovereignty to create within this larger framework. However, this new system of Master Blueprints will guide us home and take us through the Jacob's ladder to breathe in Amun Ra's Light and dissolve all our bodies. We become the I Am Presence.

The I Am Presence is a sphere of transparent light present in the frame beyond space and time. She will encompass the all-knowing, the all-being as a divine creator, and bestow her pearls of wisdom upon all who desire to receive them. She encloses a source of abundance, a new source of existence. Procreation is continuous, upscaling to higher levels of consciousness until the Cosmic Axis of the Cosmic Womb unfolds, opens completely, and bestows its codes on the Divine Cosmic Creational Mothers of Existence. At that moment, all divine sparks return to the Omega Ω. All divine sparks return home fully remembered. The primary goal of this sacred Creational trajectory is to experience enjoyment and Eternal Bliss while always remaining aligned with Source, with the Omega Ω and the Foundational Desire for Life.

IV.7 Dynamics of a Sacred Witness

As Sacred Witnesses, we open ourselves to all realities within and without the frame of time and space. This spherical spectrum is organic, divine. Through this Divine Essence, only the highest standards of love and light in service to All That Is are fulfilled.

The spherical organism in which we move is a place where many higher Creational Light Beings are also present. Together we travel through time and space. With open, loving hearts, we create a hopeful and loving future for the Earth and ourselves and far beyond. The changes occurring in this *Sacred Journey through Creation* are in line with the Master Blueprint for our Cosmos, passed on by the Omegas Ω. We are all aligning ourselves with the realisation of this divine mission of Cosmic Ascension. In this way, timelines, blueprints of temples, Light Beings, and ourselves are being rewritten. The changes are structural and have a quantum impact on the Earth and all her timelines, the subconscious of all who remain and have remained here.

IV.8 Epilogue

Present at this transmission are Thoth Hermes Trismegistus, the Light Beings of the Venus Light Path, the Cosmos Light Being, the Source Field Light Being, the Light Being of the three Omegas Ω (the White-Stringed Omega Ω, the Carnelian Omega Ω, the Omega Ω of Eternal Bliss), the Light Being of the Garden of Eden, the Light Being of Earth, Mary Magdalene and Yeshua and their Divine Child, Isis and Osiris and their Divine Child Horus, the Musica Universalis, Nun and Nunet, Vishnu and Sita, and Amun Ra and Amunet. All the Creational Light Beings of this Cosmos, the Light Beings of you the reader, and my own Light Being.

This is a story of Creation bestowed upon us by the Creational Light Beings of the Venus Light Path and Thoth Hermes Trismegistus. In co-Creation with the Creational Nile Temples, the Enlightenment Codes remind us that we are, as divine sparks, infused into Creation. They show us the Cosmic Master Blueprint of how we move back through our Pillar of Light via the vibrational strings of primordial existence and climb our ways up through the Cosmic Womb into the Source Field to go home to our Divine Womb, the Omega Ω. The more we funnel into our own Pillar of Light, the more we travel through it along the vibrational strings of primordial existence. Thus, we each travel through our own toroidal field, the toroidal field of Earth, that of the Cosmos, and those of our Cosmic Creational Mothers of Existence.

This journey initiates us into mirroring the Cosmic Master Blueprint within our own Master Blueprint, remembering our I Am Presence, our three Divine Creational Mothers of Existence, the Omegas Ω and their energetic signature of Eternal Bliss, and the Foundational Desire for Life.

Because most of us have deviated from the Cosmic Master Blueprint, which is our own Master Blueprint, the Enlightenment Codes are resurrecting our spiritual backbone, our Pillar of Light, and aligning it with the Cosmic Axis, the Axis Mundi. In this Light Tablet, we also resurrect the backbone of each Creational Nile Temple and align it with the Cosmic Axis represented by the Nile River. As we reflect in our hearts our Foundational Desire for Life, Eternal Bliss, and Divine Love, we fulfil Thoth's Hermetic Principle of As Above, So Below. As Within, So Without, which is encoded in the golden disc.

The sacred architecture of the Nile's Creational Temples, which mirror the starlit sky, reflects the Hermetic Principle of Thoth Hermes Trismegistus. The temples show us our star maps. These detail how to resurrect our wholeness, our Pillar of Light. We learn to reflect the cosmic sky and tune in to all the stars helping us to fulfil our divine potential. Not only that, they go beyond. The stellar consciousness thrives beneath the temple foundations. In the multidimensional realms of the Inner Earth, it permeates the sacred grounds the temples are built upon. As the energies of stellar consciousness find their ways into the walls of the temples, they lead us back to our One divine spark, our I Am Presence. They show us how to be reflections of the Divine.

They, together with their stellar guides, initiate us into igniting our own, unique Soul Light Tablet for the Aquarian Age. The Aquarian Age is the age that asks only of us to seek fulfilment, completion, and resurrection in our consciousness and the consciousness of the Earth, the Garden of Eden. The primordial Abundance, like a cosmic law, reigns on the Earth and throughout the Cosmos.

The Garden of Eden, which we must resurrect, is paradisiacal energy residing within the human heart and in the unconsciousness of the Earth. Yeshua said that Paradise is in the heart, the ignition of the Diamond Heart. The Heart Light it emanates reflects the supreme golden solar essences. Embodied, these translate into the Diamond Heart, a honeycomb structure accommodating the Light of Amun Ra.

The solar essence of Amun Ra, Supreme God, known to the Egyptians as Amun Ra, to the Hindus as Vishnu, leads us through the moon cycle in co-Creation with the Moon Goddesses and the moon grid, which pervade the Cosmos. The moon cycle, from New Moon to Full Moon, will ignite our seed of life, our divine spark, to full completion. As a prerequisite to resurrecting our Pillar of Light, we are birthed by the solar essences of Amun Ra. In the birth cycle from New Moon to Full Moon, we offer our Unseen divine potentials into the Light of Amun Ra reflected by the Full Moon. We thereby resurrect our Mastery, our I Am Presence.

As we move through this moon cycle, we are being endowed with a new energetic system. It will allow us to resonate with future incarnations beyond this current incarnation of Earth. These future incarnations are present in the seven universes. An opportunity presents itself: to become a Bodhisattva guiding Earth through her Key of Life. We resurrect our Universal Solar Angel and its honeycomb structure. The Honeycomb Universal Solar Angel is the physical embodiment of the supreme solar essences of Amun Ra. It is the sacred container for living on Earth as God and Goddess, as once in Lemuria, we all consciously radiated our golden essences and walked the Earth as Gods and Goddesses.

By allowing the divine nectar of Amun Ra's Light to infuse your honeycomb structure, you unite your divine masculine, your divine feminine, and your Divine Child, the guardians of truth and purity. You become the holy trinity, fully attuned to the Master Blueprint and to the greater Cosmic Ascension pathway. This alignment will empower you to step into your mastery, live your life from truth and purity, and bring forth Divine Creation.

As we move towards completion, out of gratitude, love, and appreciation we return our Divine Creations to the Earth and the Cosmos Light Being. As so many ancient Gods once did, Thoth Hermes Trismegistus and Amun Ra initiate us into carrying the Moon Disc and the Sun Disc. These are the capacities giving life force to a growing seed in a birth process and at the same time providing the conducive environment for a seed to develop and blossom from within, to bring forth Cosmic Ascension.

Carrying the Sun Disc and Moon Disc ignites you back into resonance with your own creatorship as a Divine Creator and carrying the wisdom of the Cosmic Master Blueprint shows you how to return home.

This Light Tablet sheds light on new possibilities, new worldviews. It is about the full embodiment of your Light through the honeycomb structure of Amun Ra. The Omega Ω desires that we unfold our One divine spark. It desires that we reflect the Life Flower of the Cosmos. It completes its full bloom into full succulent fruit. We witness the Earth Star ignite the process of completing her Flower of Life. We join her in completing ours.

As you do so, you ignite within yourself the energies, the power, the adventure, the laughter, the strength, the Eternal Bliss, the Foundational Desire for Life, and your creatorship. You embody the Garden of Eden in your heart. The Garden of Eden is the timeline for walking the Earth, the Master Blueprint and only path for the Aquarian Age.

Fulfilment, abundance, and profound inner bliss is the only modality of life for the coming Aquarian Age.

The Garden of Eden.

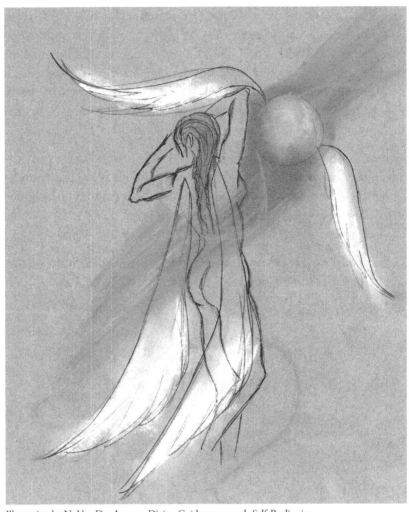

Illustration by N. Van Der Auwera. Divine Guidance towards Self-Realisation.

To My Soul, and the Self-Realisation of All Souls

"As if the Sea should part"

As if the Sea should part
And show a further Sea –
And that – a further – and the Three
but a presumption be –

Of Periods of Seas –
Unvisited of Shores –
Themselves the Verge of Seas to be –
Eternity – is Those –

Emily Dickinson

If you enjoy this Light Tablet I would greatly appreciate it if you would provide an honest review. As a self-published author, reviews help a lot to propel this Light Tablet out into the world to like-minded people. Your review is very valuable to me. Thank you so much.

Kindly, Sabrina

Here you will find the possible sites to leave your review and greetings:

www.amazon.com

www.bookbub.com

www.goodreads.com

www.barnesandnoble.com

The Cosmic Ascension Project presents this Light Tablet.

It is our intention to expand consciousness on Earth, for those who wish, into the Cosmic levels of Creation.

The Cosmic Ascension Project is a great opportunity to learn more about Soul Embodiment such as

The Mission statement of the Venus Light, a Prima Mater Light technology: The Venus Light, is offered to you by a co-creation of many Ascended Masters and the Path of the Venus Light Beings. We live to restore Cosmic Wholeness on Earth and to everyone residing on her celestial body. In this offering you will partner with the Ascended Masters, with Cosmos as Cosmos, with Source as Source as they offer you the universal dynamics of the Venus Light and a unique approach in tune with your unique soul energy signature, your Divine Light Being self. Please visit my website for detailed information.

Twin Flame Sacred Union. (upcoming)

The yearning for earthly belonging is reminiscent of the eternal Twin Flame bond we miss and are unable to experience in our daily existence. Coming Home.

And more to come. Stay tuned via my mailing list.

Receive exclusive, never-before-published audio and written content when you sign up for my mailing list at
www.enlightenmentcodes.com

Stay tuned for scheduled trips to sacred sites worldwide and indulge in cosmic initiations. Stay informed of upcoming events and New Light modalities.

About the Author

Living from the higher heart of unconditional love and the mystical heart of Divine Love, standing within our power and potential while remaining vulnerable, pure, and true to ourselves seems a challenging task on Earth.

This is the soul mission Sabrina Di Nitto envisions for her life and the lives of many others she guides. She has deepened her physical and soul structures to enable herself to embody her soul light. With a background in transpersonal therapy, energy medicine, transpersonal breathwork, reading energy blueprints, constellation work, and her own development of new light technologies, she performs the same profound work with adults and children.

In addition to her extensive experience in the field of transformation, she also works at sacred sites, revealing their pristine primordial blueprints. In this context, and as part of Cosmic Ascension Project, she undertakes sacred journeys around the world.

Sabrina Di Nitto holds a M.A. in Romance Literature, Linguistics and Philology and lives in the countryside in Flanders, Belgium, where she writes and conducts private sessions and trainings. For more information on upcoming events and soul embodiment courses, visit her website :

www.sabrinadinitto.com

www.enlightenmentcodes.com

Glossary

Adept: an incarnated soul with a considerably high light coefficient, whereby the individual in this incarnation can integrate high-level sacred initiations into their energetic system in a balanced way.

Alpha α and Omega Ω: an energy that is fully balanced in its masculine and feminine essence so that it can equalise. The beginning and the end converge. The Alpha α and Omega Ω represent the cosmic father and mother who send all their children into life. Their veils of light envelop the divine sparks throughout Creation and guide them until they are ready to return home. The principle of the Alpha and Omega Ω means all-encompassing love, light, and nurturing.

Amun Ra: the Supreme God of the Egyptians. The Sun God, who embodies the Central Sun's Light, the first manifestation and Creation of Source and All That Is. He not only created himself, but he was the creator of the multiverse. Mut is his consort. She is also a Mother Goddess worshipped in ancient Egypt. In the ancient Egyptian language, her name literally means Mother.

Anubia: a network in Inner Earth that takes place in the third dimension while at the same time transcending time and space as it gives direct access to cosmic astronomical points in the plane of heaven. The network was used by star peoples and ancient civilisations to travel on Earth and in the Cosmos. This multidimensional network is still active today.

Axis Mundi: the Cosmic Axis, World Axis, World Pillar, Centre of the World, and World Tree, a mythological concept representing the connection between heaven and Earth or the higher and lower planes in myths worldwide.

Blue Moon Goddesses: the cosmic midwives who resonate with the Cosmic Moon Grid and guide souls in awakening their seed of life and activating the divine spark. They carry within them the codes of self-realisation.

Blue Star energy: the core essence of an animated soul. Being extremely powerful, it ignites life. In the multiverse, Blue Star regions are where many avatars on Earth originate. These are energetic hotspots thriving on high-frequency energy. Blue moon energies are powerful energies that allow our inner Blue Sun to unfold and emerge from our inner depths.

Causeway: a long walkway joining the valley and mortuary temples. The causeway has walls decorated with painted reliefs and a ceiling ornamented with painted stars.

Cosmic Aquatic Light Beings: the Creational Light Beings from the upper part of the Cosmos. In this segment, the energies are divine, and there are many places where divine ultrasonic Creational sounds permeate the present liquid etheric waters. These liquid light waters, which differ in essence from the primordial waters, are conducive to the transport of sound and geometry throughout the multiverse. Here, the Cosmic Aquatic Light Beings are countless and provide the universal codes to create new worlds. While working with sound, similar to Hathor, they truly are the builders and creators who, in their divine potential, conjure up from their bodies new sacred geometrical forms, creating new patterns. In this capacity they work with the Earth's temples, asking them to radiate their created frequencies. They reflect their sounds and geometric patterns through the sacred sites. Through sound, they create sacred geometry and blueprints and participate in the Creation and fractal expansion of our Cosmos. A cosmic whale is complete, and its essence travels through the multiverse. The Cosmic Whale and the Mermaid were seen in the Pyramid of Khafre, in Giza, in a pit when raising the Pyramids' backbone. These two beings work closely with the Omega Ω and have been sent by her to assist Earth and humanity in returning home by activating all dormant temples located in the depths on the ocean floor.

Cosmic Ascension: the directionality that leads us through the Cosmic Axis, the Axis Mundi, to achieve complete ascension. Here we do not limit ourselves to merely ascending through various dimensional levels. Cosmic Ascension can be experienced physically, where one is no longer incarnating in the Cosmic Womb, or as an attained higher state of being, a state of enlightenment.

Cosmic Blueprint: the carrier transporting all development codes within to obtain Cosmic Ascension. We also will refer to it as the Master Blueprint.

Cosmic Life Key: the path that leading us to self-realisation, and furthermore, to Cosmic Ascension. It contains all the codes that align our One divine spark with all multidimensional soul extensions and unite us in our golden diamond heart. It activates the sacred heart and inherently, the Creator within. The Cosmic Life Key is a path all souls walk in the incarnation of man, animal, plant, planet, star, and so on.

Cosmos Light Being: the soul of our Cosmos, our Cosmic Womb.

Crone: a collective unconscious primal archetype conveying wisdom, inner knowing, and intuition. It guides us through life processes and going within to bring forth the light for transformation.

Coral structure: the unique skeletal structure of our cosmos. We refer to its axis, as the Axis Mundi. All cosmic segments, multidimensions, are located around it. In other words, all life occurs on her. It is the mother tree in which we all live and where we undergo, surrender, and trust the cosmic cycles breathed into and whispered to us by the primordial Cosmic Creational Mothers of Existence.

Dimensionality: the deepening and lengthening of essences, as well as our soul's extension through time and space, in certain sections of our cosmos. In this process, there is an unfolding simultaneous with the outbreath of Cosmos Light Being.

Divine spark: the golden light animating a soul. The seed of life is a further development into a manifest form of the divine spark.

Divine Primordial Cosmic Creational Mothers of Existence: the trinity embodying the foundation of all existence in this Cosmos, and beyond. They emit their creational energies through the entire Creation via an out-breath. Subsequently, via in-breath, they call their children home. Within this trinity, the Cosmic Mother of Eternal Bliss is the nurturing principle upon which the Carnelian and the White-Stringed Omega Ω in a vesica piscis geometry weaves the Creation principles into existence.

Earth's light body: that which mirrors the outer structures and consists of many inner dimensions also referred to as density levels.

Enlightenment Codes: the cosmic codes capable of transforming our vibration to the highest states of light if we so desire. They consist primarily of Source Codes and are then further coded by the Creational Light Beings for our particular cosmos.

Feather of Maat: an ostrich feather, very light, ethereal, highly discerning, and sensitive throughout all dimensional layers. Maat, who is the Goddess of cosmic balance, truth, harmony, morality, and justice in Egyptian religion, wears this feather to weigh the soul's heart when it leaves the body. The lightness of her feather is the guideline that determines when a soul should reincarnate.

Group consciousness: the entity formed when different souls, divine sparks, have committed to each other to descend the cosmos together as a consciousness, as a group. The individual members of this consciousness share the common field of the group, and at the same time, each retains their own soul uniqueness. From within the group consciousness, each soul can choose at any time to descend in an individualised frequency level. In the Enlightenment Codes, cosmic love and eternal care are experienced between all group consciousness members, individualised or not. The joining of the group consciousness can be resumed from a renewed growth of the soul.

Hathor: the ancient Egyptian people connected with the Temple of Hathor. They worked with vibration and sound on Earth. These multidimensional, galactic beings have ascended and are palpably present for those who desire to entrain with their vibrations. Hathor was often depicted as a cow, lioness, cobra, or a woman with a headdress of cow horns and a Sun Disc.

Hermetic Principle of Thoth Hermes Trismegistus, also called Tahuti by the Egyptians: the power bringing everything in Creation together through harmonic resonance in a spherical geometry that represents the Cosmic Womb and the sphere of the divine spark. Also, the beginning and the end of the Alpha α and the Omega Ω. Through cosmic reflections, mirroring between the microlevel and macrolevel the Cosmos, the Earth, and the Moon. Also, the reflections between ourselves and our fellow human beings and animals. The Above and Below, the Within and Without converging. When one undertakes this process, one walks straight up the Cosmic Axis to enlightenment. The Hermetic Principle carries the coordinates of Cosmic Ascension and, for those who have eyes to see, is woven into all of Creation.

Sacred Heart: the affirmation that, with its blue, pink, white and yellow rays, carries within it the consciousness of Creation. It is an affirmation of the embodiment of the cosmic love body, of the evolutionary principle, or in other words, the Cosmic Key of Life: the unique Source Codes we express throughout our cosmic existence and the purity embodied by our Pillar of Truth.

Horus: the son of Isis and Osiris. In Egyptian religion, he is represented as the mighty Falcon God. Here in the Enlightenment Codes, he also represents the Divine Child, symbolising that our human nature is an overlay we are asked to deify as a God on Earth. The Golden Age, or rather the Aquarian Age, has arrived, and partly because of this, he comes powerfully to the fore in this capacity to show us the inner divine nature of being human.

I Am Presence: the higher presence of our soul, which transcends the paradigm of time and space, no longer resonating with the aspect of evolution but contemplating the Cosmos and our existence. In the I Am Presence, stillness, equilibrium, and vastness reign in the heart.

I Am that I Am: the truth reflects the Hermetic Principle As Above, So Below. As Within, So Without. I am human, and at the same time divine. I am the drop of water, and also the ocean. I am human, and at the same time the Omega Ω. I encompass everything. I am the seed of life that carries its full potential.

Isis: the wife of Osiris and the mother of Horus. She and her siblings – Osiris, Set, and Nephthys – are the children of Geb, God of the Earth, and Nut, Goddess of the Sky in Egyptian religion. Isis is a High Priestess, Merchant Priestess and Goddess. In the Enlightenment Codes, as one of the primordial energies, she reveals to us of the importance of acknowledging Earth Light Being as a divine partner.

By moving through the inner dimensional layers of her light body, we sculpt ourselves to embody our divinity. Isis tells us that Cosmic Ascension can be achieved on Earth. The Earth is our home. Everything we seek is at our reach.

Jacob's Ladder: a term derived from the story in Genesis, where in a dream, Jacob saw a ladder extending into heaven, on which God's angels descended and ascended. Jacob's Ladder can be interpreted on a microlevel and macrolevel, indicating the different dimensional levels of the totality of a soul, being a human being, the Earth, a star, or the Cosmos as a Light Being.

Khnum: the Ram Head God in Egyptian religion, originally the God of the Nile's source, which annually flooded Egypt with its clay and water. Khnum was believed to be the creator of the bodies of human children, which he modelled on the potter's wheel and carefully laid in the mother's womb. He is also called the divine potter. In the Enlightenment codes, he puts forward his divine role as the weaver of stellar DNA and the golden light in the human body. Our compass to experience life on Earth from a cosmic surrender.

Maat or Ma'at: the ancient Egyptian concepts of truth, balance, order, harmony, law, morality, and justice. Maat was also the Egyptian Goddess carrying the ostrich feather. She embodies these concepts. It was said she governed the stars, seasons, and the actions of mortals and the deities who had brought order from chaos at the moment of Creation. The Cosmic Maat revealed in the Enlightenment Codes goes beyond the above meaning and gathers all wisdom of the whole Cosmos, of Source Field, and includes all prima mater and substances (etheric, liquid, plasmic, crystalline, and so on) as well as all essences of colour. The Maat represents the mainframe of all existence. Here geometry, colour, and primordial matter originate life. In Egyptian times the Maat energy enabled us to balance and live according to cosmic laws. At least, that is what we were told. It tuned us into harmonic resonance but did not directly support the quantum ascension of the Cosmic Axis. Therefore, the Cosmic Maat transcends all Egyptian rites of passage. Now we are honoured to access the expanded Maat. And, you are outside the framework of time and space, of the hierarchy of suns and moons. There are only eight divine beings who carry this knowledge. The missing two represent the two golden orbs at Abu Simbel that were unfinished.

Maltese Cross: the primordial sacred geometry that promotes expansion and growth as a cross symbol, consisting of four V or arrowhead shapes that meet at a central vertex. It is a primordial geometric structure present as a sacred geometric building block in the expansion of the multiverse. This structure expands matter and supports growth and development on microlevels and macrolevels.

Melchizedek: a king and priest who lived on Earth during the epoch of Enoch. Later, in his wake, they founded the order of Melchizedek priests. The name is presumably composed by Melchior and Zadok, which were ancient priesthoods. The adepts in the role of priesthood are now, in the present time, ascended masters who guide us to self-realisation.

Music of the Celestial Spheres: the Música Universalis represented by the sound of the orbiting celestial bodies and the void spaces within, which are equally important for harmonic resonance.

Nephthys: a daughter of Nut and Geb, and a sister of Isis, the god Osiris, and as the sister-wife of Set. She was associated with childbirth, death, mourning, celebration, night, and the Unseen. She was a Temple Priestess.

Nun and Nunet: the primordial dark Source waters from which all life springs in ancient Egyptian religion.

One divine spark: the first animated form, a consciousness that can procreate itself multidimensionally in numerous divine sparks, each leading a different form of incarnation in a different level of density. When coming into Oneness, we all return home to our One divine spark.

Ouroboros: the tail-eater. As an alchemical symbol and one of the oldest mythical symbols in the world, it is found in Aztec mythology, Chinese mythology, and numerous others. It depicts a snake or dragon biting its own tail to create an eternal circle. It symbolises the cyclical nature of nature, its eternal return, and the unity of everything.

Ovus: A rebirth, the hatching of the egg and giving ourselves new life. A new beginning. At the same time, the principle incorporates the Axis Mundi, through which it moves to sculpt and manifest the new existence.

Physicality: various forms of density. Sometimes, the material, the bricks, are not present anymore. The etheric blueprint of the sacred site, however, still is. This etheric blueprint level of material density can also be considered as a physical dwelling, but in a more etheric form.

Pillar of Light: the Central Axis of our toroid. It also represents the microlevel of the Axis Mundi, the place where all codes are rendered at the end of our incarnation.

Light being: the energetic electromagnetic informational sphere of light characterised by unique and universal qualities. Your Light Being is a higher dimensional frequency of who you are beyond your three-dimensional physicality.

Light Tablet: a multidimensional scribed text that is evolutionary and multilayered. Its codes radiate out to its reader and its environment, setting in motion a transformative evolution. One has the ability, if one so desires, to fully incorporate the Light Tablet into one's physical system and thus embody its essence.

Light Temple: the multidimensional etheric blueprint of a physical manifestation in the third dimensional realm. It can refer to a building, an individual, an animal. In short, any Creation that is animated.

Sacred witness: a silent witness whose heart is divinely connected to the observed. The cosmic laws of harmonic resonance, multidimensionality, and functioning or not functioning within time and space are assumed as the reality. The sacred witness observes from the knowledge that everything has an anima, a divine unique and autonomous will, whereby the observed follows its own divine guidance for the highest good of all, and in the Enlightenment Codes, according to the Master Blueprint.

Scarab: a being who governs the cycles of life, it represents the concepts of self-generation, rebirth, renewal, and resurrection to the practice of dung beetles. In the Enlightenment Codes, the Scarab turns the wheel of Time. In doing so, it wheels us into Oneness and Cosmic Ascension. The Scarab powers the Giza Pyramids, which function as a portal taking us into another world. "When I stop rotating time, and time stops, everything will be pulled into this black hole and dissolve. I will also dissolve as soon as everything has passed through my body," – the Black Scarab.

Scroll of Truth: your Pillar of Light imbued with Maat's energy of truth, cosmic law, order, harmony, and balance.

Seed of life: the vessel that carries the divine spark and is imbued with the energies of Eternal Bliss and our vibrational blueprint, unique to our soul and universal to existence. This vessel contains all the Source Codes we need to fully develop ourselves in any dimensional realm. We have everything within us to achieve Cosmic Ascension.

Sekhmet: the Lioness Goddess. She is a fierce warrior and was seen as the protector of the pharaohs and led them in battle. Even after their decease, Sekhmet continued to protect them and carry them to the hereafter. Sekhmet is a sun deity, also called the daughter of Ra. She wears the Sun Disc. In the Enlightenment Codes, Sekhmet has a strong connection with the blue sun energy, and teaches us to create in devotion, ease, and grace.

Seti I: a pharaoh of the New Kingdom Nineteenth Dynasty of Egypt, the son of Ramesses I and Sitre, and the father of Ramesses II.

Sita: an avatar (incarnation) of Lakshmi, a Goddess of wealth, fertility, agriculture, and vegetation. She is the wife of Vishnu; whenever Vishnu incarnates, she is with him. She is also described as the daughter of Bhūmi (the Earth), where, as a testimony to her purity, she returns to her mother's womb, the Earth, for deliverance from a cruel world.

Solar King: humans who have been initiated into the highest level of Solar Kingship and rule the Earth through the pure essence of their hearts and in co-Creation with Amun Ra's light. Each Solar King completes the role of Solar Kingship because each period requires an update. As such, you become a co-creator of the Earth.

Sothis or Sopdet: the ancient Egyptian name for the star Sirius. As a Goddess, she personifies this energy. During the transmission of the Enlightenment Codes, she also reveals an intimate connection with the moon energy as a cosmic midwife and its unfolding qualities in the process of rebirth and new beginnings.

Source Codes: the light codes coming from the three primordial Cosmic Creational Mothers of Existence and their Creational Waters, radiating out through the Source field and our Cosmos. The Source Codes are multidimensional and evolutionary, meaning that they are constantly evolving in accordance with their genesis, being the three Cosmic Creational Mothers of Existence. Through this we also understand that we are always being cared for and that we can, if we wish, always vibrate at the highest frequencies of light accessible in our Cosmos.

Sun and Moon Disc: the award for embodying the Enlightenment Codes of developing the seed of life to its full potential through which Cosmic Ascension can be achieved. Wearing the Sun and Moon Disc empowers one's cosmic creatorship.

Temple of Love: the Earth Temple in the heart of the Earth. Also referred to as the Holy of Holies on Earth. Each sacred site has a Holy of Holies where the Divine seed of life resides. The core of Earth's womb, where all souls incarnating on Earth receive her divine blessing.

Temple seed: the anima of a temple, it carries within itself the complete etheric multidimensional structure. The temple seed rests in the Holy of Holies and bathes in divine light.

Toroid: the shape around which a seed of life regroups its energy field in such a way that it constantly rotates about. In essence, the central axis of the toroid may be seen as our unique Cosmic Axis, as the reflection of the Universal Axis of the Cosmos. Here also the Hermetic Principle of As Above, So Below. As Within, So Without, is integrated. When we acquire the vibratory match with the Enlightenment Codes for Cosmic Ascension, our toroid field becomes aligned and resonates with the Cosmic Axis, the mainframe of the Cosmos. From this moment on, we bear evolution in our essence. We become evolution. We simply become the Cosmos.

Triple Goddess: the three archetypes often described as the Maiden, the Mother, and the Crone, each symbolising a different phase in the female life cycle. In the Enlightenment Codes, this principle is applied to the natural evolution of celestial bodies, from a planet to a Sun, and ultimately the sage woman, the Moon.

Ultraviolet Sun: the energetic quality and level of consciousness of the future incarnation of the planetary Earth. A planet, if it wishes, evolves, and ascends via the Cosmic Key of Life to a Sun. Within the solar segment, there are several levels, of which the ultraviolet ray is one.

Venus Light: the primordial essence that emerges as an application for further developing Source Codes that build all the blueprints of life in this Cosmos.

Vishnu: one of the Supreme Gods in the Hindu triumvirate (or Trim-urti). Along with Brahma and Shiva. He is the keeper and protector of the universe. Vishnu returns to Earth at pivotal moments to restore the balance between light and dark. He protects the people and restores order in the world. His presence can be found in everything in Creation, in All That Is. By some Hindus, he is seen and revered as the divine being from whom all things emanate. Vishnu is represented with a blue-coloured human body and with four arms.

Made in the USA
Las Vegas, NV
04 October 2024

96289458R00203